CONVICTIONS MATTER

The Function of Salvation Army Doctrines

RAY HARRIS

FOREWORD
JOHN LARSSON

In his book, *Convictions Matter*, Ray Harris states his belief that it is important to engage the future with our core convictions. In articulating and reflecting on the core convictions that guide the work of The Salvation Army and hold its communal life together, Harris has achieved that elusive but essential balance between accessibility and depth. He has put the doctrines of the Army in conversation with the Salvationist understanding of holiness for the purpose of broadly, deeply and faithfully engaging the future. The reflection questions at the end of each chapter are a perfect and thorough example of that. They challenge us to deep understanding and faithfulness and they call us forward into the creation of significance in our current context and beyond. Harris continually asks and continually answers the question of what function doctrines serve. This is a book for all Salvationists most surely, but it is also a book for the whole church.
—*The Rev. Dr. Karen Hamilton, General Secretary,*
The Canadian Council of Churches

Doctrines are like the Scriptures: they always call for interpretation and need to be understood anew in every generation. All readers of this book will stand in debt to the author for helping them do just that.

The author has been faithful to two interpretive principles that are evident from the beginning of the book. First, as he works through the doctrines, he acknowledges the authority of the Scriptures and is faithful to that authority on every page. Second, he embraces the Salvationist doctrine of holiness as our central doctrine and thereby interprets our doctrines through the lens of holiness.

Doctrines are not monuments to the past, but living testimonies to the present and hopeful signs of the future. Ray Harris adeptly looks at the formation of our doctrines. From his personal convictions and vocation, as well as his interest in our life together, he speaks about those doctrines with clarity and purpose. In order to do that, he uses a wide range of sources, beginning with the early church and moving to the 21st century, which will enrich the doctrinal conversation of the Army with the broader theological world. There is compelling theological history in this book that will engage the mind and the heart of every reader.

The reader need not fear getting lost in a maze of theology. As Ray Harris considers the 11 Army doctrines, he breaks up each chapter into three sections: forming the doctrine, engaging the doctrine and practising the doctrine. And in keeping with the biblical emphasis on theology as a community task, he provides insightful reflection questions at the end of each chapter.

Convictions Matter has stimulated my own thinking in many ways, and I know that every reader will be challenged and enriched by reading this book.

—Dr. Roger J. Green, Professor and Chair of Biblical Studies and Christian Ministries, Terrelle B. Crum Chair of Humanities, Gordon College, Wenham, Massachusetts

At the heart of *Convictions Matter* by Ray Harris is an investigation into the relationship between Salvation Army doctrine and the way in which we live out that deepening experience of Christian faith, which is known as growth into holiness. Written in a straightforward and readable style, the book describes briefly the development of each of the articles of faith before exploring ways in which it connects with the 21st-century world and with the practice of faith in the life of the believer. Each chapter concludes with questions for discussion and reflection, which could be used effectively by small groups as an aid to developing Christian discipleship. This well-researched and creative book is a valuable addition to Salvationist writing on the core tenets of our faith.

—Lieut.-Colonel Dr. Karen Shakespeare, Assistant Secretary for Personnel, United Kingdom Territory with the Republic of Ireland, and Secretary to the International Doctrine Council

Ray Harris cares about his readers. *Convictions Matter* is not a textbook in generic theology; it is a stimulus to doing theology contextually. It is a book to engage 21st-century Christians who want a faith grounded in the Bible and historical creeds, but who equally want a faith that addresses the questions of their times. It is commended to Salvationists who want convictions that mean something—that make a difference to how they live and how they help others live, too.

—Dr. James E. Read, Executive Director, The Salvation Army Ethics Centre

RAY HARRIS

FOREWORD JOHN LARSSON

Published by The Salvation Army, Canada and Bermuda Territory
2 Overlea Blvd., Toronto, Ontario M4H 1P4
Phone: 416-425-2111; fax: 416-422-6120
www.salvationarmy.ca

Cover, Layout and Design: Brandon Laird

Printed in Canada
ISBN: 978-0-88857-508-1

The assistance of these contributors in preparing this book is greatly appreciated:

Members of the Territorial Literature Council, staff of the Editorial Department (Editor-in-Chief and Literary Secretary: Geoff Moulton; Copy Editor: Pamela Richardson)

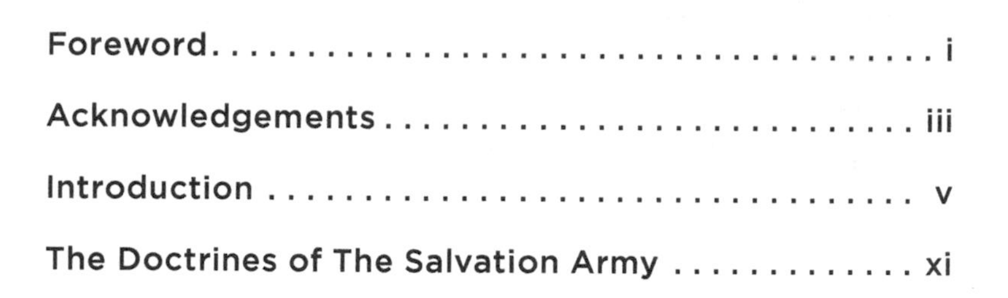

TABLE OF CONTENTS

FOREWORD

DEPARTMENTS RESPONSIBLE FOR RAISING FUNDS FOR THE Salvation Army's social and community services are not usually staffed by theologians. It therefore came as a surprise to discover in 2012 that the Army's public relations department in Great Britain had chosen a doctrinal slogan for its appeal to the public. The message that went out in the publicity was: "It's what we believe that makes us what we are!"

Whether theologians or not, the public relations people had hit the nail on the head. For it is indeed what we as an Army believe that makes the Army what it is. But the truth is even greater than that. For it is also what we as individuals believe that makes us what we personally are. It is our beliefs that make us tick.

Ray Harris would have applauded the slogan when it appeared for in a snappy phrase it sums up the thrust of *Convictions Matter*, this masterly book of his. Salvation Army doctrines serve a practical function, he says. Our beliefs make us what we are. Our core convictions, therefore, matter supremely. And for Salvationists, these core convictions are the 11 points of Salvation Army doctrine.

In providing the biblical background and discussing the historical development of each of these doctrines, the author expands our thinking in a remarkable way—a notable characteristic of the book as a whole.

But what makes this work truly distinctive is his focus throughout on the practical relevance of the 11 articles of faith for everyday living in the 21st century. Doctrines are not meant to be locked away in some musty mental cupboard for occasional reference. They are there to be lived out. They are there to be practised.

To focus their practical relevance, the author links each doctrine with the Salvationist understanding of holiness, the doctrine by which "we interpret and live out our common lives," as Roger Green reminds us. With this innovative approach, the pages sparkle with new insights as the author applies the doctrines to the living of our lives. Once more the horizons of our thinking are expanded, and never more so than when he deals with the doctrines concerning salvation. J.B. Phillips, the celebrated Bible translator, once wrote a book entitled *Your God Is Too Small.* The challenge that Ray Harris brings in these pages could well be headed *Your Salvation Is Too Small!*

The doctrine about being wholly sanctified becomes the climax to everything that has gone before. Again the author explores larger dimensions. "Without losing our emphasis on heart holiness," he writes, "we need to expand it to include social, political and even ecological dimensions."

In concluding his survey of the Army's doctrines, Ray Harris calls the present generation of Salvationists "to engage these historic core convictions with the issues of our day." The breadth of his canvas is seen in the issues he touches on in the course of the book—issues such as life in a pluralist society, interfaith dialogue, evolution, the relationship with science, the market economy, social justice, unemployment, immigration, transplant tourism and dementia.

With its twin emphases on the Army's doctrines being functional and having holiness as their common denominator, *Convictions Matter* is a groundbreaking book. It is also a scholarly work of the highest order and tackles difficult doctrinal issues head on. But with its amazing range of memorable down-to-earth illustrations and apt quotations, the author grounds the subject in daily life and makes it accessible to us.

Convictions Matter is not a handbook for theorizing about our beliefs but a handbook on how to live by them in the 21st century. We all, therefore, stand indebted to Ray Harris for his inspirational insights. And of one thing we can be sure: if what we believe makes us what we are, then nothing matters more than our convictions.

—General John Larsson (Rtd)

THIS BOOK HAS BEEN WRITTEN OUT OF A DEEP SENSE OF indebtedness to the Christian tradition as embodied in The Salvation Army. It has nurtured my life, and has given me a framework through which to serve the present age. It is my hope that Salvationists will realize that our core convictions are part of something much larger than ourselves. For this reason I have alluded to many sources that have helped to shape and challenge my own convictions. There is a huge conversation going on in our world and we belong at the table.

I have also written with a deep sense of indebtedness to others. I have learned from Salvationist congregations across Canada, from colleagues in our various Colleges for Officer Training and at Booth University College, and at the Army's divisional and territorial headquarters. I have also come to value the contribution of friends in ecumenical circles such as the Toronto School of Theology, the Canadian Council of Churches, and in multifaith circles such as the Manitoba Multifaith Council.

Personal thanks is due to those colleagues who have helped to bring this book to the light of day: Lieut.-Colonel Jim Champ, Geoff Moulton, Pamela Richardson, Brandon Laird and Major Bruce Power, and to Commissioner Brian Peddle for giving it the green light. I am most grateful, too, for those who have taken time to read the manuscript and offer personal comments: Dr. Roger Green, Rev. Dr. Karen Hamilton, Dr. James Read, Lieut.-Colonel Dr. Karen Shakespeare and General John Larsson (Rtd).

This work had its beginnings in a family where I learned the importance of convictions. It is dedicated to the memory of my parents, Herb and Grace. The book was nurtured in my own family where three kids found their greatest delight in challenging me; thanks Colin, Kristen and Alison. My special thanks is due my wife, Cathie, to whom this book is also dedicated. Her love and commitment to the importance of convictions is found all through its pages.

—Ray Harris (Major, D. Min.)
Winnipeg, Manitoba

It's the quality of one's convictions that determines success, not the number of followers.—J. K. Rowling[1]

I believe ...

Actually, I believe a number of things. I believe Canadian winters can be enjoyed. I truly believc this, but I will hibernate like a groundhog when the temperature reaches minus 35 C! I believe that exercise is important for good health, therefore I work out in the gym and run. I also exercise because I am much less disciplined when it comes to eating desserts! Personal convictions vary in importance, and how they are lived out.

We believe ...

A group's convictions can lead to important accomplishments. Habitat for Humanity believes that every person should have a safe and affordable place in which to live, so they build houses. Martin Luther King Jr. held the American civil rights movement together with his convictions about racial justice and non-violent protest. Families, teams, schools, companies and nations live purposefully when there are core convictions at work. Communal convictions play important roles.

Salvationists believe ...

Salvationists believe many things. We believe the devil shouldn't have all the good music. We believe our faith belongs in the streets. We believe that women have a rightful place in leadership. We hold these convictions and we practise them, even if inadequately. However,

Salvationists also have *core convictions* that guide our work and hold our communal life together. They are known as Affirmations of Faith, or Doctrines. Each Salvationist doctrine begins with the phrase, "We believe...." Together, the 11 doctrines of The Salvation Army are central to its identity. Salvationists around the world affirm their faith with these core convictions. We are a people committed to doctrines.

The Army's doctrines were constituted in 1878, the same year The Salvation Army was given its name. They have their roots in the Methodist Movement, but they also possess their own integrity. The doctrines are affirmed when a Salvationist becomes a soldier, and when officers are ordained and commissioned.[2] However, life in the 21st century is not the same as it was in 1878, regardless of where we live. Do these doctrines make sense in *this* world? Do these eleven statements of faith make any difference to the way Salvationists *live* in our world? What is their *function*? It seems pointless to hold on to core convictions unless they actually help us to practise our faith today.[3]

It seems pointless to hold onto core convictions unless they actually help us to practise our faith today

It is with these questions in mind that I approach this study of Salvationist doctrines. In order to explore them more fully, I will examine each doctrine under three headings:

1. Forming the Doctrine
2. Engaging the Doctrine
3. Practising the Doctrine

A few comments about each are in order:

1] Forming the Doctrine: The church's doctrines are human constructions, formed over time. The early church recognized its need for concise summaries of faith, called creeds. Years later the church was reformed through Martin Luther's emphasis on the doctrine of justification by faith. The Wesley brothers, John and Charles, transformed the face of England through their emphasis on the doctrine of grace. Years later, an itinerant evangelist named William Booth proclaimed a "boundless salvation" in the streets of England's East London, and The Salvation Army emerged from the convictions he had about his sense of calling. It's important for Salvationists to understand that our doctrines reflect the greater convictions of the church. They are not fringe beliefs; they are part of what has been called "The Christian Tradition." Like convictions in a court room, these doctrines have been formed in light of competing claims and evidence. They are critical judgments based on sustained arguments. Thus I want to give attention in these chapters to the formation of each Salvationist doctrine.[4]

2] Engaging the Doctrine: The Salvation Army's 11 doctrines were established in 1878. They were put in place before the world was aware of Google, steroids and Free Trade coffee. The 21st century is different from Britain in 1878, let alone Tertullian's Roman Empire in the fourth century. How then are these historic convictions to be heard in our day? What questions are posed to Salvationist doctrines now that weren't envisioned in 1878? To what extent do these doctrines make sense to Salvationists in Canada or Denmark or Zimbabwe? Thus I will engage each core conviction with issues at work in our time. These core convictions will matter to the degree that they make sense today.

3] Practising the Doctrine: It's a Salvationist conviction that Christian faith is *practised* faith. There is an obvious danger to thinking about practice as only a rehearsal. Teams practise in preparation for a game. Musicians practise in anticipation of a performance. But we also use the word practice when referring to a *vocation*. Surgeons practise medicine and lawyers practise law; this is what they do. Salvationists practise Christian faith; this is who we are and what we do.

In order to pursue this question, I intend to put each doctrine in conversation with a Salvationist understanding of holiness.[5] My reason for choosing this method is suggested by Roger Green, who argues that The Salvation Army's doctrine of holiness "... is the doctrine by which we interpret and live out our common life."[6] My goal is to explore the connection between The Salvation Army's affirmations of faith and its defining practice of holiness.

> The Salvation Army's doctrine of holiness is the doctrine by which we interpret and live out our common life
> —Roger Green

Convictions matter. They mattered to Abraham Lincoln, whose influence is still felt in America and beyond. Lincoln had no sooner assumed the office of president in 1861 when the tragic Civil War broke out. His unique capacity to forge a cabinet team out of men who had rivaled him for that office did much to gain trust. His ability to find humour in some of the most difficult situations helped others to feel at ease in his presence. It was Lincoln's steadfast convictions, however, that guided his leadership. In particular, "His conviction that [the United States] is one nation, indivisible, 'conceived in Liberty, and dedicated to the proposition that all men are created equal,' led to the rebirth of a union free of slavery."[7] Convictions matter because they make a difference.

Since affirming my ordination vows as a Salvation Army officer, I have come to a much greater appreciation of Salvationist doctrines. But I sense us entering a new moment in history. We may not be able to discern all that lies ahead, but I believe it's important to engage that future with our core convictions. I believe it's important to faithfully teach their transforming role for this moment. Salvationist convictions matter. With this in mind, let's begin our work together. In so doing we, too, may discover, "It's the quality of one's convictions that determines success, not the number of followers."

Reflection Questions for Introduction

1. Express one of your convictions by completing the sentence, "I believe...." Why is this conviction important to you?
2. Name a conviction you have about food. How did this conviction come to be important for you? How has this conviction changed

over the years? What difference does this conviction make to the way you live?

3. Read the 11 doctrines of The Salvation Army and the Introduction to this book.
4. Which of the Army's doctrines do you think is more important? Why?
5. Which of the Army's doctrines do you find more puzzling? Why?
6. What are some other vocations that use the word "practice" to describe their work?
7. What is one thing you hope to gain from this study of the Army's core convictions?

Endnotes for Introduction

1 Spoken by Professor Lupin in the film, *Harry Potter and the Deathly Hallows: Part 2*. Directed by David Yates. Warner Brothers. Based on the novel by J. K. Rowling, 2011.

2 When cadets are about to be ordained and commissioned, they publicly proclaim the doctrines and are asked: "Do you promise to faithfully teach these doctrines?" This question regarding an officer's convictions is part of a larger series of events which includes the Officer's Covenant, ordination and commissioning, and confirmation of the officer's initial appointment. For the most recent edition of *The Handbook of Doctrine* see, The General of The Salvation Army, *The Salvation Army Handbook of Doctrine 2010* (London: Salvation Books, 2010). The doctrines can also be found at: https://www.salvationist.org/extranet_main.nsf/vw_sublinks/a98a5a4b56a0d43a80256cd8002f8126?opendocument. Accessed February 28, 2013.

3 The disconnect between belief and practice is part of a much larger picture in the western world. The modern era, from the 1700s to the late 20th century, effectively severed their connection. Universities focused on theoretical research, but the practice of that research became the concern of others. As it relates to the church, Ellen Charry argues, "The divorce of theoretical from practical concerns ... has been maintained at a high price: Intellectual concerns have obscured the moral shaping function of Christian beliefs." This author argues that doctrine has traditionally assumed a practical function in the church, which is "the formation of character." See Ellen T. Charry, "The Moral Function of Doctrine," Theology Today 49 (April 1992): 33. The theme of healing the polarization between belief and practice is also developed by Randy L. Maddox, "Spirituality and Practical Theology: Trajectories Toward Reengagement," Association of Practical Theology Occasional Papers 3 (Spring 1999): 10-16.

4 See Earl Robinson, "The History of Salvation Army Doctrine," *Word and Deed* 2 (May 2000): 31-45. In this article Robinson traces the roots of Salvationist doctrines in the Wesleyan Movement. His contention is that "From the beginnings of The Salvation Army in 1865 as the East London Revival Society to the present, there has always been a definite creed to which the movement's members have subscribed." He also draws attention to *The Salvation Army Act of 1980* which sets out the conditions under which these doctrines may be revised. For the place of doctrines in the early church, see Catherine Gunsalus Gonzalez, "The Rule of Faith," in W. Brueggemann and George W Stroup eds., *Many Voices, One God* (Louisville: Westminister John Knox Press, 1998).

5 This is usually considered to be the Army's Doctrine 10. In order to sustain this conversation among the doctrines, I will hold off discussion of the 10th doctrine until the last chapter, and I will also include a chapter on the church, which has received attention recently in the 2010 edition of The Salvation Army Handbook of Doctrine.

6 Roger J. Green, "Facing History: Our Way Ahead for a Salvationist Theology," *Word and Deed* 1 (Spring 1999): 33.

7 Doris Kearns Goodwin, *Team of Rivals: The Political Genius of Abraham Lincoln* (New York: Simon and Shuster Paperpacks, 2012), 749.

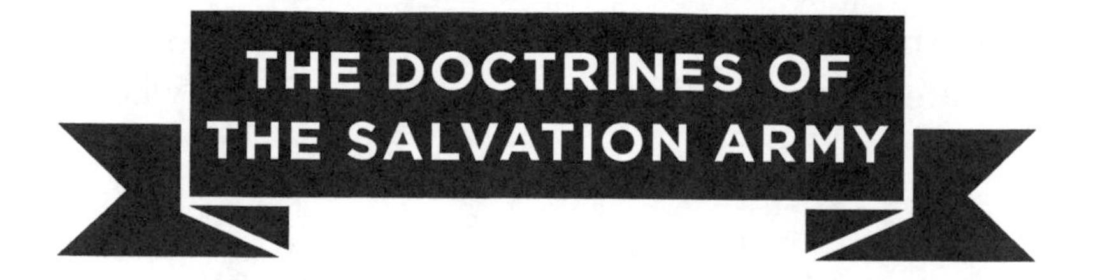

1. We believe that the Scriptures of the Old and New Testaments were given by inspiration of God, and that they only constitute the Divine rule of Christian faith and practice.

2. We believe that there is only one God, who is infinitely perfect, the Creator, Preserver, and Governor of all things, and who is the only proper object of religious worship.

3. We believe that there are three persons in the Godhead—the Father, the Son and the Holy Ghost, undivided in essence and co-equal in power and glory.

4. We believe that in the person of Jesus Christ the Divine and human natures are united, so that He is truly and properly God and truly and properly man.

5. We believe that our first parents were created in a state of innocency, but by their disobedience they lost their purity and happiness, and that in consequence of their fall all men have become sinners, totally depraved, and as such are justly exposed to the wrath of God.

6. We believe that the Lord Jesus Christ has by His suffering and death made an atonement for the whole world so that whosoever will may be saved.

7. We believe that repentance towards God, faith in our Lord Jesus Christ, and regeneration by the Holy Spirit, are necessary to salvation.

8. We believe that we are justified by grace through faith in our Lord Jesus Christ and that he that believeth hath the witness in himself.

9. We believe that continuance in a state of salvation depends upon continued obedient faith in Christ.

10. We believe that it is the privilege of all believers to be wholly sanctified, and that their whole spirit and soul and body may be preserved blameless unto the coming of our Lord Jesus Christ.

11. We believe in the immortality of the soul; in the resurrection of the body; in the general judgment at the end of the world; in the eternal happiness of the righteous; and in the endless punishment of the wicked.

The Bible: Holiness as *Biblical* Spirituality

We believe that the Scriptures of the Old and New Testaments were given by inspiration of God, and that they only constitute the Divine rule of Christian faith and practice.—Doctrine 1

With Christ as our true teacher, we are called to become people of character, a holy people, who perform the Scriptures wisely and faithfully so that God may be at home in our midst.—L. Gregory Jones[1]

THE SALVATION ARMY'S FIRST DOCTRINE IS CONCERNED with the Christian Bible. This remarkable book has had a profound impact throughout the world. Its language has made its way into public discourse, and themes of its stories have been re-created in novels, film, painting and music. For instance, when we say somebody has seen "the writing on the wall," we have alluded to the Book of Daniel; Micah's words, "They shall beat swords into ploughshares," has been inscribed into the United Nations building in New York; Rembrandt painted many biblical scenes, such as *The Return of the Prodigal,* and the jazz pianist, Dave Brubeck, composed *Forty Days,* based on Jesus' temptations in the wilderness. The Scriptures of the Old and New Testaments, so central to Christian faith, have had a remarkable influence in our world.

On the other hand, the Bible has also come under suspicion in the 21st century. Its importance can no longer be assumed. Its language is seldom recognized or understood today. Indeed its portrayal of God is seen by some as problematic. As we begin our work on the Army's core convictions, we need to understand how and why this first doctrine came to be formed, and engage it with 21st-century concerns about the Bible. Then we can ask how it contributes to our understanding and practice of holiness. Our convictions about the Christian Scriptures matter.

Forming the Doctrine

The Christian Bible is a remarkably diverse book. It contains deeply personal letters, poetry that sometimes shakes its fist at God, genealogies that teach and parables that shape our imaginations. Whatever else might be said of the Bible, Salvationists view it as sacred Scripture, both Old and New Testaments.[2] How the Bible came to be affirmed as Scripture is instructive.

A primary clue to the importance of the Bible is found in the life of Christ himself. When Jesus began his public ministry, he went to Nazareth's synagogue and read from the prophet Isaiah: "The Spirit of the Lord is upon me, because he has anointed me to bring good news to the poor. He has sent me to proclaim release to the captives and recovery of sight to the blind, to let the oppressed go free, to proclaim the year of the Lord's favour." As the congregation looked intently at him, Jesus continued: "Today this scripture has been fulfilled in your hearing" (Luke 4:18-21).[3] Luke's Gospel goes on to portray Jesus as he lives out his mission of releasing captives, giving sight to the blind and proclaiming the year of Jubilee.[4] After his crucifixion and resurrection, the risen Christ joined two grieving disciples on the road to Emmaus. As they walked together, "he interpreted to them the things about himself in all the scriptures" (Luke 24:27). Jesus viewed his mission through the interpretive lens of Israel's Scriptures.

How the New Testament itself came to be viewed as Scripture is a long and complex process. When the church moved into its second and third generations, it became clear that the voices of its foundational leaders had begun to disappear. The Apostle Paul and others were no longer alive to write letters of encouragement or criticism. Something more permanent was needed to say, "This is our story; this is who we are; this is what it means to be Christian." Many texts were in circulation, but by the second and third centuries, leaders like Irenaeus and Origen began to list various writings they considered authoritative. In the next century, Bishop Athanasius wrote an Easter letter to his flock, and in it he went on to name those 27 writings that form our present New Testament. By the end of the fourth century, the church had affirmed its authoritative collection of sacred writings.

It was an assumption of the early church that its sacred Scriptures also included the Old Testament. The church viewed its story to be continuous with Israel's story. Jesus himself taught that he had come not "to abolish the law and the prophets ... but to fulfil" them.[5] The importance of the Old Testament is endorsed by Jesus. However, some early Christians took issue with this conviction. Marcion, for instance, lived in the second century and believed that the Old Testament portrayed a wrathful God in contrast to the New Testament's God of love. As a result, he deleted the Old Testament and edited out some New Testament books that reflected a strong indebtedness to Judaism. Marcion's anti-Jewish stance was rejected by his contemporary church, but his spirit has affected the church in other periods. During the 1930s, Nazi anti-Semitism sought to eliminate the study of the Old Testament from German universities. Courageous scholars such as Gerhard von Rad resisted this movement at personal cost. Salvationists join with the greater church in authorizing the Old Testament as essential for Christian faith. The Old Testament is not "second class."[6] Salvationist faith is rooted in *both* the Old and New Testaments.

When Athanasius published his list of authoritative New Testament writings, some of its authors might have been surprised to see their work included. For instance, Luke begins his Gospel by saying that "I too decided, after investigating everything carefully from the very first, to write an orderly account" of the life of Jesus (Luke 1:3). All biblical writings spring from the minds, hearts and concerns of *human* authors. Luke composed his Gospel to instruct Theophilus. Paul wrote to the Galatians with some frustration to help get this young church back on track. The composition and collection of the biblical writings has been a fully human process. Salvationists do not claim a flawless, purely dictated text from God. The Bible comes to us through the work of its human authors and the reconstruction of its texts based on the manuscripts available. This realization is characteristic of our faith: God risks important communication through ordinary people and ordinary words.

Yet while we acknowledge the thoroughly human hand in the biblical writings, this first doctrine also expresses the view that the Bible was "given by *inspiration* of God." The classic text for this belief is 2 Timothy 3:16, which says: "All scripture is inspired by God." Literally it means that Scripture is "God-breathed." This doesn't imply that the biblical writers were passive recorders; they were in fact fully engaged in the composition. Yet so was the Spirit of God. While the Psalmists, Jeremiah, Mark and unknown editors wrote and compiled the Bible, God worked through their personalities and abilities to produce these texts. Thoroughly human, the Bible is also "given by inspiration of God."[7] When we read Luke's words we also read them as the Word of God.[8] These ancient words are also the contemporary Word of God. They are inspired Scripture.

This first core conviction of The Salvation Army authorizes not just the individual 66 books of the Bible, but their formation into one Book. The result is called the *canon* of Scripture. In other words, the various books of the Bible were not simply thrown together like tossed salad. They were sequenced in a particular way. The Christian Bible begins with the phrase, "In the beginning when God created the heavens and the earth" (Genesis 1:1) and concludes with John of Patmos's vision: "Then I saw a new heaven and a new earth" (Revelation 21:1). The whole of the Bible is ordered as a singular story, which is a story of good news or gospel.[9] And while there are dissonances between the various books of the Bible, this tension is welcomed as part of the whole biblical symphony. Each individual book can be properly understood only in light of the greater story, which centres on the person of Jesus of Nazareth.

When we say that the Bible *alone* guides our faith and practice, it's a way of affirming Scripture as the *primary* voice for Christian faith and practice, not the *only* voice. Salvationists also listen to the church's tradition as it bears on any matter. We listen to the contemporary voices of oppressed peoples, the insights of the sciences and arts, believing that God's grace is at work in the experiences of our world today.[10] The Bible may sing the melody, but it's not solo work. The Scriptures are part of an ensemble voicing truthful perspectives.

Bringing these various threads together, Salvationists affirm the Bible as its authoritative sacred Scripture. "We believe" this along with Athanasius, Martin Luther and John Wesley. We hold this core conviction with Catherine Booth who, when she argued with Reverend Rees regarding the place of women in Christian ministry, wrote, "Hence, drawing our weapon, mainly, from the Word of God, we shall proceed to combat them."[11] Salvationists believe the Christian Bible to be sacred Scripture.

Engaging the Doctrine

We live at a time when our faith convictions can no longer be taken for granted. This is especially true of the doctrine of Christian Scripture. Western culture has been shaped to a large degree by the language and stories of the Bible, such as David and Goliath or the Good Samaritan. However, the Bible is effectively absent from public conversation today. Salvationists in the West practise their faith in a biblically illiterate culture. A visit to any bookstore will show that the word "bible" in our culture tends to mean a kind of do-it-yourself instruction manual, like "The Golfer's Bible" or "A Bible for House Renovation." Let's engage this first affirmation of faith with some issues at work in the 21st century so that we can view the Bible as sacred Scripture for our times.

First, the modern age has raised an important question regarding the *adequacy of language* in matters of faith. With words alone it is difficult to convey the deep affection of a parent for a child, let alone God's love for us. Surely, it is argued by some, any meaningful experience of God is beyond the capacity of words to express. There is merit to this argument. And yet it is with words that a judge declares immigrants to be citizens and pronounces two people to be married. Words are what we have to work with in some of the most important areas of life.

For this reason it's helpful to understand how words work. Observe what happens when a child begins to grasp the meaning of words such as juice, ball, airplane and "No!" It isn't long before a vocabulary forms, and with it the child imagines a world that makes sense. Words enable a child to interpret her place within the world. Words create worlds. We learn to live through language worlds. This is true of any language, but our lives are also formed by such language worlds as computer, sport and business. The Christian Scriptures invite us into a language world. With biblical words such as grace, hope, sin and salvation, we are invited to imagine our world as a place where God is present and active. Biblical words are adequate for their task.

> Deprive children of stories and you leave them unscripted, anxious stutterers in their actions as in their words
> —Alasdair MacIntyre

Second, one of the implications of the Salvationist doctrine of Scripture is that we live not only in the language world of the Bible, but within its *story world*. Stories create identity. They help us to understand who we are. "Deprive children of stories and you leave them unscripted, anxious stutterers in their actions as in their words."[12] Research demonstrates that adults with dementia are best helped when time is taken to learn their stories. One concern of the 21st century, though, is the loss of a story that defines us all. It is commonly argued that there are fragments of stories, but no overarching story. Yet as Robert Fulford notes, "The need to shape the past as a coherent narrative will not leave us, no matter how many disappointments we endure."[13] We yearn for a story that helps to make sense of the whole of our world. The yearning for meaning is embedded deep within us.[14] It's a core conviction of Salvationists that the canon of the Old and New Testaments constitutes our *defining story*. The biblical story has to do with life's meaning. We are formed by other stories, such as family, ethnicity, nation and vocation. But the Bible's story situates us within a larger narrative of God's story in relation to our world.

Third, while this first core conviction affirms the Bible as the story of God's ways in the world, it also affirms the *authority* of the Bible as Scripture. This notion of authority poses difficulties in our culture. Some expressions of authority *are* dangerously coercive, such as that of an abusive parent or drug trafficker. However other expressions of authority invite dialogue, such as a piano teacher with her student. Prior to the modern age, the Bible's authority was virtually unquestioned. But with the maturing of a scientific mindset, all authority came under question, including the authority of the church and the Bible. This is not to be lamented; much good has come with the rejection of authority that is not open to question. But it is also the case that scientists themselves work within the authority of the *scientific tradition*. Scientists practise their vocation within the authority of accepted convictions, questions, symbols and personalities.[15] Lesslie Newbigin draws out the implication of this for the Christian Scriptures:

The need to shape the past as a coherent narrative will not leave us, no matter how many disappointments we endure —Robert Fulford

> When we are received into the Christian community ... we enter into a tradition which claims authority. It is embodied in the Holy Scriptures and in the continuous history of the interpretation of these Scriptures ... This tradition, like the scientific tradition, embodies and carries forward certain ways of looking at things, certain models for interpreting experience.[16]

While The Salvation Army's first doctrine affirms the authority of the Bible, it is not a coercive authority but one that invites genuine dialogue.

Finally, a proper understanding of this doctrine is particularly important as we *converse with other world faiths in the 21st century*. Soon after he assumed the office of General in 2006, Shaw Clifton addressed the United Kingdom's Three Faiths Forum. He did so acknowledging that "as a Salvationist ... I am deeply committed to my own faith as a Christian and to that part of the Christian body known as Salvationism ... However, I am equally committed to the ever-present work of deepening our understanding of the other great faiths of the world and of forming lasting friendships across faith boundaries."[17] Our world no longer grants favoured status to the Christian faith. Christians need to live within a world of many faiths. One way of doing this is to look for shared language. In recent years it has been noted that the phrase "to love God and neighbour" is found not only in the Bible but in the Muslim's Koran. Muslim, Jew and Christian share "common words." This realization has prompted some Muslim and Christian leaders to begin a dialogue around these "common words."[18] They realize that in a global world such as ours, it is absolutely essential that we find ways to understand and work with each other. This doesn't mean compromise in matters of difference between faiths. The Christian community will understand "God" differently than a Muslim. We may even understand the meanings of "love" and "neighbour" differently. But the fact that these words are shared words in our sacred Scriptures opens up important opportunities for conversation and understanding.[19] Our commitment to the Bible as Scripture invites us to engage in conversations of integrity around "common words."

I want to see a new translation of the Bible into the hearts and conduct of living men and women
—William Booth

Thus, while Salvationists acknowledge the full humanity of the Bible's composition, we also believe the Bible to be the Word of God. We value the ethnic, national and vocational narratives that contribute to our sense of identity, but we look to the Bible as our defining narrative. And while we know that the Bible's authority can be misused, we seek a healthy and appropriate expression of its authority in our personal and communal life. When the *Revised Standard Version* of the Bible appeared in the 1880s, William Booth welcomed its arrival but said, "I want to see a new translation of the Bible into the hearts and conduct of living men and women."[20] In his view, the Bible was intended to be made visible in the lives of Salvationists.

Practising the Doctrine

The Bible has played a central role in the life of The Salvation Army. The reading of the Bible at the end of a meal has been an important aspect of family life for many. The public reading of the Bible has characterized Salvationist worship. The rigorous study of the Bible in small groups and schools has proved helpful to many of us. The importance of the Bible prompted Commissioner Gunpei Yamamuro to write a series of commentaries in order to "familiarize people of all classes within Japanese society with biblical teaching."[21] Bob and Ruth Chapman, Canadian Salvationists, followed God's calling to work with Wycliffe Bible Translators, until their tragic death in an air disaster off the coast of West Africa.[22] It is difficult to imagine Salvationists without the Bible having a prominent place.

We need to ask, however, what role should the Bible play in shaping our lives now? When the Apostle Paul expressed his conviction that "All scripture is inspired by God," he went on to say that it "is useful for teaching, for reproof, for correction, and for training in righteousness."[23] The Bible exists not simply to inform but to *form*. John and Charles Wesley affirmed this conviction when they set out to renew the Church of England in the 18th century through the Methodist Movement. They became convinced that God had called the Methodists to "spread *scriptural* holiness throughout the land."[24] But what of the 21st century? A close look at our own age suggests that there is renewed interest in spirituality in western culture. From a Christian perspective, spirituality is best understood as our *lived experience of God*.[25] The spirituality suggested by this doctrine is a *biblical* spirituality. The Christian Scriptures show us what it is like to live in relationship with God, who is disclosed in the biblical story. This is biblical spirituality. With this in mind, I want to suggest there are at least four practices that help to cultivate holiness understood as biblical spirituality: we are to *read, pray, preach and perform the Bible as Scripture*. Let's explore each of these practices.

First, the practice of biblical spirituality means that we will *read the Bible as Scripture*. There are many ways to read the Bible, just as there are many ways to read the script of a play. A theatre critic will read the script one way, and an actor will read the script another way. It depends on the purpose for which they read. Salvationists come to the Bible for the purpose of hearing God address us in the 21st century. The Bible is an ancient text, but it is also God's contemporary word to us. Thus we read the Bible with a view to understanding our world through its world. Convinced that words create worlds, we read the Bible slowly and prayerfully, paying attention to such words as grace, wilderness, atonement, covenant, holiness, hope and salvation. We do not assume that our culture's use of these words means the same thing when used in the Bible. We also pay attention to the story worlds of the Bible. Through these stories we envision what it means for us to meet with God as friend with friend, as did Moses.[26] We imagine a world where Jesus washes our feet with basin and towel, just as he did the feet of his disciples, even over their protests.[27] These stories, and others, give us a glimpse into the character of God and what it means to relate to God today as disciple and friend. They are, however, not just examples; they are models for us to imitate.[28] For this reason we not only read the Bible personally, we read the Bible in community. The Bible is the church's book and is intended to be read in the meeting of God's people.[29] This first doctrine points to the practice of *reading the Bible as Scripture* in order to be formed in biblical holiness.

The Bible is an ancient text, but it is also God's contemporary word to us

Second, we will learn to *pray the Scriptures* as we practise biblical spirituality. This is not to say that prayer is limited only to the texts of the Bible, but there are spiritual disciplines that draw on Scripture as we pray. For instance, the Lord's Prayer is drawn from the Gospels, and the benediction spoken by Moses in Numbers is used often in worship, as is Paul's closing benediction to the Corinthian church.[30] While much of the Bible lends itself to prayer, this is especially true of the Psalms. There are times of tragedy or joy when we can't seem to find words to pray. Praying the Psalms can help us in those moments. They utter lament with images that voice our own losses; they praise with resounding chords that take us out of our superficiality; they question God in ways we are reluctant to address God; they express trust in ways that we find difficult.[31] During the 1930s when the Nazis came to power in Germany, Dietrich Bonhoeffer created an alternative seminary to train Lutheran pastors. They began each day praying a Psalm together. In opposition to Nazi policy, Bonhoeffer wrote a small book connecting the Lord's Prayer to the Psalms. His instructions then are relevant to us now: "The richness of the Word of God ought to determine our prayer, not the poverty of our heart."[32]

The richness of the Word of God ought to determine our prayer, not the poverty of our heart
—Dietrich Bonhoeffer

Praying the Bible also includes artistic expressions of its texts in worship. It has been argued that if we were to suddenly lose access to the Bible, we could recover it through the 6,000 hymns of Charles Wesley because they are saturated with the language of Scripture.[33] Praying the Bible includes choral and instrumental music, mime and dance. It's difficult to imagine The Salvation Army without music.[34] We are shaped by the biblical world when we play and sing music that resonates with that world. The European Reformation was impacted deeply by Martin Luther and his songs, such as *A Mighty Fortress Is Our God,* based on Psalm 46. The word "hallelujah" virtually rings when spoken, but when sung to the music of George Frederic Handel's *Hallelujah Chorus*, it is electrifying. *Praying* the Christian Scriptures becomes an important way to be formed in biblical holiness.

As we seek scriptural holiness we will attend to the practice of *preaching biblically.* The Salvation Army places an emphasis on preaching in its worship, given its roots in the Reformation.[35] But preaching has come upon hard times in our culture. "Don't preach at me," tends to mean, "Don't criticize me." The depiction of preaching in television and movies often deals with stereotypes and seldom does justice to good preaching in the Bible or in the Christian tradition. It was argued earlier in this chapter that the Bible is the church's book. Thus it is read publicly in our worship, and sermons form an important part of that worship. In Fred Craddock's view, "Preaching brings the Scriptures forward as a living voice in the congregation. Biblical texts have a future as well as a past, and preaching seeks to fulfil that future by continuing the conversation of the text into the present."[36]

Salvationists are practitioners of biblical spirituality

One important role the Bible can play in preaching is to help *shape the form* of our preaching. Sermons have a structure or form, just as a building has architectural form. The form of biblical texts can suggest the form of a sermon. Parables tease the imagination, but if we turn the parable of the Good Samaritan into a three-point sermon we risk victimizing the parable itself. The Psalms are intended to teach us, and a sermon on a Psalm will instruct, but like the Psalm it will also pray. Biblical texts can inform the structure of our sermons. An important contribution of the Bible to preaching is the *biblical canon*. There is a point to the Bible being organized from Genesis to Revelation. The spirituality that the Bible portrays has its twists and turns, but it moves towards a goal, as does our personal spirituality. We will learn much about spirituality from preaching Esther, Ecclesiastes and Ephesians. But we will also want to preach with the biblical plot in mind. Salvationists will experience little narrative plot when our preaching leaps from Paul one Sunday to Jonah the next and Revelation the next. Such disjointed readings can create a disjointed spirituality. Leaders of Salvationist worship need to sit down and plan with the Bible's narrative structure in mind.[37] Biblical holiness has a story, and we do well to keep its overall plot in mind as we prepare to preach it.

Finally, we will learn to practise holiness as biblical spirituality as we *perform the Scriptures*. L. Gregory Jones has expressed it this way: "With Christ as our true teacher, we are called to become people of character, a holy people, who *perform the Scriptures wisely and faithfully* so that God may be at home in our midst."[38] Certainly there are dangers in thinking of the Christian life as performance; it can too often imply lack of sincerity. But we also use the word to describe the way cars drive on the highway, or Olympic athletes compete during the Games. In other words, the notion of performance has to do with the way we take scripts and bring them to life. Salvationists have performed biblical texts artistically, such as with the John Larsson and John Gowans' musicals like *Hosea*. But this image of performance goes beyond our worship into lived faith. As noted earlier in this chapter, Jesus began his public ministry by reading from Isaiah, and then went about freeing the oppressed and embodying the Year of Jubilee. In other words, *Jesus performed the Scriptures* in his public ministry.[39] Like musicians and actors, Christians take the biblical script and perform it before a watching world. Salvationists perform the biblical text when we practise hospitality with new immigrants, provide sanctuary for abused women and engage in healthy conversation with our Muslim or Hindu neighbours.[40] A wise and faithful performance of the Bible will make God's saving grace visible in our world. Scriptural holiness involves the intentional performance of the Bible.

Salvationists thus have an important heritage that values the Christian Scriptures. Our commitment to scriptural holiness lies at the heart of our identity. This is who we are. This core conviction matters! We are practitioners of biblical spirituality. The Salvationist tradition is important; our personal experiences are valued; but the integrity of our spirituality will be governed by the degree to which it really is a *scriptural* holiness. Lynn Deshazo has composed a song that reflects the transforming influence of the Bible. It's an appropriate prayer as we approach Scripture, and prepare our hearts to hear it as the Word of God:

> Holy word long preserved for our walk in this world;
> They resound with God's own heart, O, let the ancient words impart;
> Words of life, words of hope, give us strength, help us cope;
> In this world where're we roam, Ancient words will guide us home.
>
> *Ancient words, ever true, changing me, and changing you;*
> *We have come with open hearts, O let the ancient words impart.*

Holy words of our faith handed down to this age,
Came to us through sacrifice; O heed the faithful words of Christ;
Holy words long preserved for our walk in this world;
They resound with God's own heart; O let the ancient words impart.[41]

It is important that the Army's core convictions begin with a doctrine of Scripture. It signals that each doctrine is grounded in the Bible. The Christian Scriptures have given rise to the doctrines that constitute Salvationist identity. The next three doctrines will focus our attention on core convictions about the God of the biblical story.

Reflection Questions for Chapter One

1. How were you introduced to the Bible?
2. If you are studying this book with a group, read the chapter together.
3. What phrase or section caught your attention? Why?

Forming the Doctrine:

4. What role has the Bible played in your life over the years?
5. What parts of the Bible are you drawn to? What parts of the Bible do you tend to avoid?
6. Read Luke 1:1-4 and 2 Timothy 3:16. What do you think Luke would say if he thought his work would be included in sacred Scripture? Have there been occasions when God has taken your efforts and used them far beyond your imagining?

Engaging the Doctrine:

7. What titles have you come across in bookstores that use the word "bible"?
8. What biblical words are important to you? Why?
9. What biblical story or book have you found helpful in your spiritual growth?

10. How do you respond to the suggestion that there are constructive and destructive forms of authority? Can you think of ways the Bible has been used destructively?

Practising the Doctrine:

11. What is your practice of *reading* the Bible?
12. What role does preaching play in the life of your congregation?
13. How do you respond to the image of "performing Scripture"?
14. In what ways have you, personally and communally, sought to *perform* the Bible? With what results?

Conclude: Pray a Psalm or the Lord's Prayer.

Endnotes for Chapter One

1 L. Gregory Jones, "Formed and Transformed by Scripture," in *Character and Scripture*, ed. William P. Brown (Grand Rapids: Eerdmans Publishing, 2002), 33.

2 I am conscious of current discussions about the language of "Old" and "New" in connection with the Testaments of the Bible. Some have begun using "First" and "Second" Testament in order to overcome the suggestion that "New" is better than "Old." Others use the phrase "Hebrew Bible" instead of "Old Testament." What needs to be kept in mind is that *both* Testaments together constitute Christian Scripture.

3 All biblical references will be taken from the *New Revised Standard Version,* unless otherwise noted.

4 It should be noted that "the year of the Lord's favour" is an allusion to Leviticus 25 and the year when slaves were granted freedom and property was restored to its original owners. This came to be known as the Day of Jubilee.

5 See Matthew 5:17-20.

6 Donald E. Burke, "Second-Class Scripture?" *Salvationist* (August 2010): 20-21.

7 " ... most Christians recognize that inspiration is not dictation, and there is nothing in Scripture to indicate that God obliterated the human personalities of the authors and turned them into copyists. Their individual styles of writing, habits of thinking, cultural background and human limitations can be seen in the biblical text." See *The Salvation Army Handbook of Doctrine* (London: Salvation Books, 2010), 5.

8 It should be noted that the phrase "Word of God" is a metaphor, and metaphors live with the tension between what the image "is" and "is not." See Sandra M. Schneiders, *The Revelatory Text: Interpreting the New Testament as Sacred Scripture* (New York: HarperCollins Publishers, 1991), 27-33.

9 Mark's Gospel begins with the heading: "The beginning of the good news of Jesus Christ" (Mark 1:1), where the phrase "good news" means "gospel."

10 It will be apparent to some that I am pointing to what is often called the "Wesleyan Quadrilateral." The phrase was coined by Albert Outler, to describe his understanding of John Wesley's approach to theology. It involves appropriate reasoning of biblical faith, with the *tradition* of the church and contemporary *experience*. I take *tradition* in the sense spoken by Alasdair MacIntyre as "an historically extended, socially embodied argument." In other words, the church seeks to embody the argument that God's grace has been expressed fully in Jesus of Nazareth.

11 Catherine Booth, *Female Teaching* (London: G. J. Stevenson, 1861 Edition), 7. For a detailed account of Catherine Booth's approach to the Bible, see Gillian E. Brown, "Catherine Booth: Faithful Interpreter of Scripture" (Master of Religion Thesis, Wycliffe College and University of Toronto, 2004).

12 Quoted in Robert Fulford, *The Triumph of Narrative* (Toronto: Anansi Press, 1999), 33.

13 Fulford, *The Triumph of Narrative*, 61.

14 "To be human is to ask the question, 'Why?' " See Jonathan Sacks, *The Great Partnership: Science, Religion, and the Search for Meaning* (New York: Schocken Books, 2011), 25.

15 This awareness was articulated in a most important book in the 1960s: Thomas S. Kuhn, *The Structure of Scientific Revolutions, 2nd Edition* (Chicago: The University of Chicago Press, 1970).

16 Lesslie Newbigin, *The Gospel in a Pluralist Society* (Grand Rapids: Eerdmans Publishing, 1989), 49.

17 Shaw Clifton, *Selected Writings: Volume 2 – 2000-2010* (London: Salvation Books, 2010), 36. Since moving to Manitoba in retirement I have become involved with the Manitoba Multifaith Council. This group brings together a number of different faith traditions and seeks common ground especially in issues of health and justice.

18 Matthew 22:34-40; Deuteronomy 6:5; Leviticus 19:18. The dialogue mentioned here was initiated by Muslim scholars in 2007. See Miroslav Volf, Ghazi bin Muhammad and Melissa Yarrington, *A Common Word: Muslims and Christians on Loving God and Neighbor* (Grand Rapids: Eerdmans Publishing, 2010).

19 Miroslav Volf states his Christian conviction this way: "Deep faith expresses itself in love, and love, understood as active care, leads to respect of and struggle for others' rights. Put differently ... *commitment to the properly understood love of God and neighbor makes deeply religious persons...into dedicated social pluralists.*" See *A Common Word*, 24.

20 Quoted in *The 2010 Salvation Army Handbook of Doctrine*, 10.

21 R. David Rightmire, *Salvationist Samurai: Gunpei Yamamuro and the Rise of The Salvation Army in Japan* (Lanham: The Scarecrow Press, 1997), 65.

22 Their story is told by Robert Chapman, *In Heavenly Love Abiding* (Belleville: Guardian Books, 2001).

23 See 2 Timothy 3:16.

24 As the Methodist Movement matured, its Minutes of 1763 responded to the question: "What may we reasonably believe to be God's design in raising up the Preachers called Methodists?" And the answer given was: "To reform the nation and, in particular, the Church; to spread scriptural holiness over the land." See Richard P. Heitzenrater, *Wesley and the People Called Methodists* (Nashville: Abingdon Press, 1995), 214.

25 "By Christian spirituality I mean the lived experience of Christian faith." Sandra Schneiders, "Biblical Spirituality," *Interpretation* (April 2002): 134.

26 See Exodus 32-34.

27 See John 13:1-20.

28 Schneiders, "Biblical Spirituality,"134

29 Joel Green argues that "the single most important practice to cultivate is

involvement in reading scripture with others who take its message seriously and who meet regularly to discern its meaning for life and faith." See Joel B. Green, "Scripture and Theology: Failed Experiments, Fresh Perspectives," *Interpretation* 56 (2002): 19.

30 See Matthew 6:9-13; Numbers 6:24-26; 2 Corinthians 13:13.

31 For helpful introductions to praying the Psalms, see Bruce A. Power, *Conversations with God: Psalms as a Resource for Prayer and Meditation* (Toronto: The Salvation Army, 2005), and Walter Brueggemann, *Praying the Psalms* (Winona, MN: Saint Mary's Press, 1986).

32 See Dietrich Bonhoeffer, *Psalms: The Prayer Book of the Bible* (Minneapolis: Augsburg Publishing House, 1970), 15.

33 See John Rattenbury's comments in John R. Tyson, *Assist Me To Proclaim: The Life and Hymns of Charles Wesley* (Grand Rapids: Eerdmans Publishing, 2007), 258.

34 However, "it is not enough to say music is an expression of identity; it is part of the way identity is formed. In short, we do not simply make music, to some extent music makes us." Jeremy S. Begbie, *Resounding Truth* (Grand Rapids: Baker Academic, 2007), 46.

35 For a recent and important treatment of preaching in the Salvationist tradition, see Julie A. Slous, *Preaching a Disturbing Gospel* (Toronto: The Salvation Army Canada and Bermuda, 2012).

36 Fred B. Craddock, *Preaching* (Nashville: Abingdon Press, 1985), 27.

37 Fred Craddock sounds his own concern: "A preaching program is a servant not a master ... However, if a preacher has no plan ... then the slightest noise in the community will sound like a cannon in the homiletically empty ear and the slightest ripple in the congregation will register like an earthquake on that blank paper on the minister's desk. Into the vacuum of no advance planning, with nothing against which to measure the emergency's right to the pulpit, rushes the hasty topic and another journalistic sermon is soon to be preached." See Fred B. Craddock, *Preaching*, 103.

38 L. Gregory Jones, "Formed and Transformed by Scripture," 33, emphasis mine.

39 It is instructive to note that the image of performance is emphasized in biblical scholarship. "In recent study of the nature of NT interpretation ... there is one metaphor that is particularly appropriate for articulating what NT interpretation involves. It is the metaphor of *performance*." See Stephen C. Barton, "New Testament Interpretation as Performance," *Scottish Journal of Theology* 52 (1999): 179.

40 Note that hospitality is an important theme of Luke's Gospel, such as Luke 19:1-10; sanctuary is an important biblical concern to protect the vulnerable.

41 *Ancient Words* by Lynn Deshazo (C) 2001 Integrity's Hosanna! Music/ASCAP.

One God: Holiness as Integrity

We believe that there is only one God, who is infinitely perfect, the Creator, Preserver, and Governor of all things, and who is the only proper object of religious worship.
—Doctrine 2

A person's conception of holiness is governed by the character of God he [or she] worships.—Frederick Coutts[1]

THE SALVATION ARMY'S SECOND DOCTRINE TURNS ITS attention to God. To speak of God in our times, however, risks the accusation of "delusion"[2] on the one hand, or the emptiness of Twitter's "omg" on the other. Certainly there are legitimate questions regarding God: What God are we speaking about? What is the source of our knowledge about God? In light of our multi-faith world, is there a distinctively Christian way of speaking about God? While not claiming to be exhaustive, this second core conviction contributes to this discussion.

Salvationist faith affirms that God is ultimately beyond human grasp, but has taken the initiative to make himself known.[3] With the Apostle Paul, we are aware that "For now we see in a mirror, dimly, but then we will see face to face. Now I know only in part; then I will know fully, even as I have been fully known" (1 Corinthians 13:12). Yet we affirm that God *can* be known because of God's self-disclosure in the history of Israel, and particularly in the person of Jesus of Nazareth. This self-disclosure of God is not exhaustive, but it is graciously true. It will become clear that there is a distinctive way to speak of God Christianly, which is to name God as Father, Son and Holy Spirit. However, the church has never lost sight of its confession that God is one, which has important implications for our understanding and practice of holiness. In order to give attention to God's identity, let's look first at this core conviction regarding God as one.

Forming the Doctrine

The second doctrine begins with the phrase, "We believe that there is only one God." The phrase "one God" is fundamental to this core conviction, and forms the heart of biblical faith. The background to this conviction lies with the Book of Deuteronomy: "Hear, O Israel: The LORD our God, the LORD is one. Love the LORD your God with all your heart and with all your soul and with all your strength" (Deuteronomy 6:4-5 *NIV*).[4] The conviction that God is one also underlies New Testament faith. Jesus was asked by a scribe, "Of all the commandments, which is the most important?" His response drew from Israel's confession: " 'Hear, O Israel, the LORD our God, the LORD is one ... ' The second is this: 'Love your neighbour as yourself.' There is no other commandment greater than these" (Mark 12:28-31). The whole of biblical faith assumes the conviction that God is *one*.

A couple of observations are in order, however. First, it's important to realize that the Hebrew language underlying our translations of Deuteronomy 6:4-5 can be heard in two ways: "The Lord is our God, the Lord alone," or "The Lord our God, the Lord is one."[5] There are differences in meaning between the two translations, both with significance for our doctrine. When Israel confessed that God was "the Lord alone," it drew attention to their loyalty. They would have "no other gods." Their worship, love and obedience would be directed to "the Lord alone." On the other hand, by expressing the conviction that "the Lord is one," Israel drew attention to God's loyalty. Patrick Miller notes the implication:

> To confess, therefore, that the Lord is "one" is to claim that [God] ... is faithful, consistent, not divided within mind, heart, or self in any way ... The presence and involvement of God in the world and in shaping history and human destiny is not in

one guise now and in another guise elsewhere. In purpose and being, God is one.[6]

To speak of God as "one" has everything to do with God's character. The actions of God in the biblical story disclose God's faithfulness and integrity.

To speak of God as "one" has everything to do with God's character

As we attend to the rest of this second doctrine, we will keep God's character in mind. Because God is one, God creates, preserves and governs all things with integrity and faithfulness.

We believe in one God ... Creator of all things

It's a Christian conviction that we live in a *created* world: "In the beginning God created the heavens and the earth" (Genesis 1:1 *NIV*). The Book of Genesis unfolds the relationship of Creator to creation through the story that follows. As early as the second century CE, however, voices suggested a distinction between the God who created the world and the God who redeemed humanity. According to the Gnostics, an inferior creator produced a material world. The superior God of the New Testament redeemed this material world through spiritual actions. These convictions raised red flags for church leaders like Irenaeus. Eventually the battle to overcome this polarization between creation and redemption found its way into the early creeds. The Nicene Creed in the fourth century begins with the affirmation: "We believe in one God, the Father, the Almighty, the maker of all things seen and unseen." All things! The refusal to separate creation from redemption finds expression in Joachim Neander's hymn: "Praise to the Lord, the Almighty, the King of *creation*; O my soul, praise him, for he is thy health and *salvation*; All ye who hear, Brothers and sisters draw near, Praise him in glad adoration."[7] Thus in Scripture, creed and song, the Christian church has emphasized this world as a created world. The one God creates and saves with integrity and faithfulness.

We believe in one God ... Preserver of all things

God not only created our world but actively sustains it in the present. Some of the Psalms sing of God's sustaining work in creation. Psalm 145, for instance, draws on poetic language to depict this relationship: "The LORD is faithful in all his words, and gracious in all his deeds. The eyes of all look to you, and you give them their food in due season. You open your hand, satisfying the desire of every living thing" (Psalm 145:13, 15-16). What this Psalm affirms, along with the greater Christian tradition, is that all of creation is sustained by God. God preserves the universe through his ongoing relationship with it: "He's got the whole world in his hands!"[8] A word that captures God's sustaining work in history is "providence."[9] It's a way of affirming that God has a hand in guiding events and people to his ultimate purposes. The Book of Ruth narrates such a story. Ruth is an alien, an outsider. Out of concern for her mother-in-law, Naomi, Ruth goes into a field to glean its harvest. "As it happened" Ruth gleaned from the crops of its owner, Boaz. This "chance" meeting eventually leads to marriage, and a son who becomes the grandfather of David. It becomes evident that even in these difficult times God is working out his purposes through deep losses, the agricultural custom of gleaning, a conniving mother-in-law, sexual advances, an old marriage custom and the faithfulness of individuals to their promises. In faithfulness, God *preserved* his purposes with Israel in and through free human actions. Thus it is an important conviction that God did not simply give the world a beginning, and then stand back to watch it unfold. Without undermining humanity's freedom, God's preserving, providential presence is ongoing.

> God's faithful integrity governs God's exercise of sovereign power

We believe in one God ... Governor of all things

When we speak of God as "the Governor of all things," we acknowledge God's sovereign rule over the world. We insist however that God's sovereignty is governed by God's character. The Bible portrays God as the world's sovereign ruler: "The LORD is king, he is robed in majesty; the LORD is robed, he is girded in strength. He has established the world; it shall never be moved; your throne is established from of old; you are from everlasting" (Psalm 93:1-2). The early creeds emphasize belief in "God the Father, *Almighty.*" It's important that we read the Bible carefully to discern what is meant by God's power, because it is a Christian conviction that the cross of Christ ultimately defines "the power of God" (1 Corinthians 1:18). The cross expresses God's utterly unique, holy, love. Parents realize that love does not always get its way. Love is vulnerable, risky. As Bette Midler sings it:

> You've got to give a little, take a little,
> And let your poor heart break a little.
> That's the story of, that's the glory of love.[10]

The "give and take" of love plays out in the biblical story. God's creative and sustaining purposes animate the story. But when we affirm God as Governor of all things, we affirm God's intention and ability to bring all things to their final realization. Because God is sovereign, all other forms of power are relative: "Belief in God has historically been the only way to establish the moral limits of power."[11] Only the sovereign God, vulnerable in love, is worthy of our worship and trust. God's faithful integrity governs God's exercise of sovereign power.

One God. Infinitely perfect. The only proper object of religious worship.

The Lord is one! The Lord alone!

Engaging the Doctrine

This core conviction about one God was formed over long periods of time. When we attend to this affirmation of faith today, we hear its emphasis on God's creative and governing love in the wake of global wars and in the face of deep ecological concerns. We also wonder about its relevance alongside other world religions. There is no merit in burying our heads in the sand. Let's engage this doctrine with some of the issues that have emerged in our time.

First, the framers of the Nicene Creed had not heard about continental shifts or atom colliders when they confessed belief in "one

God, the Father, the Almighty, the maker of all things seen and unseen." Nor had the framers of The Salvation Army's doctrines heard about DNA or the Hubble telescope. It's essential, therefore, that we *engage this particular doctrine with scientific understandings of the world and universe*. The church has not always had a comfortable relationship with science. Its resistance to the findings of Copernicus and Galileo took time to overcome. The fallout from Darwin's work continues to occupy good minds today. If the church should have learned anything from the history of this perceived conflict between science and faith, it is the need to trust the integrity of *both* scientific and faith convictions. The implication of this doctrine is that the creator of our universe is also the author of faith's story. Science views our world through one lens and religious faith through another. Each has its separate task, but both are required to complete the picture. Jonathan Sacks offers this distinction: "*Science takes things apart to see how they work. Religion puts things together to see what they mean.*"[12] For instance, scientists can describe much that contributed to the sinking of the Titanic in the spring of 1912, such as the movement of icebergs in the North Atlantic, the quality of steel used in the building of the ship, and the communications used on board. But for the meaning and significance of this disaster we have to look beyond science to the story of shipbuilding and the values embodied in the sailing of this "unsinkable" ship. Scientific disciplines contribute much to our understanding of the world. Through their work we are coming to understand our universe to be something in the vicinity of 13.7 billion years old, having begun from virtually nothing to expand to a distance that is beyond our grasp. At the same time, it is composed of such small atomic building materials that 500 trillion protons can fit on the dot of this "i" without having to go on a diet! Our own planet earth is the result of enormous forces in our solar system, and came into being around 3.8 billion years ago.[13] Because this "one God" is creator of all, Christians of all people will respect the integrity of science. Its explanatory role is powerful and deeply moving. But the sciences do not have the capacity to tell the whole story. The Christian Bible is sparse in its account about creation: "In the beginning God created the heavens and the earth" (Genesis 1:1 *NIV*). What fills our libraries with volumes of scientific descriptions is covered in the Bible's opening with a scant couple of pages. This should help us to realize that the Bible is not a scientific account of the beginnings of our world, let alone of our universe. What Genesis and the rest of the Bible is concerned with is God's assessment of creation—"It is good!" (Genesis 1)—and with the *relationship* between Creator and creation. What happens when God brings into existence something other than himself, especially when part of that creation is given the capacity to respond freely to God? Convinced that God is one, we trust the integrity of both science and the Bible. They need each other to be complete.

Convinced that God is one, we trust the integrity of both science and the Bible

Salvationists affirm God's providential care, but we *cannot turn a blind eye to the realities of suffering and evil in our world*. We praise God because "The oceans move at Thy Command,"[14] and then face the devastating power of a tsunami in the Indian Ocean. We affirm God's sustaining power with chemicals, and then shudder at the horrors of gas ovens in Auschwitz. We marvel at the dynamics involved in flight, and then realize that God's sustaining power of flight was used to destroy the Twin Towers in New York City. From global suffering to personal loss, it is difficult to square any notion of God's providential care with lived realities. We must never offer glib responses to suffering. It is true that we can learn something about ourselves from what we suffer, but the rape of a child cannot justify whatever might be learned. It is affirmed that God created the world purposefully, but what purpose is served by ethnic cleansing? Acknowledging the painful mystery of suffering, how can we approach it with Christian convictions in view? One thing we can do is to recognize that the biblical writers themselves don't turn a blind eye to suffering. The Psalmists, for instance, face God with suffering's reality: "Why, O Lord, do you stand far off? Why do you hide yourself in times of trouble?" (Psalm 10:1). The prophet Habakkuk agonizes over the suffering that has come upon his people: "O Lord, how long shall I cry for help, and you will not listen? Or cry to you 'Violence!' and you will not save? Why do you make me see wrong-doing and look at trouble?" (Habakkuk 1:2). However, a more complete Christian response to God's sustaining work and suffering's reality necessitates viewing it through the life, death and resurrection of Christ. It is clear that Jesus of Nazareth engaged suffering in his public ministry. He brought healing to bodies and communities; he sat down for meals with the outcasts and excluded; he provided for widows and hungry crowds. Matthew's Gospel portrays Jesus' actions as fulfilling "what had been spoken through the prophet Isaiah, 'He took our infirmities and bore our diseases' " (Matthew 8:17).[15] In the person of Jesus Christ we understand God to be one who has embraced suffering in all its dimensions. There are times when a Christian can only weep at the depth of suffering encountered. But a Christian weeps in hope. We trust that God's sovereign grace will one day resolve the dissonances of history into his harmonic peace and justice. We worship the one God who works his purposes in a wounded world, bears the marks of that wounded world and invites us to engage that world with our own wounds.

Finally, the doctrine of "one God" has important *implications for interfaith dialogue in the 21st century.* One of the contested issues today is what different world faiths mean by the phrase, "one God." In particular it is often claimed that Christians cannot be committed to "one God" because of our trinitarian understanding of God. We need to be clear about our depiction of God as "one" in our conversations with other faiths. It's important to keep in mind that our language about God will be pushed to its limits. Miroslav Volf argues that "to affirm that there is one God means that there is only one, unique, and incomparable divine being, on a different plane of existence from everything that is not God."[16] The Christian faith will certainly insist that God's oneness does not cancel out God's trinitarian nature, but there is at least a shared language for purposes of discussion. The Salvation Army's second doctrine invites interfaith dialogue. If God is "one," and we are required to "love God and neighbour," there is no person who stands outside the sphere of that love.

Doctrine Two thus points us to an understanding of God whose faithfulness underlies the movements of atoms and stars, and contributes to a meaningful history. Tensions are there, but so is the conviction that the faithfulness and integrity of one God sustains our world towards its ultimate purposes.

Practising the Doctrine

"There's probably no God. Now stop worrying and enjoy your life!" This sign appeared on buses travelling the streets of London, England, in 2008.[17] Whatever we might think about the opening statement, the sign does have something right: Our view of God impacts the way we live. Salvationists call it holiness. I want to suggest ways that this second core conviction contributes to our understanding and practice of the holy life. Our conviction about God's oneness matters.

We begin with the Army's eighth General, Frederick Coutts, who claimed that "A person's conception of holiness is governed by the character of God he [or she] worships."[18] As we worship this one God who creates, sustains and governs the world in faithfulness, how does this translate into our daily lives?[19] Let's consider what it means to worship this "one God" and thus to exhibit a life that is different, holy.

A view of holiness impacted by this doctrine will shape our *view of the world as one*. It will refuse to polarize this world into sacred and secular compartments. It is thought by some that the secular spirit of our age keeps God out of the picture, therefore what Christians need to do is focus on the sacred. This tends to create a deep division between secular learning and sacred learning, and between sacred music and secular music. In contrast, Salvationist musicians learn to perform the music of Tschaikovsky and The Beatles alongside that of Joy Webb and Robert Redhead. Musically speaking, God's world is one world. Horatius Bonar's song expresses the conviction well: "So shall no part of day or night, From sacredness be free; But all my life, in every step, Be fellowship with thee."[20] Holiness will be found in "all things," not just in what we think is sacred. Most of us will have a special place where we have been overwhelmed by the presence of God in creation. For some it may be a view of the Northern Lights in the Prairies or the north shore of Lake Superior. For my wife, Cathie, it came during a vacation in Newfoundland and Labrador:

> The contrasts and diversity of God's creation have become more evident to me since coming to Newfoundland ... I still

get excited each and every time I see a whale, gigantic creatures that they are. I stood on the side of a boat and watched a mother and baby humpback whales jumping and playing and swimming underneath the waves. Their size and their playfulness brought to mind God's power and the fullness of joy He wants us to have. And for the first time this summer I've seen the delightful Atlantic puffin, a distinctive bird only 12 inches tall, fluttering its wings and bounding along the top of the water in a most humourous way, but with the ability to dive 150 feet into the ocean to fish ... But it is in the people of Newfoundland that I have experienced God most deeply. Their circumstances and persevering spirit have pushed them to redefine themselves over and over again throughout their history ... I am an "upalong," a "come-from-away." But I am beginning to sing the *Ode to Newfoundland* with tremendous feeling, and pray from the bottom of my heart as I sing: "God guard thee, Newfoundland." We can all see God in the places and the people where we live—wherever that might be. We just need to pay close attention with eyes, ears, hearts and minds wide open.[21]

This doctrine invites us to worship the God who creates, sustains and governs all things. Our creative arts, our learning, our preaching are all in the service of the worship of God. Because God is one we practise the presence of God in the whole world, this one universe.

Holiness is cultivated in the world God creates and sustains, therefore *time* plays an important role. The first occasion the Bible uses the word "holy" is in relation to time. When God's creative work came to completion, "God blessed the seventh day and made it holy, because on it he rested from all the work of creating that he had done."[22] Our playful imaginations might enjoy envisioning God resting! But the implications of this text are important for Salvationists in the western world. We live in a culture that values time differently. We are told that "time is money." We are constantly encouraged to "save time." Yet despite the boom in time-saving devices, Canadians have been described as "time poor." Reginald Bibby points to two factors that have contributed to this: a technology that works around the clock, and rising expectations that we be accessible all the time. This has given rise to the assumption that we live in a world of 24/7, where time has become a commodity in short supply.[23] In contrast, while all time is sacred, Salvationists hold to the conviction that the Old Testament's concept of Sabbath gives special attention to time's holiness.[24] The Sabbath invites us to *come to a stop* from those things and activities that define us. To shut off the computers and cellphones to which we are addicted; to think twice about shopping; to leave school assignments off to the side for a period of time. This holy time also invites us to worship and play, to do what our culture considers harmless and unimportant. There is a qualitative aspect to time. The practise of Sabbath helps to keep all time holy.

> The need for integrity in our culture is especially important because we live in what is called a cheating culture

This core conviction also points us to a view of holiness which takes seriously our role as *stewards* of God's creation. This doctrine argues that God retains an active involvement with his creation. God is concerned with the whole of his creation, not simply with us creatures who are made in his image. God's active love extends to the survival of cod in the North Atlantic, birds on the Prairies and melting ice caps. We have increasingly become aware of the word "sustainability." This is what the word "preserver" in our doctrine means. God sustains his creation; God sustains his purposes for our world. When we take seriously the notion of sustainability, and engage in ecological issues, we reflect the interactions of a holy God with his world. A concern for the holy life will take Salvationists into ecological projects in their community. The architectural designs of Salvation Army buildings have to do with holiness, because they can contribute to sustainable cities. The degree to which we contribute to a sustainable world reflects our understanding of God's character. We are called to be stewards of the planet, not its exploiters.[25]

This second doctrine also voices the conviction that holiness must be related to personal and corporate *integrity*: "In purpose and being,

God is one."[26] The need for integrity in our culture is especially important because we live in what is called *a cheating culture*. Recent years have been characterized by major financial institutions that have compromised their balance sheets, athletes who competed having used performance-enhancing drugs, students who cheated on essays and examinations, and internet services that provide alibis for spouses who want to deceive the other partner. These are not isolated instances of cheating, but have taken on cultural dimensions: "available evidence strongly suggests that Americans are not only cheating more in many areas but are also feeling less guilty about it. When 'everybody does it,' or imagines that everybody does it, a cheating culture has emerged."[27] This has important implications for the corporate life of The Salvation Army: "Integrity has never counted for more. With everybody watching, you'd better be on track to deliver what you promise. You'd better be who you say you are."[28] Financial audits have to do with holiness. Employee policies and their implementation have to do with holiness. Preaching your own sermon, rather than one downloaded from the internet, brings integrity into worship. Integrity means that we act with consistency, whether the microphone is on or off. Such character keeps actions and words bound together; the person and the organization can be trusted. Holiness will be characterized by personal and communal integrity.

The year 1929 was a watershed for The Salvation Army. What began as a small revivalist movement in the 1870s had become a most significant international Movement within 50 years. And within that period of time a constitution that had been designed for a small company of Salvationists was being stretched beyond its capabilities. The lightning rod for constitutional reform was directed to the issue of how the General would be succeeded in office. William Booth named his successor in a sealed envelope, and expected this person to do the same. But when Bramwell Booth succeeded his father on August 20, 1912, it would be the last time a General was put into office this way. While Bramwell believed it was his duty to follow his father's wishes and name his own successor, a growing number of international leaders opposed this method of succession. Times had changed, and they were not comfortable with the process set out by William Booth. It was a difficult moment. These respected leaders were torn between their love for Bramwell, whose health was failing from the stress of the office, and their commitment to the health of the wider Salvation Army. Behind the scenes and in public, they exercised leadership with a costly love. The voices of Edward Higgins and Samuel Logan Brengle demonstrated what it means to lead with integrity, to lead with concern both for the person and the organization. Lived holiness became a factor in the decisive move towards the first High Council and an "elected General" within this Army.[29]

The Salvation Army's second doctrine voices the conviction that God is one. God's oneness is expressed within God's creative, providential and sovereign work. It is this one God who is "infinitely perfect," meaning that God's integrity and faithfulness lie at the heart of God's character. Whatever else might be said, holiness has to do with our sustained practices of faithfulness and integrity. This core conviction matters! How God's oneness relates to God's triune nature assumes the focus of the next doctrine.

Reflection Questions for Chapter Two

1. This chapter introduces the notion of "character." What observations have you made about the importance of character in our world?
2. If you are studying this book with a group, read the chapter together.
3. What phrase or section caught your attention? Why?

Forming the Doctrine:

4. Read the texts mentioned in different translations—Deuteronomy 6:4-5; Mark 12:28-31—and note the differences.
5. When you hear the word "God" what images come to mind?
6. What other biblical texts or songs come to mind when you think of God as Creator?
7. How have you witnessed God's providential hand in your own life?

Engaging the Doctrine:

8. What are some areas where you think there is tension between a scientific understanding of things and your faith?
9. What examples of suffering in our world give you concern? How might you respond on the basis of this doctrine?
10. How have you engaged in conversation with people of other faiths? How does this discussion of "one God" help with those discussions?

Practising the Doctrine:

11. How do you seek to make *time* special in your life?
12. What value do you think there is in the church's seasons of Advent and Lent?
13. In what parts of the world do you feel a special sense of beauty and sacredness?
14. What are some issues of integrity in our world? What do you think it means personally and as a church to be people of integrity?

Conclude: Read Psalm 19.

Endnotes for Chapter Two

1 Frederick Coutts, *The Call to Holiness* (St. Albans: Campfield Press, 1957), 24.

2 See Richard Dawkins, *The God Delusion* (New York: First Mariner Books, 2008). It should be noted that the Bible makes no attempt to "prove" God's existence. Its concern is with the story and character of God in relation to humanity. For a response to Richard Dawkins and the "new atheists" see Alister McGrath, *Why God Won't Go Away* (London: SPCK Publishing, 2011).

3 I will use pronouns like "him" and "himself" throughout this study to refer to God. As noted in the third chapter, God is beyond gender, thus it is inadequate to envision God as male. The purpose of using words like "him" is to retain the personal dimensions of God's being rather than resorting to impersonal language.

4 This text is often called the *Shema*, taken from the first Hebrew phrase, "Hear, O Israel."

5 The first translation is from the *New Revised Standard Version*, and the second from the *New International Version*.

6 Patrick D. Miller Jr., *Deuteronomy* (Louisville: John Knox Press, 1990), 101.

7 J. Neander, "Praise to the Lord," *The Song Book of The Salvation Army: American Edition* (Verona, N.J.: The Salvation Army National Headquarters, 1987), No. 19, emphases mine. (Hereafter this edition of the Song Book will be cited as SBSA 1987).

8 See http://en.wikipedia.org/wiki/He's_Got_the_Whole_World_in_His_Hands. Accessed Feb 1, 2013.

9 The word "providence" combines two related words: *pro*, or before, and *video*, or view.

10 http://www.lyricstime.com/bette-midler-the-glory-of-love-lyrics.html. Accessed November 5, 2012.

11 Jonathan Sacks, *The Great Partnership: Science, Religion, and the Search for Meaning* (New York: Schocken Books, 2011), 290.

12 J. Sacks, *The Great Partnership*, 39, emphasis his.

13 For a most readable treatment of this, see Bill Bryson, *A Short History of Nearly Everything* (Toronto: Anchor Canada, 2004).

14 A. Wiggins, "Thine is the Kingdom, Lord," *SBSA 1987*, No. 171.

15 Matthew's Gospel names Jesus as "Emmanuel ... God is with us" (Matthew 1:23). This raises the issue of Christology, which will be discussed more fully in Chapter Four.

16 Miroslav Volf, *Allah: A Christian Response* (New York: HarperCollins Publishers, 2011), 142.

17 It could be argued that the timing of the sign is somewhat ironic in that it appeared the same year as the global financial crisis!

18 F. Coutts, *Call to Holiness*, 24.

19 Volf makes an important observation when he says, "To know whom people worship, we cannot just look at what they say about God; rather, we need to pay attention above all to how they live." See Volf, *Allah*, 113.

20 H. Bonar, "Fill thou my life," *SBSA 1987*, No. 7.

21 Cathie Harris, "Seeing God in Newfoundland," *The War Cry* (October 2004): 4-5.

22 Genesis 2:3 *NIV*.

23 Reginald W. Bibby, *The Boomer Factor* (Toronto: Bastion Books, 2006), 78.

24 "The Sabbath itself is a sanctuary which we build, *a sanctuary in time*." See Abraham Joshua Heschel, *The Sabbath* (New York: The Noonday Press, 1951), 29. This is not to suggest that there is only one particular day in the week when Sabbath can be experienced, especially when modern cities and nations require people to be working seven days a week.

25 The Salvation Army Ethics Centre in the Canada and Bermuda Territory has produced the *Green Toolkit* for this purpose. See http://www.wegogreen.ca/. Accessed July 3, 2013.

26 See Patrick Miller above.

27 David Callahan, *The Cheating Culture* (Orlando: Harcourt Books, 2004), 13.

28 Robert A. Watson and Ben Brown, *The Most Effective Organization in the U.S.* (New York: Crown Business, 2001), 89.

29 See John Larsson, *1929: A Crisis That Shaped The Salvation Army's Future* (London: Salvation Books, 2009). Note that the issue of succession has been at work in the British Parliament's decision in 2013 to pass a law making it possible for either a boy or girl to claim succession to the throne.

Trinity: Holiness as the Practice of Missional Love

We believe that there are three persons in the Godhead—the Father, the Son and the Holy Ghost, undivided in essence and co-equal in power and glory.—Doctrine 3

The Trinity is at the very center of the day-to-day practice of the Christian life. Because human beings are created in the image of the triune God, we are called to live into *God's triune life, insofar as that is possible.*—David Cunningham[1]

THERE ARE TIMES WHEN NEW WORDS ARE NEEDED TO depict new realities. The introduction of the computer into modern life has required a new vocabulary. Words such as internet, cyberspace and e-mail had little meaning until just a few decades ago. Now we understand that a virus can mean something other than a biological organism! As the early church grappled with the implications of its faith, it became evident that new words were needed. If Jesus Christ was in fact the "Word made flesh,"[2] and if the Holy Spirit was understood to be God's active presence in the world, then a new language was needed to speak about God. The North African Christian, Tertullian, coined some of these words in the third century. He loved language so much that he created close to a thousand new words! Among them was the Latin word, *Trinitas*, or Trinity. Without losing sight of God as one, the

Christian church also spoke of God as Father, Son and Holy Spirit: Trinity![3]

We may not realize it, but the word *Trinity* is not in the Bible. That does not, however, make the word unbiblical. It's important to understand that this core conviction developed over time, and from biblical roots. Like the development of Da Vinci's sketches into paintings and machines, the biblical sketch of God as triune developed organically until it became a cornerstone conviction of the church's creeds. This understanding of God has had its critics, both in the past and in the present context. But there is a sense that this view of God as triune is timely, not least because of its implications for understanding God as holy. This conviction matters! Thus we want to trace its formation, engage it with particular questions in the 21st century, and then consider ways it impacts our understanding and practice of holiness.

Forming the Doctrine

When considering the biblical roots of the Trinity, we need to be careful not to isolate one or two texts, or of reading this conviction back into the Bible. Integrity is needed to read Scripture so as to respect its voice, and not turn it into a ventriloquist's puppet.

As has already been noted, the early church affirmed the *oneness* of God. The central text of Deuteronomy 6:4-5 is also affirmed by Jesus. When he was approached with the question, "Which commandment is the first of all?" he responded, "The first is, 'Hear, O Israel: the Lord our God, the Lord is one' " (Mark 12:28-29). Whatever else might be said of God, the Christian conviction assumes God's oneness. The Lord is one, the Lord alone.

It wasn't long though before the identity of Jesus of Nazareth became a crucial question. Mark's Gospel notes a turning point when Jesus posed the question to his disciples: "Who do people say that I am? Who do you say that I am?" (Mark 8:27-30). Others had already raised similar questions: "Why does this fellow speak in this way? ... Who can forgive sins but God alone?" (Mark 2:7). "Who then is this, that even the wind and the sea obey him?" (Mark 4:41). As Jesus carried out his public ministry, questions about his identity stirred public controversy. The humanity of Jesus was not in question, but the conviction grew that in the person of Jesus, God was being encountered.[4]

Similarly, as the early church found itself animated by the Holy Spirit, the conviction developed that the Spirit's work was also the active presence of God. The Book of Acts portrays the Holy Spirit animating the church in its mission from the Day of Pentecost to the Apostle Paul's imprisonment in Rome. Paul may have been held captive, but the Holy Spirit was not. The Holy Spirit was God's presence pushing the church out from Jerusalem to the edges of the empire. Beverly Roberts Gaventa draws out the implication of this for a trinitarian understanding of God:

> With respect to God, Jesus, and the Spirit, then, they are so identified with one another in Acts that explicitly Trinitarian language seems an inevitable development. Although Luke is not concerned with later church councils, *his story nevertheless moves in a direction that can only be called Trinitarian.*[5]

The Apostle Paul points us in a similar direction when he responds to tensions regarding spiritual gifts in the Corinthian church: "Now there are varieties of gifts, but the same Spirit; and there are varieties of services, but the same Lord; and there are varieties of activities, but it is the same God who activates all of them in everyone" (1 Corinthians 12:4-6). Richard Hays comments:

> Paul of course had no explicit doctrine of the Trinity; this doctrine was not articulated formally by theologians until hundreds of years later. This passage shows, however, that he *experienced* God as Trinity; he can describe the activity of God in the community in three synonymous parallel clauses as the working of the Spirit and of the Lord Jesus and of God.[6]

While these texts imply the doctrine, there are more explicit trinitarian texts in the New Testament. As Paul comes to the end of his Second Epistle to these same Corinthians, he closes with the familiar benediction: "The grace of the Lord Jesus Christ, the love of God, and the communion of the Holy Spirit be with you all" (2 Corinthians

13:13). And Matthew's Gospel closes by noting that some "worshipped" Jesus who said to them, "All authority in heaven and on earth has been given to me. Go therefore and make disciples of all nations, baptizing them in the name of the Father and of the Son and of the Holy Spirit."[7] The relationship between these foundational sketches and subsequent development has been expressed by Alister McGrath:

A word that was coined to describe the internal relationships of Father, Son and Holy Spirit is perichoresis, a word closely related to the English word choreography, or dance

> The doctrine of the Trinity can be regarded as the outcome of a process of sustained and critical reflection on the pattern of divine activity revealed in Scripture, and continued in Christian experience. This is not to say that Scripture contains a doctrine of the Trinity; rather, Scripture bears witness to a God who demands to be understood in a trinitarian manner.[8]

The "process of sustained and critical reflection" to which McGrath refers brings into play the role of the early church.

As Tertullian and others considered the church's convictions about the Trinity, they developed what might be called "rules of engagement." If I want to drive a car on Canadian streets and highways I will need to drive with its traffic rules in mind, not those of Great Britain! These are rules of engagement. When considering God as triune, one "rule of engagement" stated that *all* persons of the Trinity are involved in the acts of *any one* person. Thus when we speak of the Father's work in creation, we need to realize that the Son and Spirit are also involved in forming the galaxies. We give attention to the life, death and resurrection of the Son, believing that the Father and Spirit are also deeply involved in these moments. This becomes especially important in the atoning work of the cross, so as not to set the Father in opposition to the Son. We speak of the Spirit's transforming work in holiness, believing that this, too, is the work of the Father and Son. This rule of engagement is called the *rule of appropriation*, where each person of the Trinity has appropriate work to do, but it is done in concert with each other. The rule of appropriation reflects the conviction that "God is one."

Another "rule of engagement" stated that God's ways *in our world* are consistent with *God's life prior to the world's existence*. The triune God existed before the universe began 13.7 billion years ago. In the words of Daniel Migliore, "When Christians speak of God as eternally triune, they simply affirm that the love of God that is extended to the world in Jesus Christ by the Holy Spirit is proper to God's own eternal life in relationship."[9] A word that was coined to describe the internal relationships of Father, Son and Holy Spirit is *perichoresis*. It's a word closely related to the English word choreography, or dance. There has been a loving relationship between each person of the Trinity from even before creation. But Christians acknowledge that our primary understanding of God's love comes from history: "God's love was revealed among us in this way: God sent his only Son into the world so that we might live through him" (1 John 4:9). We come to know God through his interactions of love in our world. This trinitarian rule expresses the conviction that God's love expressed with Israel, and in Bethlehem, Galilee and at Calvary is consistent with the love that has characterized God eternally.

As the church developed this biblical sketch, it put the trinitarian mystery of God into confessional language. It spoke of God as "one in essence, distinguished in three persons." Despite pressures to lean in the direction of either side of this affirmation, the church held onto its trinitarian understanding of God. From the work of Augustine to Anselm, from the Eastern Orthodox Church to the hymns of Charles Wesley, the affirmation of God as triune is deeply embedded in Christian faith and practice:

> Holy, holy, holy, Lord God Almighty!
> All thy works shall praise thy name in earth and sky and sea;
> Holy, holy, holy, merciful and mighty,
> God in three persons, blessed Trinity![10]

Engaging the Doctrine

This core affirmation of God as triune is central to a Christian understanding of God, but has its critics. Some challenges focus on language, while other challenges fault it for being unreasonable. Let's engage this doctrine with these concerns so that we might hear it more clearly in our times.

One challenge levelled against this core conviction involves its use of *language*. Critics view human language as inadequate to speak of God at the best of times. As argued by some, however, the depiction of God as *Father, Son* and Holy Spirit conveys too much of a patriarchal view of God. Its implication has been bluntly stated: "If God is male, then we live with the disastrous implication that the male is god!" This would be a disastrous implication! However, consider first the role of language in human experience. Whatever their inadequacies, with words we sign contracts, coach teams, swear in new citizens and order food in a restaurant—unless it's food from another culture! We also use words to imagine things we can't see. Scientists speak of black holes, economists project a bear or bull market, and runners say they hit the wall. Words are essential in all aspects of life.

Similarly, the Bible employs many words and images to speak of God: Shepherd, Rock, Fortress, Friend, Potter, King, Mother and Father. No one image is exhaustive; they all contribute some understanding of God. Note that some of these images are impersonal, such as Rock, while others are personal, such as Friend. It's a Christian conviction that while something important is conveyed by the impersonal images, God is essentially personal. In Jesus Christ we have the most complete personal disclosure of God: "No one has ever seen God. It is God the only Son, who is close to the Father's heart, who has made him known" (John 1:18). Thus we draw upon personal language to speak of God. When the language of Father is used of God, this does not imply that God is male. God is beyond any notion of gender, but we use this word to emphasize God's *personal* nature. It can be observed that this reflects the language of Jesus himself when speaking of God. "When you pray, say: Father, hallowed be your name" (Luke 11:2). Jesus continues: "If you, then, who are evil, know how to give good gifts to your children, how much more will the heavenly Father give the Holy Spirit to those who ask him!" (Luke 11:13).

Similarly, Paul employs the language of God as Father in his letter to the Galatians:

> But when the fullness of time had come, God sent his Son, born of a woman, born under the law, in order to redeem those who were under the law, so that we might receive adoption as children. And because you are children, God has sent the Spirit of his Son into our hearts, crying, "Abba!, Father!" So you are no longer a slave but a child, and if a child then also an heir, through God.[11]

It's not that the concept of God as Father is the only image of God in the Bible. It is however an image that dominated the language world of Jesus, and other writings in the New Testament. A danger, of course, is that when we speak of God as Father, we assume it means the same as our own personal or cultural experiences of father. For some the experience of father has been one of neglect or even abuse. It has been observed that the early Army tended to draw on Victorian understandings of "father." The result was that "God, as Father, laid claim to absolute obedience and submission."[12] But a more biblical understanding of God's fatherhood should inform and restore human fatherhood to its vulnerable and compassionate dimensions. This conviction is expressed in the words of John Gowans' song:

> If human hearts are often tender,
> And human minds can pity know,
> If human love is touched with splendor,
> And human hands compassion show,
>
> *Then how much more shall God our Father*
> *In love forgive, in love forgive!*
> *Then how much more shall God our Father*
> *Our wants supply, and none deny!*[13]

If one challenge confronting the Trinity concerns its language, another concerns its *reasonableness*. The affirmation of God as Three-in-One is viewed simply to be "incomprehensible." And if we attempt to state the doctrine of the Trinity in mathematical terms alone it *is* incomprehensible. Three just doesn't equal one. The difficulty though is that we fail to ask, three what? And one what? First, let's acknowledge that reason *is* important. We are commanded to love God with our minds, not to check them at the gate when we step into the arena of Christian faith. Our faith is not a private faith where we live with all kinds of intellectual nonsense. Our convictions about the Trinity must function in the public world, open to any argument and criticism. While we acknowledge the mystery that we face, we are required to think as clearly as we can. We reason within the disclosure of God that has been given in Scripture, and developed by the church. Rather than being an irrational doctrine, however, a triune understanding of God can make sense, and it does have significance for our times. For instance, it has been observed that trinitarian language is not individual but *relational.* A father can only be a father when there is a son. The experience of being a parent is caused as much by a son or daughter as by mom or dad. Thus it's important to think of the relationships within the Trinity, for they depict God who is one and at the same time diverse. Within God's trinitarian life there is both unity and diversity. David Cunningham has drawn attention to a musical analogy that reflects this simultaneous unity and diversity. In western music it's known as *polyphonic* music—*poly* meaning many, and *phonic* or sound. In this form of music, different melodies are sung or played at the same time. But they do so in such a way as to interweave with each other to form a unified sound:

Our convictions about the Trinity must function in the public world, open to any argument and criticism

> Christianity proclaims a polyphonic understanding of God—one in which difference provides an alternative to a monolithic homogeneity, yet without becoming a source of exclusion. Attention to any one of the three does not imply a diminished role for the others; all three have their distinctive

melodies, and all are "played" and "heard" simultaneously without damage to God's unity.[14]

At a time when our world is seeking ways to embrace its diverse peoples within some form of unity, this relational view of God as triune is most important. The Salvationist conviction that God is trinitarian is open to challenges in our time. However, far from simply responding to challenges, this core conviction is a gift for our times: diversity within unity constitutes the character of God.

Finally, this core conviction that God is named Father, Son and Holy Spirit is crucial for distinguishing a Christian understanding of God in *interfaith dialogue*. It is often argued that Christians believe in three gods while Muslims believe in one God. This is not the case. In holding to a triune understanding of God, Christians still maintain our commitment to God as one. The rule of appropriation means that we do not divide God's essence. Because each person of the Trinity is involved in the action of the others, God's unity remains intact, undivided. We can continue to dialogue with people of different faiths given our commitment to God as one. However, the point of God's triune nature is that it helps us to understand not simply that God loves, but that "God *is* love."[15] Before the universe was created, God loved: "The doctrine of the Trinity is a way of explaining why we say that God *is* love, not only that he shows love."[16] God's gracious actions in creating our world flow from a love that is known deep within the life of Father, Son and Holy Spirit. Because God is love from eternity, we live in a world where that love has been made visible in time. This core conviction of God as triune both distinguishes a unique Christian understanding of God and invites dialogue with people of other faiths.

Thus while a trinitarian understanding of God may appear to be problematic in our times, it is nonetheless quite relevant. The conviction that God is triune holds importance and hope for the 21st century. This core conviction matters!

Practising the Doctrine

Having paid attention to this doctrine's formation and its meaning in our context, let's ask what kind of direction it gives to Christian living. What contribution does this core conviction bring to our understanding of holiness and its practice? Attempts to comprehend God as "three persons in one nature" can seem distant from the realities of shoveling snow, studying for a biology exam or visiting a friend in the hospital. It's jarring then when David Cunningham expresses the conviction that "The Trinity is at the very center of the day-to-day practice of the Christian life. Because human beings are created in the image of the triune God, we are called to *live into* God's triune life, insofar as that is possible."[17] In this section we will give attention to particular ways that the Holy Trinity impacts our holy living.

The Trinity and God's Holiness

Before we consider any implications for Christian living, let's inquire how a trinitarian understanding of God affects our view of *God's* holiness. The church has too often drawn from isolated texts in the Bible to speak of God's character, such as wrath, love, jealousy or holiness. Instead, "Our reflections on the triune reality of God point to the need for a thorough rethinking of the doctrine of the attributes of God, which have all too often been presented and debated without any reference to the life, death, and resurrection of Jesus Christ, or to the doctrine of the Trinity, which is simply a summary redescription of the God of the gospel."[18] This is especially important when cultivating a trinitarian understanding of God as holy.

It has been noted that a triune understanding of God helps us to say that "God is love" (1 John 4:8), not simply that God loves. Before the dawning of creation, loving relationships existed between Father, Son and Holy Spirit. However, while it is true that "God is love" there is a danger in emphasizing God's love to the exclusion of God's holiness. L. Gregory Jones has expressed his concern that:

> ... we emphasize God's love as a counterbalance to images that many people have of an excessively austere, judging, wrathful God. We want to know that God ultimately loves us, redeems us, forgives us; we want to know that mercy does indeed triumph over judgment. But in the process, have we domesticated God? Have we lost sight of God's majestic holiness?[19]

An initial reaction might be to say that these are almost mutually exclusive descriptions of God. Both Old and New Testaments portray God as holy, to be approached only with caution, like coming close to an active volcano. Yet both Testaments also agree that God loves, and love is vulnerable and open to rejection. So we seem caught between God's holiness on one hand, with its emphasis on separateness, and God's love on the other, with its emphasis on closeness.[20] One way forward is to speak of God as characterized by *holy love*. The Bible narrates God's story, where each person of the Trinity is deeply involved. And when the whole biblical story is heard, we discern God's character to be that of holy love. God is holy, distinct. But God's distance from us did not prevent him from becoming vulnerable in love. Neither, however, is God's love precisely what we understand by love. God's is a holy love, a distinct love. Thus our core conviction that God is Trinity becomes integral to our understanding of God's holiness. But what contribution does this make to the way Salvationists practise this conviction in our daily lives?

The Trinity and Our Holiness

One implication of the Trinity for Salvationists is that we are called to *practise relational holiness*. We have argued that God lives in dynamic relationship. God is not a solitary ruler, but experiences eternal giving and receiving of love between Father, Son and Holy Spirit. What is true of this holy God is intended to be true of God's holy people: holiness is fundamentally relational. It was this realization that prompted John Wesley to declare that "Christianity is essentially a social religion, and that to turn it into a solitary religion is indeed to destroy it."[21] We learn to participate in the love of God by active involvement within our congregational life. Here we learn to "look not to [our] own interests, but to the interests of others" (Philippians 2:4). It's in our congregational life that we learn to embrace differences of musical taste, dress, language and understandings of faith. It's within the diversity of these differences we learn to create a "new humanity,"[22] a community that participates in God's love.

Another feature of trinitarian spirituality is that it *embraces complexity*. We have spoken of God as a polyphonic God, one who embraces difference in unity. Even within God's story these differences can be filled with ambiguity and tension. Think of that moment in the Garden of Gethsemane when Jesus prays to the Father that this cup might pass, only to be met with silence. Each person of the Trinity weaves their own distinctive melody within the biblical story, and there are times when they sound dissonant. Complexity is part of the Bible itself. The four Gospels, for instance, do not always sound the same melodies. They form a polyphonic choir within the New Testament. One of the difficulties in forming a view of Salvationist spirituality is that we tend to simplify complexity. We sing, "There is a message, a simple message."[23] There *is* simplicity to the gospel, but it is not the kind of simplicity that eliminates complexity.

It is often thought that when John Wesley's heart was "strangely warmed" his doubts and anxieties were also resolved. The difficulty is that Wesley's doubts and anxieties did not leave him, and his life after Aldersgate left much to be desired, especially his relationship with women.[24] Roberta Bondi frames the matter this way:

> The true Wesleyan model of spirituality encourages reflection on the external and internal complexities of our lives as central to Christian life. Far from encouraging us to fear our complexity, it helps us to regard even our most painful family situations, our most devastating doubts, and our worst tragedies as food for growth in the love of God and neighbour.[25]

The practice of holiness that is grounded in the triune God will embrace complexity in our own lives.

Holy love grounded in the triune God will engage us in the *practice of missional love*. It is the nature of God's love to move beyond itself. The Trinity has created a universe out of love and has become involved in humanity's story out of that same love. The Trinity's love for our world reflects an understanding of God as a missional God. David Bosch argues that before we speak of the church's mission, we need to understand God as a God of mission. Critical to this understanding of God is the Christian conviction about God as Trinity:

> Mission was understood as being derived from the very

> nature of God. It was thus put in the context of the doctrine of the Trinity ... God the Father sending the Son, and God the Father and the Son sending the Spirit was expanded to include yet another 'movement': Father, Son, and Holy Spirit sending the church into the world.[26]

> To participate in mission is to participate in the movement of God's love toward people, since God is a fountain of sending love
> —David Bosch

The church's mission is grounded in its conviction that God is a sending God, a missional God. God's mission conveys his holy love to our world. "To participate in mission is to participate in the movement of God's love toward people, since God is a fountain of sending love."[27] Holiness and mission are inseparable: "The holy life ... is the life of Christ which we live out in mission. God sanctifies his people not only in order that they will be marked by his character, but also in order that the world will be marked by that character."[28] Salvationists are called by God to "seek the welfare of the city" (Jeremiah 29:7). It is this understanding of mission that prompts The Salvation Army to engage in its ministry of emergency disaster response. From our responses to hurricanes such as Katrina and Sandy, to our work at Ground Zero in 9/11, to floods in Manitoba and Alberta, Salvationists respond to suffering in disasters because of our conviction that the triune God has engaged the suffering of our world. A trinitarian understanding of God requires a close connection to mission. Thus we sing:

> For thy mission make me holy,
> For thy glory make me thine,
> Sanctify each moment fully,
> Fill my life with love divine.[29]

This third doctrine is crucial for the identity of Salvationists and our practice of holiness. "The doctrine of the Trinity is central to the

Christian account of God and to the Christian faith as a whole, not an optional extra. Take away the trinitarian nature of God, and the Christian belief about Christ as the incarnation of God collapses, and with it, the whole Christian faith."[30] With these words we turn our attention to the Salvationist core conviction about Christ. It was the church's understanding of Christ's identity that prompted a fully trinitarian view of God who is one.

Reflection Questions for Chapter Three

1. This chapter is about God as Trinity. What questions come to your mind when thinking about God as triune?
2. If you are reading this book with a group, read the chapter together.
3. What phrase or section caught your attention? Why?

Forming the Doctrine:

4. This chapter argues that the doctrine of the Trinity is developed from the Bible, like a painting is developed from a sketch. What is your response to this?
5. How important do you think are the "rules of engagement" set out by the early church?
6. In what ways do you hear God spoken of as Trinity in worship?

Engaging the Doctrine:

7. What objections do you encounter with others when thinking of God as triune?
8. How helpful is the analogy of "polyphonic music" to connect with God as triune?
9. How do you respond to the suggestion that the Trinity helps to make sense of the conviction that "God *is* love," and not simply that "God loves"?

Practising the Doctrine:

10. What are some differences between people in your congregation? How does this view of God as triune affect your approach to those differences?
11. In what ways does your Christian life experience complexity?
12. What helps a congregation to be mission minded instead of only inward looking?

Conclude: Read 2 Corinthians 13:13.

Endnotes for Chapter Three

1 David S. Cunningham, "The Holy Trinity: The Very Heart of Christian Ministry," *Quarterly Review* 22 (Summer 2002): 126.

2 John 1:14.

3 Note that I am using the more contemporary language of Holy *Spirit*, rather than the older phrase, Holy *Ghost*.

4 This matter of Christ's identity will be explored more fully in the chapter on Doctrine 4.

5 Beverly Roberts Gaventa, *The Acts of the Apostles* (Nashville: Abingdon Press, 2003), 39—emphasis mine. Note that the assumption here is that the author of Acts is Luke, the author of the Gospel by that name.

6 Richard B. Hays, *First Corinthians* (Louisville: John Knox Press, 1997), 210.

7 Matthew 28:18-19. It has been noted that the word "the" before each person of the Trinity is emphasized in the Greek, linking each person to "the name."

8 Alister E. McGrath, *Christian Theology: An Introduction, 4th Edition* (Malden: Blackwell Publishing, 2007), 249.

9 Daniel L. Migliore, *Faith Seeking Understanding: An Introduction to Christian Theology, 2nd Edition* (Grand Rapids: Eerdmans Publishing, 2004), 70.

10 Reginald Heber, "Holy, Holy, Holy," *SBSA 1987*, No. 220.

11 Galatians 4:4-7; note the trinitarian dimensions of this text in Paul.

12 Barbara Robinson, "Neither Fearful nor Familiar: Imaging God the Father," *Word and Deed* 4 (Fall 2001): 36.

13 J. Gowans, "If human hearts," *SBSA 1987*, No. 50.

14 Cunningham, "The Holy Trinity," 129.

15 1 John 4:16, emphasis mine.

16 Quoted in Miroslav Volf, *Allah: A Christian Response* (New York: HarperCollins Publishers, 2011), 148.

17 Cunningham, "The Holy Trinity,"126.

18 Migliore, *Faith Seeking Understanding*, 82.

19 L. Gregory Jones, "God's holiness," *Christian Century* (October 20, 1999): 1004.

20 This tension between "holy" and "love" is developed further in the chapter on Doctrine 10.

21 This phrase is taken from John Wesley's fourth sermon based on "The Sermon on the Mount." See Theodore Runyon, "Holiness as the Renewal of the Image of God in the Individual & Society," in *Embodied Holiness: Toward a Corporate Theology of Spiritual Growth*, Samuel M. Powell and Michael E. Lodahl eds., (Downers Grove: InterVarsity Press, 1999), 81.

22 Ephesians 2:15.

23 John Gowans, "There Is A Message," *SBSA 1987*, No. 270.

24 Reflecting on John Wesley's relationship with Sophy Hopkey in the New World, Ronald Stone says, "He knew neither the ways of women nor his ways with women. This flaw would haunt him the rest of his life." See Ronald H. Stone, *John Wesley's Life and Ethics* (Nashville: Abingdon Press, 2001), 75.

25 Roberta C. Bondi, "Aldersgate and Patterns of Methodist Spirituality," in *Aldersgate Reconsidered*, ed. Randy L. Maddox, (Nashville: Kingswood Books, 1990), 26.

26 David J. Bosch, *Transforming Mission: Paradigm Shifts in Theology of Mission* (Maryknoll: Orbis Books, 1992), 390.

27 Bosch, *Transforming Mission*, 390.

28 *The Salvation Army Handbook of Doctrine* (London: Salvation Books, 2010), 198.

29 Brindley Boon, "Thou Hast Called Me," *SBSA 1987*, No. 463.

30 Volf, *Allah*, 145.

Jesus of Nazareth: Holiness as Christlikeness

We believe that in the person of Jesus Christ the Divine and human natures are united, so that he is truly and properly God and truly and properly man.—Doctrine 4

Holiness is the unfolding of Christ's own character in the life of the believer.—Frederick Coutts[1]

SOME THINGS CAN BE SEEN WITH THE NATURAL EYE, SUCH AS an approaching storm on the prairies or the beauty of an Eastern Canada autumn. Other aspects of life are not so clearly visible, such as justice or courage. So it is that when Canadians want to talk about courage we often tell the story of Terry Fox. Terry was diagnosed with cancer at a young age and had one of his legs amputated below the knee. However, Terry had a dream to run across this land that covers five-and-a-half time zones. At the age of 22, Terry started his run from the harbour of St John's, N.L., but had to conclude it prematurely when his lungs filled with cancer. He died soon after in 1981. A magnificent monument to Terry overlooks Lake Superior near Thunder Bay, Ontario, where his run came to a finish. The section of the Trans-Canada Highway nearby is called the Terry Fox Courage Highway. This young Canadian made courage visible.

It's a Christian conviction that Jesus of Nazareth has made God visible: "the Word became flesh" (John 1:14). Christians do not claim that what is known of Jesus exhausts all there is of God, but what is known of Jesus is truly God. And because Jesus has made God visible, he has also made holiness visible. In his life, death and resurrection we see more clearly what holiness looks like, and how it might be replicated in our lives. In this chapter I want to explore the doctrine of Jesus Christ, to recall its formation, to engage it with issues in our own context, and to suggest ways this doctrine contributes to an understanding and practice of holiness in our time. The very notion of *Christian* holiness grounds our discussion in the person of Christ. This core conviction matters!

The very notion of Christian holiness grounds our discussion in the person of Christ

Forming the Doctrine

The Salvationist's fourth doctrine centres on the *identity* of Jesus of Nazareth. His identity is constructed from the biblical writers and its continued reflection in the church. It's not possible to exhaust the attempts to fashion this identity, but we can indicate its key elements.

Let's begin with Luke's Gospel which, with other New Testament writings, never questions the humanity of Jesus. But when Mary went into labour at Bethlehem's inn, the Lord's angel jolted shepherds on a Bethlehem hillside with a message: "Do not be afraid; for see—I am bringing you good news of great joy for all the people; to you is born this day in the city of David a *Saviour*, who is the *Messiah*, the *Lord*."[2] This startling news contains a number of key words regarding the identity of the child in the manger, which are then developed in the whole of Luke's Gospel and the Book of Acts.[3]

The title "Saviour" has its background in the Old Testament. God's liberation of Israel from slavery was an act of salvation (see Exodus 15:2). Israel's national vocation was to live out the conviction that "There is no other god besides me, a righteous God and a Saviour" (Isaiah 45:21). In the Mediterranean world of Jesus, saviours not only rescued people from potential disaster, they brought medical healing. "People might even refer to their physicians as 'saviors.' People other than physicians, who contributed to the welfare of a city, for example, could also be thought of as bringing salvation."[4] So it was that on a number of occasions Jesus turned to people he had just healed saying, "Your faith has saved you."[5] Jesus' mission is summarized with the words, "For the Son of Man came to seek out and to save the lost" (Luke 19:10). The child who was given the title "Saviour" carried out God's mission of salvation.

The shepherds also heard that the child born in the manger was "the Messiah," which means "an anointed person."[6] Israel's hope came to be centred on a king who would be anointed by God so that Israel might fulfil its vocation. A critical moment comes in Luke's Gospel when Jesus questions his twelve apostles about their perception of his identity: "Who do the crowds say that I am? ... Who do you say that I am?" Peter responds, "The Messiah of God." Jesus "sternly ordered and commanded them not to tell anyone," not because it wasn't true, but because his understanding of Messiahship necessitated suffering, rejection and death (see Luke 9:18-21). This was not the popular expectation. Jesus accepted the title, but refused its contemporary understanding.

When the angel proclaimed the child in the manger to be "Lord," the worlds of both the Old Testament and the Roman Empire inform its meaning. After God commissioned Moses to return to Egypt to free the Hebrew slaves, Moses anticipated their question: "What is the name of this God?" And God responded to Moses saying, "My name is YHWH."[7] However, when the Hebrew Bible was translated into Greek, the word *kyrios* was used for Yahweh. And while *kyrios* could be used as a title of respect, like our word "sir," it also carried overtones of divinity from the Old Testament. Luke's Gospel attests to the child who was born in a manger, was called "Lord" in his public ministry (see Luke 7:13), and was eventually "worshipped" (see Luke 24:52). For this reason, Peter's first sermon after Pentecost draws attention to this new reality: "Therefore let the entire house of Israel know with certainty that God has made him both Lord [*kyrios*] and Messiah, this Jesus whom you crucified" (Acts 2:36).

The naming of Christ as Lord forms a critical part of Paul's Letter to the Philippians. Concerned that the young Philippian church look to the interests of others and not simply their own, he writes:

> Let the same mind be in you that was in Christ Jesus, who, though he was in the form of God, did not regard equality with God as something to be exploited, but emptied himself, taking the form of a slave, being born in human likeness. And being found in human form, he humbled himself and became obedient to the point of death—even death on a cross. Therefore God also highly exalted him and gave him the name that is above every name, so that at the name of Jesus every knee should bend, in heaven and on earth and under the earth, and every tongue should confess that *Jesus Christ is Lord* [*kyrios*] to the glory of God the Father.[8]

This text narrates the story of Christ in a unique manner. Paul draws attention to Christ Jesus who "was in the form of God" but took "the form of a slave." The audacious claim is not simply that Jesus gave "form" to God, but gave *God* the "form of a slave."

According to Paul, Jesus did not use his equality with God "for his own advantage." Instead, Jesus "emptied himself." The word Paul uses here is from the family word, *kenosis*. Charles Wesley understood the original Greek when he penned the words:

> He left his Father's throne above,
> So free, so infinite his grace,
> *Emptied himself* of all but love
> And bled for Adam's helpless race.[9]

This self-emptying of Christ is not simply a reference to his birth when he took on humanity. It characterizes his whole life, especially with the realization that he "became obedient to the point of death—even death on a cross."[10] Paul continues his unique narration of Christ with an abrupt shift: "*Therefore* God also highly exalted him." Giving Jesus "the name that is above every name" is a way for Paul to refer to the Old Testament name for God, Yahweh. In so doing, Paul draws from the Book of Isaiah, which alludes to the exclusive "oneness" of God:

> Turn to me and be saved, all the ends of the earth! For I am

> God, and there is no other. By myself I have sworn, from my mouth has gone forth in righteousness a word that shall not return: "To me every knee shall bow, every tongue shall swear."[11]

What Isaiah envisioned, Paul ascribes to Christ, who emptied himself, who lived obediently, who died on a Roman cross. It is this Christ who is exalted at the right hand of God, who shares in God's sovereign rule and is worshipped.

At no point do New Testament writers actually come out and say, "This Jesus of Nazareth is truly and properly God." But they do point to this conviction with different expressions, such as: "In the beginning was the Word, and the Word was with God, and the Word was God"; "My Lord and my God!"; "For in him all the fullness of God was pleased to dwell"; "He is the reflection of God's glory and the exact imprint of God's very being, and he sustains all things by his powerful word."[12] However, as these convictions about Christ took shape in the early church, they raised new questions. "If Jesus is worshipped, how is he like or unlike God? And if Jesus is both human *and* divine, how are these two realities connected?" The whole discussion took on a Twittering effect, so that by the fourth century Gregory of Nyssa complained that,

> If you ask for change, the shopkeeper philosophizes to you about the Begotten and the Unbegotten. If you ask the price of a loaf, the answer is "the Father is greater and the Son is inferior"; if you say, "is my bath ready?" the attendant declares that the Son is of nothing.[13]

It's hard to imagine that kind of chatter in our culture. But it was a reality in Gregory's world.

By the early fourth century, the real point of debate centred on the divinity of Christ. Earlier attempts to discount the humanity of Christ were strongly rejected.[14] Any hint of a Christ who was considered less than human was unacceptable. What the church did struggle with, however, was the manner by which it would speak of Jesus as fully divine. The tensions in the debate were felt in the centre of the

Empire. Constantine had recently been installed as emperor, and he did not want these debates to create fault lines in the Empire. Thus he called for a meeting of church bishops in the city of Nicea, near the Black Sea. This was the first Ecumenical Council, held in CE 325. It would not be the last. After intense discussion, the Council produced the Nicene Creed, which states:

> I believe ... in one Lord Jesus Christ, the only-begotten Son of God, begotten of His Father before all worlds, God of God, Light of Light, very God of very God, begotten, not made, *being of one substance [homoousios] with the Father*, by whom all things were made.[15]

While other doctrines underwent changes, this core conviction did not. Jesus of Nazareth is confessed by the historic church as "fully human, fully divine." Or in the words of our Salvationist doctrine, "the Divine and human natures are united, so that he is truly and properly God and truly and properly man."[16] It was this conviction that led the church to rethink its understanding of God, resulting in its doctrine of God as Trinity: Father, Son and Holy Spirit.

Engaging the Doctrine

Much has happened since the early confessions of faith were formulated. As human constructions they always need to be examined and engaged with questions of our own day to be faithful. Let's consider a few of these challenges and questions.

One challenge confronting this core conviction about Jesus Christ is the accusation that *it has been imposed on the New Testament*. To use a more contemporary image, the church's doctrine about Christ has been photoshopped onto the pages of the New Testament and doesn't truly reflect the Bible's portrait of Christ. In particular, the Nicene Creed's language of Jesus "being of one substance with the Father" is not the language used by any of the biblical writers, and therefore is not acceptable. This is a serious and important challenge, and needs to be acknowledged. However, just because the early creeds use language that is not expressed in the New Testament does not of necessity mean that their *judgment* is different. For instance, many people have attempted to express their judgment of the significance of Abraham Lincoln. As Lincoln lay on his deathbed, one of his former rivals for the presidential office said, "Now he belongs to the ages." Writing 20 years after Lincoln's assassination, the poet Walt Whitman said, "Abraham Lincoln seems to me the grandest figure yet, on all the crowded canvass of the Nineteenth Century." Years later still, the Russian Leo Tolstoy wrote that Lincoln "was not a great general like Napoleon or Washington; he was not such a skilful statesman as Gladstone or Frederick the Great; but his supremacy expresses itself altogether in his peculiar moral power and in the greatness of his character."[17] There are differences in language, but consistency in judgment. While later creeds may use different words to speak of the identity of Jesus, they express a judgment consistent with the New Testament.[18] Thus there is integrity between the New Testament's portrayal of Christ and the later confessions of the church, including the Army's core conviction.

A second concern in our time is how a *particular* person, living in a particular culture and historical moment, can have *universal* significance. How is it that this one individual, Jesus of Nazareth, can take on significance for Asians and Africans and South Americans? This is the scandal of history that lies at the heart of Christian faith. It is a biblical conviction that God has disclosed himself and his purposes through the particular life of Israel, and especially through the life, death and resurrection of Christ.[19] It is through the particular story of Christ that the universal love of God has been made known. However, just as there are four Gospels in the New Testament, each bearing unique witness to Christ, there is need for an understanding of Christ that relates to the cultures of Latin America, Sri Lanka and Japan. The conviction that "the Word became flesh," means that God takes human cultures seriously. There is something about each culture in our world that has the capacity to gain insight into the incarnation. No culture will exhaust its meaning. Having said this, we also need the wider story of the church's confession of faith to keep local insights faithful. The Salvation Army can make a unique gift to the church as we bring together various cultural understandings of Christ through our international life and combine it with the wider witness of the church.

Related to this is the fact of living and working in a *pluralist society*. Salvationist students in Canada study alongside Muslims wearing the hijab, or Hindus enjoying naan for lunch. The families of the earth have come to our own nation. How are we to hold convictions about Christ with integrity, yet respect those who have quite different convictions? My own view is that our Salvationist convictions are always open to new questions and challenges. They are more than private religious convictions. If Christ is "Lord of all" this includes the public life of our nations. But it also means that we listen to the critiques and challenges of our time, such as those that come from other faith traditions. It means that we honour the language of the past, but recognize the need to speak this conviction in terms that are meaningful in the present. Thus when Frederick Booth-Tucker dressed himself in Indian garments and went barefoot, he took seriously the incarnation and helped God's gift of Christ to be recognized.[20] We confess Christ to be God incarnate in a pluralistic world. We do so because the incarnation means that God has taken the world seriously, with all of its cultures. We seek to make that gift of grace visible to our world and its various cultures. The international Salvation Army has a unique opportunity to draw out the many dimensions of that gift.

Finally, we need to understand what we mean when we affirm the conviction that Jesus Christ is "truly and properly God." It is not possible to fully comprehend God. It is the Christian claim however that "God was in Christ" (2 Corinthians 5:19, *NRSV* footnote). *It is in and through Jesus that we comprehend God's character and ways.* We need to be careful how we express this. In saying that Jesus is "truly and properly God" we are not claiming that Jesus is all there is to God. But through the life of Jesus we glimpse the ultimate mystery of God and God's love for us. In other words, as we view Jesus healing the leper with his touch, we see God in action. As we watch Jesus wash the feet of his disciples, we are led to the remarkable awareness of the God who serves. As we hear Jesus pray forgiveness for his oppressors on the cross, we are also hearing the voice of the God who was in Christ reconciling the world to himself. As we look at the wounded hands of the risen Christ, we glimpse the wounded God. Michael Arthur Ramsey has expressed it this way: "The importance of the confession

'Jesus is Lord' is not only that Jesus is divine, but that God is Christlike."[21] The important thing for Salvationists is that we do not speak about God without reference to Jesus Christ.

This fourth doctrine focuses primarily on the identity of Jesus Christ. We believe him to be "truly and properly God, and truly and properly human." This is not, however, a conviction that is relevant only to the past. Who Jesus is for us *today* is tremendously important. How we relate his identity to the issues of our time is the stuff of Christian faith. It is an ongoing task to comprehend Christ's identity and mission in light of the 21st century, and to comprehend our century in light of his identity and mission.

Practising the Doctrine

Frederick Coutts became the eighth General of The Salvation Army in 1963. Just like Terry Fox made courage visible, it was Coutts' conviction that Jesus "makes holiness visible."[22] Because holiness became visible in the person of Christ, Coutts understood personal holiness as "the unfolding of Christ's own character in the life of the believer."[23] Character is most often inferred from the actions we see or the words we hear. The tree is known by its fruit.[24] There is much we could pursue in seeking to understand Christ's character, but let's begin with these biblical stories and how Christ's character might unfold in our lives today.

Christ's Character and Ours

As we explore the Gospels, it's important that we keep in mind the unity of Jesus' divine and human natures. It's not helpful to ask whether a particular action demonstrates his humanity or divinity. His character is not compartmentalized. Thus as we read through the Gospels we will simply inquire what it means to think of his unfolding character. It's all of a piece.

Even before he began his public ministry, "Jesus ... was led by the Spirit in the wilderness, where for forty days he was tempted by the devil."[25] The temptations focus on his identity: "If you are the Son of God." The temptations are not wrong in themselves. Jesus *will* feed a multitude with bread; he *will* know the Father's provision but he will not presume upon it; he *will* inherit the kingdoms of the world, but not in the way suggested by Satan. In each instance Jesus has the capacity and discipline to say, "No." His character disposes him to reject immediate possibilities for God's greater purposes. Holiness often begins with the capacity to refuse even good things for the sake of something greater. Christlikeness is characterized by the self-discipline that can say, "No!"

Christ's compassionate character doesn't play favourites

Jesus crossed social boundaries in his public ministry. Much like social boundaries that existed in Britain's early 20th century, they served to mark the identity and worth of people.[26] He accepted an invitation for a meal from Simon the Pharisee, and from Levi and other tax collectors. He expressed his healing ministry *impartially,* and this often evoked opposition. The Salvation Army's second General, Bramwell Booth, negotiated the tensions of the Army's internationalism at the outbreak of the First World War. At a time when Germany was a marked enemy, this General encouraged Salvationists to drive ambulances for British troops, but he also encouraged the visitation of German prisoners of war in Switzerland. His practice of impartial compassion evoked opposition in his homeland, but it held the Army's international world together. Christ's compassionate character doesn't play favourites.

On one occasion Jesus entered a synagogue on the Sabbath and encountered a man with a "withered hand." Jesus realized that there were some who watched with suspicion to see if he would heal on the Sabbath day. He called the man front and centre, and then posed the question: "Is it lawful to do good or to do harm on the sabbath, to save life or to kill?" His question was met with silence. Jesus "looked around at them with anger [and] was grieved at their hardness of heart" (Mark 3:1-6). In the ministry of Jesus we understand God's engagement with the suffering of humanity. Through Jesus we understand that God is not detached from human suffering. There is an appropriate holy anger that springs from a concern for those obstructions to God's healing presence. And there is an appropriate holy anger to be cultivated in response to the evils of the 21st century.

Approaching the town of Nain one day, Jesus encountered a funeral procession.[27] A widow's only son had died. She had lost a son far too soon, thus also losing her only means of economic support. Luke tells the story, "When the Lord saw her, he had compassion for her and said to her, 'Do not weep.' " Then, risking his own uncleanness, Jesus touched the bier and spoke to the young man who then sat up, began to speak, and was given back to his mother. Out of a *heart of compassion*, Jesus brought life where death cast its shadow. Jesus' character empathized with the widow and gave her a future. The need for empathic compassion in our time has been well articulated by Martha Nussbaum. In her view, "We are in the midst of a crisis of massive proportions and grave global significance."[28] This "silent crisis" is one where we have lost "the ability to imagine sympathetically the predicament of another person."[29] Jesus had that capacity. And as Salvationists meet to study and hear the Word of God, we engage our imaginations in such a way as to evoke that capacity in our own lives.

At a turning point in the synoptic Gospels, Jesus turns to his disciples with a question and then new instruction. After asking who they thought he was, Jesus "began to teach them that the Son of Man *must* undergo great suffering."[30] There are many dimensions to this little word, but it speaks to Christ's sense of *obligation*. Jesus recognized a claim upon his life. He understood himself to be responsible, accountable, obligated. This sense of obligation goes against the grain of western culture. With respect to public conversations,

> The idea of reasoning together was dealt a fateful blow in the twentieth century by the collapse of moral language, the disappearance of 'I ought' and its replacement by 'I want', 'I choose', 'I feel'. Obligations can be debated. Wants, choices and feelings can only be satisfied or frustrated.[31]

Christ's character is marked by a sense of obligation to something greater, "I must."

Luke's Gospel describes a critical moment in Jesus' ministry by stating that Jesus "set his face to go to Jerusalem" (Luke 9:51). The subsequent chapters in Luke portray Jesus' determination to stay on that path and not deviate from it. The character of Jesus was not driven by external circumstances. He didn't waver in his purposes, but was settled in his own mind. Here is the person of Psalm 1 who is like a "tree, planted by streams of water," and not like "chaff that the wind drives away." The unfolding of Christlike character includes *stability.* In the sixth century, Benedictine monks took a "vow of stability." This vow meant that they would remain in one place with the same community in order to live out their faith. It entailed geographical stability. This is not always possible for Salvationists today, who are often on the move because of employment. But there is a kind of "stability of the heart" whose character creates stability for others. Claire McGinnis writes that "the vow of stability implies a long-term commitment to persons and situations. And at a deeper level it involves accepting 'this particular community, this place and these people, this and no other, as the way to God.' "[32] Holiness is characterized by resolute steadfastness, stability.

John's Gospel contains an episode not found in the other Gospels. It happened in the hours just prior to Jesus' arrest and crucifixion. Alone with his disciples, Jesus took a towel and basin and washed their feet, including Judas. Peter objected, but Jesus insisted. Then he drew out the implication of this sacred moment: " 'Do you know what I have done for you? You call me Teacher and Lord—and you are right, for that is what I am. So if I, your Lord and Teacher have washed your feet, you also ought to wash one another's feet. For I have set you an example, that you also should do as I have done for you.' "[33] Christ's character is marked by *humble service.* In contrast, journalists have drawn attention to a *sense of entitlement* that characterizes our culture. Students in school feel entitled to a passing grade simply by showing up to class. CEOs of large corporations feel entitled to bonuses for meeting financial goals, even if it has meant cheating in order to accomplish those goals. Holiness as Christlikeness is expressed by humility, not entitlement. Edward Read has penned lyrics to express this sacramental moment:

> The basin and the towel
> And God upon His knees.

What graciousness is here,
What holy mysteries!
How needs of mine assail me when
I watch the master and His Men.[34]

New Testament writers envision their readers being "conformed to the image of [God's] Son" (Romans 8:29). Out of some exasperation Paul writes to the young Galatian church: "My little children, for whom I am again in the pain of childbirth until *Christ is formed in you*" (Galatians 4:19, emphasis mine). Jesus makes holiness visible, and through the Holy Spirit's presence creates in us the capacity to make holiness visible in our time. This fourth doctrine points to the conviction that holiness is the unfolding of Christ's character in our personal and communal life as Salvationists. For good reason Salvationists pray:

My little children, for whom I am again in the pain of childbirth until Christ is formed in you
—The Apostle Paul

To be like Jesus!
This hope possesses me,
In every thought and deed,
This is my aim, my creed;
To be like Jesus!
This hope possesses me,
His Spirit helping me,
Like him I'll be.[35]

As we bring this chapter to a close, let's summarize our work thus far. Salvationists believe that the Christian Scriptures provide a lens through which to best view our lived relationship with God. The biblical story centres on the person of Jesus Christ, who makes God visible. And as the church reflected on his identity, the conviction grew that in Christ we come to know one who is fully human and fully divine. This realization prompted a more complete expression of God's identity from a Christian perspective. Without losing a commitment to the conviction that "God is one," the church also came to express that oneness in a trinitarian manner: Father, Son and Holy Spirit. Each of these core convictions impact the spirituality that is shaped in relation to this triune God. Each of these core convictions helps us to understand God's identity. They matter. We move from these core convictions about God to doctrines related to humanity, and then to God's mission of salvation.

Reflection Questions for Chapter Four

1. If you are studying this book with a group, read the chapter together.
2. What phrase or section caught your attention and why?
3. In what ways do you see character disclosed in the actions of others?

Forming the Doctrine:

4. Read John 1:1-18 and the story of Thomas after the resurrection in John 20:24-29. What do you find significant in his confession, "My Lord and my God"?
5. What other biblical texts come to your mind when you think of the identity of Jesus?
6. What Christmas carols give attention to the identity of Christ?

Engaging the Doctrine:

7. What has been your experience in sharing something of the story of Jesus with people of other faiths?
8. What other questions do you think our culture poses concerning the person of Jesus?
9. Why do you think it is important to say that Jesus is "fully human"?

Practising the Doctrine:

10. This section draws on several incidents in the life of Jesus to draw out references to his character. What is your response to

the importance of these in our culture?

11. What other stories about Jesus shed light on his character and, potentially, ours?
12. Is there an aspect of character that you think is especially important in our times?

Conclude: Pray the chorus of John Gowans, "To Be Like Jesus" (*SBSA 1987*, No. 107 Chorus Section).

Endnotes for Chapter Four

1 Frederick Coutts, *No Continuing City* (London: Salvationist Publishing, 1978), 62.

2 Luke 2:10-11, emphases mine.

3 These two New Testament books are considered together because they have been composed by the same author, and are linked by language and themes.

4 Joel B. Green, *Salvation* (St. Louis: Chalice Press, 2003), 36.

5 See Luke 7:50; 8:48; 17:19.

6 The Greek word *christos* means *anointed,* and translates the Hebrew word for *Messiah.*

7 The Hebrew word *YHWH* has come to be translated with the word *Yahweh* in most modern English translations. The Hebrew word has no vowels, and means something like, "I will be whoever I will be," such as expressed by God to Moses at the burning bush—see Exodus 3:14.

8 Philippians 2:5-11, emphases mine.

9 C. Wesley, "And can it be," *SBSA 1987,* No. 283. Note that the *Authorized Version* in Wesley's day translated this verse, "Made himself of no repute." But Charles Wesley knew his Greek, and the meaning of *kenosis.*

10 The word *kenosis* has also come to portray God's triune character in creation, providence and governance. See for instance, John Polkinghorne ed., *The Work of Love: Creation as Kenosis* (Grand Rapids: Eerdmans Publishing, 2001).

11 See Isaiah 45:22-23.

12 See John 1:1; 20:28; Colossians 1:19; Hebrews 1:3.

13 Quoted in Mary Cunningham, *Faith in the Byzantine World* (Downers Grove: InterVarsity Press, 2002), 122.

14 The word *docetism* comes from a Greek word (*dokeo*) which means, "It appears to be." Thus according to this view, Jesus only "appeared to be human."

15 The controversy centred around two words, differentiated by an iota! Athanasius and his supporters advocated that Jesus was *homoousios,* of the *same* stuff, as God. Arius argued for the word, *homoiousios,* Jesus was of *like* stuff. One vowel, yet there was a world of difference between the two words.

16 The word "man" in this instance needs to be understood as referring to humanity, not male gender.

17 See Doris Kearns Goodwin, *Team of Rivals: The Political Genius of Abraham Lincoln* (New York: Simon and Schuster Paperbacks, 2005), especially pp. 747-748.

18 "It is essential ... to distinguish between judgements and the conceptual terms in which those judgements are rendered. We cannot concretely perform an act of judgement without employing some particular, contingent verbal and conceptual resources; judgement-making is an operation performed with words

and concepts. At the same time, however, the same judgement can be rendered in variety of conceptual terms, all of which may be informative about a particular judgement's force and implications." See David S. Yeago, "The New Testament and the Nicene Dogma" in Stephen E. Fowl ed., *The Theological Interpretation of Scripture* (Malden: Blackwell Publishers, 1997), 93. The Australian Salvationist Dean Smith has drawn attention to the concern that the church has been adversely affected by concepts drawn more from the Hellenistic world rather than the biblical story, such as the concept that God is impassible, or immune to suffering. He has given special attention to its impact on Christology. See Dean Smith, "Christology in Crisis: An Assessment and Response" (PhD Thesis, The University of Queensland, 2009). http://espace.library.uq.edu.au/view/UQ:203098, accessed February 1, 2013.

19 "God's way to universality is through the particular." Daniel L. Migliore, *Faith Seeking Understanding, 2nd Edition* (Grand Rapids: Eerdmans Publishing, 2004), 198.

20 See Robert Sandall, *The History of The Salvation Army: Volume Two, 1878-1886* (New York: The Salvation Army, 1950), 272-281.

21 Quoted in Alister E. McGrath, *Christian Theology: An Introduction, 4th Edition* (Malden: Blackwell Publishing, 2007), 275.

22 Frederick Coutts, *The Call to Holiness* (St. Albans: Campfield Press, 1957), 9.

23 Coutts, *No Continuing City,* 62. Coutts was strongly influenced by the writings of C.H. Dodd who said: "We may fairly say that it is never safe to emphasize the call to holiness as part of Christian teaching, unless the idea of the Holy is understood by constant reference to the Jesus of the gospels, His example and teaching." See *No Continuing City*, 61.

24 See Luke 6:43-45.

25 See Luke 4:1-13.

26 The sense of social boundaries has been expressed in the television series, *Downton Abbey,* with its notion of "upstairs and downstairs."

27 See Luke 7:11-17.

28 Martha Nussbaum, *Not For Profit: Why Democracy Needs the Humanities* (Princeton: Princeton University Press, 2010), 1.

29 Nussbaum, *Not For Profit*, 6. Nussbaum's argument is that modern education in the West and India has permitted the sciences to supplant the arts in the curriculum, thus taking away from the development of an empathic imagination. The pursuit of dollars for education is, in her view, undermining the capacities needed for democracy.

30 Mark 8:31, emphasis mine.

31 Jonathan Sacks, *The Dignity of Difference: How to Avoid the Clash of Civilization* (London: Continuum, 2002), 3. When Sacks was invited to address the opening of the European Parliament in 2008, this religious leader said, "Rights without responsibilities are the sub-prime mortgages of the moral world."

32 See Claire Mathews McGinnis, "'Yea, the Work of Our Hands, Establish Thou It': On Stability in Academic Life," in *The Scope of Our Art*, L. Gregory Jones and Stephanie Paulsell eds., (Grand Rapids: Eerdmans Publishing, 2002), 182.

33 John 13:12-15.

34 The lyrics for this song can be found in Edward Read, *In the Hands of Another: Memoirs of Edward Read* (Toronto: The Salvation Army, 2002), 117-118. The song was intended to be used with the melody, "Lennox," which is well known in the Province of Newfoundland and Labrador where the song was composed. It should also be noted that the original lyrics used the words, "And Jesus upon his knees," but Edward Read's son, James, has discovered different manuscripts, one of which has the lyrics quoted here, "And God upon his knees"! Edward Read understood the implications of this fourth doctrine.

35 J. Gowans, "To Be Like Jesus," *SBSA 1987,* No. 107 Chorus Section.

CHAPTER 5

Humanity: Holiness as Restoring the Image of God

We believe that our first parents were created in a state of innocency, but by their disobedience they lost their purity and happiness, and that in consequence of their fall all men have become sinners, totally depraved and as such are justly exposed to the wrath of God.—Doctrine 5

There is only one thing capable of defeating tragedy, which is the belief in God who in love sets his image on the human person, thus endowing each of us with non-negotiable, unconditional dignity.—Jonathan Sacks[1]

VICTORIAN ENGLAND WAS A NATION OF CONTRASTS. ITS emerging Empire in the late 1800s brought significant wealth to individuals, and yet many men, women and children lived in extreme conditions of poverty. William Booth addressed this social chasm with a jarring comparison. Those living in poverty, he argued, were worse off than "cab horses." At least when a taxi cab horse stumbled under exhaustion, its owners provided "a shelter for the night, food for the stomach, and work allotted to it by which it can earn its corn." But, he continued, this provision was "absolutely unattainable by millions of our fellow men and women." Creatures made in the image of God were treated with less dignity than cab horses.[2]

The Salvation Army's fifth doctrine focuses on the question of what it means to be human. It holds in tension the conviction that while we are created in the image of God, we have also defaced that image through the realities of sin. Holding this tension between humanity's dignity and destructiveness has not always been maintained in the church. But it is a core conviction of importance in the 21st century, and has significant implications for our understanding and practice of holiness.

Forming the Doctrine

Among its many features, the Bible narrates the stories of people. Some persons are named, such as Esther, Martha and Timothy. Others are anonymous, such as the widow who gave money to the temple despite her poverty. Some are powerful, such as Solomon and Caesar Augustus. Others are vulnerable, such as the woman who anointed Jesus in the home of Simon the Pharisee. And others are fictional, such as the Samaritan in the parable who came to the aid of the victim of thieves. The Bible's view of individuals and society has helped to form this doctrine.

We begin where the Bible begins, with its opening chapters in the Book of Genesis. They set the tone not only for Genesis but for the rest of the biblical story. The Bible is clear that humankind stands in continuity with the rest of creation. In many respects we share creaturely life with "living creatures of every kind."[3] What makes humanity different comes with the sixth day of creation: "Then God said, 'Let us make humankind in our image, according to our likeness' ... So God created humankind in his image, in the image of God he created them; male and female he created them."[4] While humanity shares much with the rest of creation, we are distinct because of being made in God's image. And both male and female share that capacity. Genesis unfolds the various dimensions of being made in God's image. Humanity's relationship to God is fundamental, since man and woman alone are addressed by God. Human relationships constitute a critical element since it is "not good"[5] that Adam is alone; the relationship between Adam and Eve is necessary to this image. This is not primarily about marriage; it's about the importance of community. Finally, humans have a vocation in relation to God's created order. We are called to exercise "dominion" in relation to it, not to dominate it but to care for it as God cares for it. We are made in the image of God, or using its Latin terminology, the *imago Dei*. Joel Green concludes, "The concept of the *imago Dei*, then, is fundamentally relational, or covenantal, and takes as its ground and focus the graciousness of God's own covenantal relations with humanity and the rest of creation."[6] When we speak of the uniqueness of humanity, we do so in relational terms: to God, to others and to the created order.

We do not sin because we are human; we sin because we are less than human

However, while Genesis opens the biblical symphony with chords that vibrate with the *imago Dei*, it also introduces dissonance: we are *sinful* creatures and live in a world deeply infected by sin. No sooner has creation's "goodness" been introduced when something goes wrong. The first man and woman were given boundaries—they could eat from most of the garden's fruit, but not from a particular tree. In their freedom they chose to ignore the boundary that had been set out. And there are consequences to their actions. They hide from God, mistrust each other and feel the shame of nakedness. The death alluded to in Genesis 3 is a relational death, not biological. The problem is that their actions do not stay contained; they begin to pollute their world like a defective oil rig in the Gulf of Mexico. It doesn't take long before "The Lord saw that the wickedness of humankind was great in the earth, and that every inclination of the thoughts of their hearts was only evil continually. And the Lord was sorry that he had made humankind on the earth, and it grieved him to his heart" (Genesis 6:5-6). The Bible makes little attempt to offer explanations for the origin of evil, and we are wise not to go down that road. The Christian tradition uses the language of "fallen" to note that what was intended for creation has not been realized. We live in a fallen world, a bent world, a polluted world, a fragmented world, a lost world. Sin results when creatures made in God's image use their freedom to decide against God. Humanity's sinfulness affects our relationship with God, between ourselves, within ourselves and with the created world. This intrusion into God's world touches the very core of a person's character, or heart, and works its way into all relationships and the various cultures of our world. We do not sin because we are human; we sin because we are less than human.

> In his ministry, Jesus demonstrated the dignity and value of each person he met and for whom he cared

Having set the tone in Genesis, the biblical story develops from the conviction that humanity is made in God's image, and while sin is present in the human heart and society's structures, it has not completely destroyed that image. We hear these opening themes of Genesis played out in the integrity of Joseph and the duplicity of Jacob; in the courage of Esther and the denials of Peter; in the generosity of the Philippian church and the lukewarm church of Laodicea. It is especially apparent in the public ministry of Jesus as he relates to people of all standings in life. He touched the leper, healed a Roman centurion's servant, defended a woman taken in adultery, restored the life of a synagogue leader's daughter and associated with tax collectors. Jesus cared for *all* because he understood *all* to be endowed with the image of God. In his ministry, Jesus demonstrated the dignity and value of each person he met and for whom he cared.

As has happened with other core convictions, the biblical understanding of humanity underwent changes during the church's story. Randy Maddox has observed that the polarization of the church between the East and West resulted in a particular emphasis in the doctrine's understanding of *imago Dei* and sin.[7] In his view, the western church in its Catholic and Protestant forms put more emphasis on the *fall* of humanity rather than the image of God. The Eastern Orthodox Church, in contrast, emphasized the created *image of God* rather than our sinfulness.[8] This Salvationist doctrine gives more attention to humanity's sinfulness, but it is helpful to note that our roots lie with the work of John and Charles Wesley who found *both* of these traditions helpful.[9] Thus it is essential that we hold in tension the fact that despite humanity's sinfulness, we are created in the image of God who has been disclosed most fully in the person of Christ.

In light of this we can touch on a couple of phrases in this doctrine that may be problematic. One phrase expresses the conviction that humanity is "totally depraved." These words are sometimes understood to mean that none of us can do any good. But even Jesus acknowledged that we "who are evil, know how to give good gifts to our children."[10] *The Salvation Army Handbook of Doctrine* adds that the phrase "does not mean that every person is as bad as he or she can be, but rather that the depravity which sin has produced in human nature extends to the total personality.... No area of human nature remains unaffected."[11] Another phrase of concern in the doctrine is that humanity is "justly exposed to the wrath of God." Wrath or anger is an appropriate way to speak of God as long as it is heard as part of the whole biblical story. This story has God's holy love at the heart of anything else that might be said of God, including God's anger. God's wrath gives notice that God is not indifferent to sin in our world. Yet despite our sinfulness, God acts in grace to restore us to his image and likeness. For this reason, "salvation means nothing less, but nothing more, than our becoming fully and genuinely human."[12]

This fifth core conviction of The Salvation Army is grounded in the whole of the biblical story and reflects the important traditions of the church. As we turn to its hearing in the 21st century, we want to keep its emphasis in mind: humanity is made in the image of the triune God, and despite our sinfulness that image determines the worth and significance of all people. This core conviction matters!

Engaging the Doctrine

The 1980 film, *The Elephant Man*,[13] is based on the true story of John (Joseph) Merrick. Living in Victorian England, Merrick was disfigured at birth. His facial distortions prompted others to taunt him as the "Elephant Man," and led him eventually to become part of circus side-shows. He was on display and dehumanized by virtually everyone who met him. Dr. Frederick Treves, however, took an interest in Merrick. Initially that interest had to do with medical research, which itself may have viewed Merrick as an object and not a person. About to give up attempts at communication, Treves hears Merrick reciting Psalm 23. This moment helps the doctor to begin to see Merrick as a human being. Others, however, were not so considerate. On one occasion, Merrick is trapped by those who would trample his humanity. In desperation, he yells out, "I am not an animal! I am a human being! I ... Am ... A ... Man!" The film portrays the moving story of how some individuals, including Merrick himself, begin to understand what it means to be human. This issue is of paramount importance in the 21st century.

Science and Imago Dei

After a long personal struggle, Charles Darwin published his book, *On the Origin of Species,* in 1859. This exacting scientist, moved by the illness of his own daughter, finally made public his thinking about the development of biological life. His work on evolution met with ridicule from some, but was warmly embraced by others. The tremors from his work are still being felt, especially in the way we seek to understand the significance of being human. It is argued by some that if humanity has evolved over millions of years, we can no longer view ourselves as being unique, or important. Humanity is simply the result of blind forces at work over a long period of time. How then might we give full respect to the work of Darwin and retain the integrity of our core conviction that we are also made in God's image? I want to argue here that belief in evolution is not only compatible with belief in God's creative work, it also tells us something very important about God.

It is essential in this, as in any discussion, to understand terms being used. The word "evolution" can raise all kinds of unnecessary red flags. The sciences have helped us to understand that the universe has a story. If we imagine something like a big bang as its beginning, this took place about 13.7 billion years ago. In time our own planet formed and cooled about four billion years ago. As it did, new forms of matter gradually emerged and gave rise to biological life, including human life. Arthur Peacocke summarizes: "On the surface of the Earth, new forms of *living* matter (that is, living organisms) have come into existence by this continuous process—that is what we mean by evolution."[14] Evolution describes the story by which life, including human life, came into existence on our planet. What needs to be recognized, of course, is that while this scientific description is accurate, it doesn't tell the whole story. What the Bible and subsequent Christian convictions express is a view of God that is deeply involved in the evolutionary process. It is not that God intruded into creation with special acts to bring about humankind. We have already spoken of the one God who is constantly creating and sustaining this world.[15] This requires a different language, but not one in opposition to science. It is appropriate to create a genetic map of human beings; it is also appropriate for the Psalmist to offer poetic praise to God: "For it was you who formed my inward parts; you knit me together in my mother's womb. I praise you, for I am fearfully and wonderfully made."[16] Maps of Canada help to navigate its huge expanse, but in order to really comprehend Canada we need to ski the Rockies or fish off Cape St. Mary's. What scientists *have* helped us to understand is that the evolutionary process has involved the death of some forms of life in order to create and sustain new forms of life. However, if God has in fact been deeply involved in the processes of evolution, *God has also participated in death that life might emerge.* Peacocke argues that,

> ... for any concept of God to be morally acceptable and coherent ... we cannot but tentatively propose that *God* suffers in, with, and under the creative processes of the world with their costly unfolding in time. In other words, the processes of creation are immensely costly *to God* in a way dimly shadowed by the ordinary experience of the costliness of creativity in multiple aspects of human existence—whether it be in giving birth, in aesthetic creation, or in creating and maintaining human social structures.[17]

This suggestion leads us back to the notion of a self-giving God. Paul's description of Jesus who "emptied himself"[18] depicts not simply *his* self-giving, but the character of the triune God who has become deeply involved in the evolutionary processes. Far from diminishing humanity's significance, evolution *actually* deepens it, and enhances our understanding of God who suffers in order to give life.

Humanity as Commodity

It is increasingly said that "Everything has its price." The truth of this statement has taken on new forms in our time. For a price a person can be hired to wait in line for those wanting to attend a congressional hearing in Washington. Married couples in the West can pay a woman in India to carry a pregnancy on their behalf. Civic parks are named after wealthy donors. In Michael Sandel's view, we have "drifted from *having* a market economy to *being* a market society." He argues, "Today, the logic of buying and selling no longer applies to material goods alone but increasingly governs the whole of life. It is time to ask whether we want to live this way."[19] It is appropriate to speak of a car or internet service as a commodity. But when a person or community is viewed as a commodity, it radically changes things. Is a child a commodity? Would we entertain the practice of selling votes in an election? Should rich nations be able to sell off their environmental responsibility to poorer nations? The question that needs to be asked is: "Are there some things that money should *not* be able to buy?" The Salvation Army's fifth doctrine matters in light of this trend to commodify life, such as the following examples show.

We may not find it advertised in government publications, but there is a new form of tourism. It's called *transplant tourism*. Human organs, such as kidneys, are bought and sold on an international black market. More Canadians need a kidney transplant than there are kidney donors available. For a large sum of money, however, arrangements can be made to travel to parts of Southeast Asia where illegal clinics provide one. Tragically the donors most often come from situations of deep poverty, and the medical procedures are poorly supervised. It is clear that the donors themselves become a commodity. They give an important organ to someone they don't know, in exchange for a small amount of money. The provision of human organs this way is one instance of treating people as a commodity, an object.

According to Chris Hedges, the world of *pornography* "is a world without pity. It is about reducing other human beings to commodities, to objects."[20] It is estimated that there are more than four million porn websites, with teenagers being the largest users. There are more than 13 million porn films made every year in the United States and in 2006, porn revenues around the globe exceeded $97 billion. Porn is a leading global "industry." Market dynamics thus play a role in this area of life, and the demand has increasingly turned to the desire for violence in porn. One director of porn films describes his actresses as "a throwaway commodity in a throwaway world."[21] The reasons why women become involved in the porn industry are complex, but the consequences are destructive. Their lives often come to exhibit mannerisms similar to military personnel who suffer from post-traumatic syndrome. On the other hand, those who become addicted to viewing pornography lose a capacity for intimacy. They have difficulty distinguishing the difference between pornographic fantasies and real relationships. Porn reduces women to objects that can be discarded and relationships that are defined by power and money. In the words of Chris Hedges, pornography "extinguishes the sacred and the human to worship power, control, force, and pain. It replaces empathy, eros, and compassion with the illusion that we are gods."[22] Porn has its own manifestations of sin; it has little comprehension of what it means to be in the image of God.[23]

The cultural acceptance of sex as commodity has resulted in the pernicious form of *human sex trafficking*. This global empire takes women and children from their homes, either by deception or force, and transfers them to places where they are confined for purposes of sex. It is a multi-billion dollar operation. The United Nations estimates that at least 2.5 million persons at any given moment are trafficked globally. It has been estimated that at least 800 women are brought into Canada each year by human traffickers. The demand for this "commodity" creates the "pull" for human trafficking, and issues of poverty "push" some women into this trade. Trafficking persons for sex takes place within national boundaries, but it also crosses those boundaries to become a global issue. This treatment of women and children violates their worth and dignity, and demonstrates systemic and global dimensions of evil. The biblical understanding of "principalities and powers" finds one of its contemporary expressions in this modern form of slavery. Its tentacles reach from the heart of a parent willing to sell one of his children, to the brutality of organized crime. It is for this reason that Salvationists pray, "Deliver us from evil."[24]

This fifth doctrine bears upon important issues in our day. It does not exhaust the way we understand our humanity, but it does provide a religious framework. Jonathan Sacks expresses our conviction well: "There is only one thing capable of defeating tragedy, which is the belief in God who in love sets his image on the human person, thus endowing each of us with non-negotiable, unconditional dignity."[25] We recognize the value and beauty of individuals and cultures, yet become painfully aware of the evils that take shape through the tools and technologies available. Salvationists value the various academic disciplines that help us to understand these dynamics, all the while keeping the conviction that people are not a means to an end. All people are endowed with the image of God, even within the depths of a very sinful world.

Practising the Doctrine

In one of his many sermons, John Wesley expressed a core conviction: "Ye know that the great end of religion is to renew our hearts in the image of God."[26] Whatever else might be said of Wesley's views of holiness, our renewal in God's image was central. New Testament writers would agree. The Apostle Paul, for instance, exhorted the Colossian believers not to lie to one another, seeing that they have clothed themselves "with the new self, which is being renewed in knowledge according to the image of its creator" (Colossians 3:10). Similarly, Paul instructed the Ephesians to put away their former way of life "and to be renewed in the spirit of your minds, and to clothe yourselves with the new self, created according to the likeness of God in true righteousness and holiness" (Ephesians 4:22-24). For Paul and other writers in the New Testament, the image of God has been fully expressed in the person of Jesus Christ: "He is the image of the invisible God..." (Colossians 1:15). Christian holiness involves becoming fully human. Like the restoration of a damaged Rembrandt painting, Christians are privileged to undergo the triune God's transforming grace in such a way that we reflect its embodiment in Jesus of Nazareth. This work of restoration is intended to take place both personally and communally. What *practices* then are related to this renewal in God's image? Let's outline a few.

Renewal in the image of God takes place as we *practise gifting in a commodified world.* It was noted earlier that we live in an age when virtually all relationships have been reduced to a commodity. While this impacts all of life, it has a profound effect on children. Tragically they learn that they are valued only when they succeed or win. So from designer labels to high intensity competitive sports, children have little opportunity to be valued for the persons of worth they are. M. Douglas Meeks, however, makes an important point: "What is common to children in all places and times is that children can only survive and flourish if they are *given* what is necessary for life and life abundant. Children live by gifting."[27] The gifts of respect, playful sports and laughter enable a child to learn her intrinsic worth. Turn the child into an object for advertisers or the ambitions of a coach and that intrinsic worth will die. Gifts evoke life. The Salvation Army begins a child's life with a ceremony of dedication. It is one way to acknowledge the child as a gift. This ceremony is rooted in the deeper understanding that Christian faith centres on a gifting God: "Thanks be to God for his indescribable gift!" (2 Corinthians 9:15). We are valued and treasured by God simply because of who we are. We are gifted by God, and we are called to be a gifting community. In the words of Meeks, "Holiness means the practice of love in justice as the return of the gift of God's love."[28] When Salvationists play floor hockey with neighbourhood kids, when we teach them the basics of music, when we provide meals for impoverished students and call them by name, we practise holiness. We gift young people with the conviction that they, too, are made in the image of God. They are not commodities but creatures capable of loving God and themselves.

Renewal in God's image takes place when we *practise friendship in a world of differences.* History knows too many tragedies where humanity has been unable to live with difference. The ovens at Auschwitz were built to deal with threatening differences. Ethnic cleansings, whether in Bosnia or Rwanda, have devised their own responses to difference. Racial prejudice reacts to those who are different. Today we see difference all around us in language, abilities and disabilities, sexual orientation, food, architecture, music, and in the games we play. Differences can be threatening to our sense of identity. Neighbourhoods and nations become mistrustful as people move in with their differences. Differences can divide, but this

Salvationist doctrine of humanity responds to questions posed by Jonathan Sacks: "Can we find, in the human other, a trace of the Divine Other? Can we recognize God's image in one who is not in my image?"[29] It is our conviction that each person we meet reflects something of God's image. Each person has the capacity to care for others, to care for creation, to appreciate beauty, to act courageously and sacrificially, to engage in conversation. Conversations don't require agreement of viewpoints. But they do seek understanding. This can only occur as we listen and trust, face to face. "Thus the LORD used to speak to Moses face to face, as one speaks to a friend" (Exodus 33:11). The nurturing of this kind of friendship takes seriously the relational dimensions of the *imago Dei*. There is a present danger of letting Facebook define the nature of friendship. It may help, but it too easily admits and dismisses friends. Friendship is hard work. Perhaps that is why it is only at the *end* of his time with the twelve disciples that Jesus says, "I do not call you servants any longer ... but I have called you friends, because I have made known to you everything that I have heard from my Father" (John 15:15). Jesus didn't give "status updates" to everyone. But he did see in the leper, the hemorrhaging woman and the Samaritan something of the image of God. He befriended the other and so practised the holy dimensions of this doctrine. Salvationists are called to broaden their understanding of God by finding God's image in those who are different. The practice of holiness involves living out "the dignity of difference."[30]

Renewal in the image of the triune God requires us to *practise attentiveness in a world of distraction*. The biblical story of Martha and Mary's hosting of Jesus has its humourous moments.[31] Martha busied herself preparing a meal while her sister listened to Jesus. Finally Martha exploded and criticized Jesus for failing to see the obvious. Jesus responded, "Martha, Martha, you are worried and distracted by many things." His words blindsided Martha, but she is not the only one who is easily distracted. Maggie Jackson has explored the nature of distraction in our own age. Our personal digital assistants, our constant multitasking and Twittering impact the depths to which we relate to others. In her words, "The way we live is eroding our capacity for deep, sustained, perceptive attention—the building block of intimacy, wisdom and cultural progress ... Put most simply, attention defines us and is the bedrock of society ... Yet, increasingly, we are shaped by distraction."[32] In this world of distraction, Salvationists are called to practise attentiveness. When we gather as a worshipping community we learn to be attentive to the difference in the other; we seek to hear God's word to us that day; we listen deeply to the traditions of the Army. It is also required that we be attentive to the depths of evil, beyond the shallow reports of tabloids. It is necessary to look deeper than the entertaining confessionals of celebrities on television talk shows. We need to look for the grace of God in the other person who is the stranger. We need to put away our digital devices when conversing with another person, and especially when we join others in worship of the God who is attentive to us, who is mindful of us (see Psalm 8).

As we worship God, whose character is expressed in the biblical story, we ask for courage and wisdom to fight those evils that plague our time and context. In this respect, Salvationists understand the Christian life to be one of combat. Because we take sin seriously in all its dimensions and glimpse the image of God, we fight to restore that image in the personal and social worlds we inhabit. How appropriate it is, then, to sing this song as we worship:

Ev'ry nation under heaven, Ev'ry colour ev'ry tribe,
All created in your image, By your will and by your design,
Ev'ry single human being, Ev'ry child of ev'ry race,
All are offspring of your pleasure, Bearing likeness of your face.

We are one Lord, by your making, And in you we find our worth.
You have called us all your children In your Kingdom here on earth.

Ev'ry language ever spoken, Diverse tongues from diverse lands,
Each reflecting something diff'rent In the beauty of your plan.
Ev'ry nation under heaven, Ev'ry colour, ev'ry tribe,
All created in your image, By your will and by design.[33]

Having introduced our core conviction about humanity, we are now in a position to give more sustained attention to God's response to the human condition. In a word, it is called *salvation*. And all of the remaining doctrines touch on some aspect of this *immense* salvation.

Reflection Questions for Chapter Five

1. What is one way you learned to be valued as a child?
2. If you are studying this book with a group, read the chapter together.
3. What phrase or section caught your attention and why?

Forming the Doctrine:

4. Who are some of the people in Scripture who interest you and why?
5. Read Luke 13:10-17. How do the issues of this doctrine show up in this text?
6. How is the word "sin" commonly used in our culture?
7. What is your understanding of the phrase, "the wrath of God"?

Engaging the Doctrine:

8. It can be argued that if we are only the result of blind evolutionary forces, then there is nothing preventing the strong from dominating the weak so that life becomes "the survival of the fittest." How does this fifth doctrine respond to this concern?
9. In what ways do you see people dehumanized in our culture?
10. What difference does it make to view *all* people as made in the image of God?

Practising the Doctrine:

11. If it is true that "Children live by gifting," what gifts do you recall receiving from others in your childhood? How is your Christian community expressing gifts to young people?

12. What differences between people do you notice in your city or town? What will it mean to practise friendship with such people?
13. What have you observed about the attentiveness of other people?

Conclude: Pray Psalm 8 together.

Endnotes for Chapter Five

1 Jonathan Sacks, *The Great Partnership: Science, Religion, and the Search for Meaning* (New York: Schocken Books, 2011), 38.

2 See William Booth, *In Darkest England, and the Way Out* (London: International Headquarters of The Salvation Army, 1890), 20.

3 Genesis 1:24-25.

4 Genesis 1:26-27.

5 Genesis 2:18.

6 Joel Green, *Salvation* (St. Louis: Chalice Press, 2003), 19.

7 See Randy L. Maddox, *Responsible Grace* (Nashville: Kingswood Books, 1994), 65-67.

8 It should be noted that the different traditions of the church emphasized different images for sin, but the Wesleys combined them. John Wesley, in one of his sermons, spoke of sin with multiple images: "Our sins, considered in regard to ourselves, are *chains of iron and fetters of brass*. They are *wounds* wherewith the world, the flesh and the devil, have gashed and mangled us all over. They are *diseases* that drink up our blood and spirit, that bring us down to the chambers of the grave. But considered ... with regard to God, they are *debts*, immense and numberless." Similarly, Charles Wesley penned these lines in one hymn: "He breaks the power of canceled sin, His sets the prisoner free." And in another he sang: "The whole of sin's disease, Spirit of health, remove." Rather than view these different images as in opposition, they point towards a more complete understanding of humanity's sinfulness.

9 During their studies at Oxford University, the Wesleys were introduced to the writings of the Patristics who emphasized the *imago Dei*.

10 Luke 11:13.

11 *The Salvation Army Handbook of Doctrine* (London: Salvation Books, 2010), 114.

12 Joel Green, *Salvation*, 13.

13 *The Elephant Man* (1980). Directed by David Lynch. Paramount Pictures.

14 Arthur Peacocke, "The Cost of New Life," in *The Work of Love*, ed. John Polkinghorne, (Grand Rapids: Eerdmans Publishing, 2001), 23. Note that humanity's relationship with nature is expressed with the phrase, "then the Lord God formed man (*'adam*) from the dust of the ground (*'adamah*)." Nancey Murphy captures the play on words in English: "we are *humans* made from *humus*," in *Reconciling Theology and Science* (Kitchener: Pandora Press, 1997), 64.

15 See Chapter Two.

16 Psalm 139:13-14.

17 Peacocke, "The Cost of New Life," 37. The danger, of course, is turning evolution into something not intended by science, and that is the domination of one group of people by another, such as Nazi Germany's treatment of the Jews.

18 Philippians 2:6-7. See discussion in Chapter Four.

19 Michael J. Sandel, *What Money Can't Buy: The Moral Limits of Markets* (New York: Farrar, Straus and Giroux, 2012), 6.

20 Chris Hedges, *Empire of Illusion* (Toronto: Alfred A. Knopf, 2009), 73. Data in this section is taken from the chapter, "The Illusion of Love."

21 Hedges, *Empire of Illusion*, 78.

22 Hedges, *Empire of Illusion*, 87.

23 See The Salvation Army Position Statement on Pornography: http://www.salvationarmyethics.org/position-statements/pornography/. Accessed February 8, 2013.

24 For further information see, http://salvationist.ca/action-support/human-trafficking/. Accessed February 8, 2013.

25 Jonathan Sacks, *The Great Partnership: Science, Religion, and the Search for Meaning* (New York: Schocken Books, 2011), 38.

26 John Wesley Sermon #44, "Original Sin" – see http://wesley.nnu.edu/john-wesley/the-sermons-of-john-wesley-1872-edition/sermon-44-original-sin/. Accessed February 8, 2013.

27 M. Douglas Meeks, *Trinity, Community and Power: Mapping Trajectories in Wesleyan Theology* (Nashville: Kingswood Books, 2000), 19.

28 M. Douglas Meeks, *Trinity, Community and Power*, 27.

29 Jonathan Sacks, *The Dignity of Difference*, (London: Continuum, 2002), 17.

30 The title of Sacks' book. It is important to note that a Salvation Army officer's covenant includes the promise to "befriend the friendless."

31 See Luke 10:38-42.

32 Maggie Jackson, *Distracted: The Erosion of Attention and the Coming Dark Age* (New York: Prometheus Books, 2008), 13.

33 Lyrics and melody composed by Leonard Ballantine, "Every Nation Under Heaven," *Hallelujah Choruses: Volume 4* (Des Plaines: The Salvation Army USA Central Territory, 2010), No. 194.

Atonement: Holiness as the Cross-Shaped Life

We believe that our Lord Jesus Christ has by his suffering and death made an atonement for the whole world so that whosoever will may be saved.—Doctrine 6

For execution by crucifixion to become the criterion of holiness, and God's holiness at that, became the supreme scandal.—Paul Minear[1]

If there is one symbol considered central to the Christian faith, it is the cross. Church buildings have been designed in the shape of a cross and some of the greatest works of music and art focus on the crucifixion of Christ.[2] Crosses mark important battlefields and scenes of tragedy. Crosses become the focus of attention the world over on Good Friday, and are carried into worship services to mark the centrality of this symbol to Christian faith. The symbol of the cross, however, has also become problematic in our time. As European nations explored the New World in the 1500s, crosses were used to symbolize the conquest of its indigenous peoples. Burning images of a cross have been used to symbolize fearful expressions of racism. This symbol that is so important to faith has tragically become a source of oppression for many. Yet it is a core conviction that the crucifixion of Jesus of Nazareth lies at the heart of Christian faith. Salvationist doctrine states that the crucifixion of Christ has profound significance because it is an *atoning* death. This core conviction argues that the heart of God's character is found in the cross, thus the heart of holiness for God's people.

Forming the Doctrine

The whole of the New Testament is consistent in one conviction: Jesus died! Some Gospel writers say simply that he "breathed his last" (Mark 15:37). Others, such as Paul, state that Jesus "humbled himself and became obedient to the point of death—even death on a cross" (Philippians 2:8). An early creed states that Jesus "suffered under Pontius Pilate, was crucified, dead and buried." The Christian tradition does not dispute the *fact* of Jesus' death. Where it differs is how we are to understand its *meaning*, to make sense of it. It has been observed that the church has not held up any one explanation as the only interpretation of his death. The arms of the cross embrace many meanings. Let's explore then what it means to speak of his crucifixion as an atoning death.

First, it's important to *connect Jesus' death to his life*. One of the baffling things for modern readers of the New Testament is why Jesus was crucified in the first place. How is it that this person "filled with compassion" seemed to pose a threat to others? Briefly put, the compassionate ministry of Jesus threatened a particular view of holiness in Jesus' social world. Recall that the Jerusalem temple was built with a space called "the holy of holies" at its centre. Entrance to this holy space was permitted only to a single male high priest, and only on one day of the year, the Day of Atonement. Boundaries extended outwards from the "holy of holies" permitting access first to other priests, then to other men, and then to women and Gentiles. The blind and disfigured were not welcome in the temple because they were "unclean." Israel's understanding of holiness governed not only the architectural design of the temple, but the social world that extended beyond it. When Jesus healed a leper and "touched" him, he crossed a social boundary. When Jesus ate meals with tax collectors, he violated the rules of the table. Compassion could be expressed, but only as long as it took the form of reinforcing social purity, upholding a view of holiness understood as separation from what was unclean. So it was that after Jesus healed a man's withered arm on the Sabbath, his opponents "were filled with fury and discussed with one another what they might do to Jesus" (Luke 6:11). This opposition gathered steam throughout Jesus' life until such time as he was accused before Pilate, "We found this man perverting our nation" (Luke 23:2). The compassionate ministry of Jesus came to be seen as a threat to God's holiness. For this reason he was turned over to Roman authorities, who also viewed Jesus as a threat to their power.[3] While there is much more that could be said, we can begin to sense that Jesus' horrific death was deeply connected to his compassionate ministry.[4]

Unless I see the mark of the nails in his hands ... I will not believe
—Thomas,
the Disciple

If there is a danger in seeking the meaning of Jesus' death apart from his life, there is a corresponding *danger of separating the cross from his resurrection*. This sixth affirmation of faith says nothing about the resurrection of Jesus. Yet as Paul said, "If Christ has not been raised, your faith is futile" (1 Corinthians 15:17). It can be argued that the importance of Jesus' resurrection comes *before* the significance of his death. That is, without his resurrection the death of Jesus would be meaningless. It is the resurrection that vindicates all that he said and did. Having been raised from the dead infuses his death with significance. It is the resurrection that gives birth to Christian faith and the production of the New Testament. John's Gospel, like the others, paints a picture of confusion on the first day of resurrection. Word filters through that Jesus is alive, and had shown himself to some of his followers. Thomas was not so sure, and counters with the condition, "Unless I see the mark of the nails in his hands ... I will not believe." One week later, the risen Christ appears to his followers and Thomas is invited to see the marks of crucifixion. He responds, "My Lord and my God!" (John 20:24-28). We cannot understand God apart from the risen Christ. And we cannot understand the risen Christ apart from the wounds on his hands. We worship a wounded God. For this reason Salvationists come to Easter morning singing:

> Crown him the Lord of love;
> Behold his hands and side,

Those *wounds yet visible above,*
In beauty glorified ....[5]

Thus any meaning of the death of Jesus needs to be approached from two directions. His death is an outgrowth of his life, and his death finds meaning precisely because it is not an ending.

Early Christians recognized that allegiance to the crucified Christ made little sense in their culture. In one of his letters to the young church at Corinth, Paul acknowledged that it was perceived by others as both a "stumbling block" and "foolishness" (1 Corinthians 1:23). Yet early Christians were transformed by the conviction that "the stone the builders rejected ... has become the cornerstone."[6] How, then, did the early church express the meaning of the cross? In what ways did they make sense of this dark hour?

A reading of the New Testament will show that its writers drew on multiple images and concepts to probe the meaning of Jesus' death. Mark's Gospel calls it "a ransom for many" (Mark 10:45). Luke's Gospel speaks of Jesus' approaching death as his *exodus,*[7] so that the liberation of Israel functions as a way to understand his death. When Jesus ate his final meal with his disciples, he broke bread with the words, "This is my body, which is given for you ... This cup that is poured out for you is the new covenant in my blood" (Luke 22:19-20). His death is "for you," and it relates to the hope of Israel, "the new covenant." John's Gospel sees in Jesus "the Lamb of God who takes away the sin of the world!" (John 1:29); "... as Moses lifted up the serpent in the wilderness, so must the Son of Man be lifted up" (John 3:14); Jesus is "the good shepherd [who] lays down his life for the sheep" (John 10:11). And when Jesus finally dies on the cross he says, "It is finished" (John 19:30). Each Gospel writer offers a unique perspective on the meaning of Jesus' death. Similarly, other writers in the New Testament portray his death with a wide variety of words: "sacrifice of atonement" (Romans 3:25); "he died for all" (2 Corinthians 5:15); "a curse for us" (Galatians 3:13); "redemption" (Ephesians 1:7); "triumphing" over the "rulers and authorities" (Colossians 2:15); "by his wounds you have been healed" (1 Peter 2:24); and Revelation's vision is of the Lamb by whose blood "you ransomed for God saints from every tribe and language and people and nation" (Revelation

5:9). There is no one way to view the death of Christ from a biblical perspective. Each writer in the New Testament contributes something to an event whose meaning cannot be exhausted. If there is a consistent message, it lies with the First Epistle of John: "In this is love, not that we loved God but that he loved us and sent his Son to be the atoning sacrifice for our sins" (1 John 4:10). By this is meant that his death has saving significance for humanity.[8] His atoning death accomplished something humanity itself could not do. It is central to our salvation.

As the early church interacted with its surrounding cultures, however, the multiplicity of these biblical images began to cluster into a few dominant images. One of those dominant images stressed the meaning of the cross as a *victory*. In this view, the crucified Christ defeated the principalities and powers of the world.[9] At a personal level, humans are in bondage to sin. It is the death of Christ that ransoms us, liberates us. If the cross constituted a ransom, an obvious question is to whom the ransom was to be paid. Origen and others in the early church believed that the devil was holding God hostage. But the New Testament doesn't respond to that detail; it simply speaks of the cross as a victory. This emphasis of the cross as victory developed at a time when the powers of the world were very real. To confess "Jesus is Lord" went in the face of the Empire's confession that "Caesar is Lord." However, once the church became part of the powers of the Empire in the fourth century, it had little need for this image of the atonement. Only in modern times has its importance been recovered.

Another dominant image of the atonement was first developed by Anselm of Canterbury in the Middle Ages. Because he lived in medieval times, Anselm wanted to relate the meaning of the cross to *his* social world. In this world a knight or lord was obliged to provide protection to those under his authority, and in return a serf gave obedience and loyalty. In this world, the honour of the lord needed to be *satisfied*. Anselm believed that humanity stood in a similar relation to God, our Lord. Because we failed to completely obey God, his honour needed to be satisfied. A penalty had to be paid in order to restore the relationship. The *obligation* to pay this penalty was ours, and yet it was beyond our capacity to do so because of our sinfulness. Only

God has the *ability* to accomplish this. In Anselm's view, the death of Jesus satisfies the honour of God because he is both God and human.[10]

Thus while the New Testament offers many images and narratives to unfold the meaning of the cross, we run into difficulty when we try to gather those images into a single explanation. It is for this reason that The Salvation Army's doctrine book argues:

> There is no single comprehensive way to interpret the Atonement through the sacrifice of Christ. But in the New Testament, helpful analogies and images, *when taken together*, provide insight into its meaning.[11]

How, then, can the atonement make sense to contemporary ears and be faithful to the biblical story? This is a crucial task as we engage the meaning of Jesus' death for the 21st century.

Engaging the Doctrine

The word "atonement" has found its way into the vocabulary of our world, but its meaning has shifted. Journalists speak of an athlete "atoning" for her poor performance in a game or a politician "atoning" for his indiscretions. In each instance, it means that the athlete or politician has found a way to "make up for" something that was inadequate. This emphasis fails to capture the Christian conviction that atonement is what God has done *for us*! In order to hear this doctrine today, it needs to be both grounded in its biblical roots and responsive to contemporary issues.

Making Sense of the Cross

One way of viewing the cross as atonement is to see it as a victory, but a *victory of a different kind*. Most victories can be determined by declaring a winner. One political candidate gains more votes than the others; an Olympic runner crosses the finish line first; a group of nations subdue other nations in battle and require a peace treaty. Such victories are most often the result of a conquest of sorts. Yet victory can come in other ways, undermining our concepts of power. Such a victory took place in North American baseball in the 1940s. Until the 1940s, Major League Baseball was a white man's sport.

Black players played baseball, but they had to play in a separate league for blacks only. Branch Rickey owned the Brooklyn Dodgers and recognized the need for change. He found a possible black player to break the racial barrier in Jackie Robinson. Rickey interviewed the young athlete and asked him what kind of player he thought he needed to be in order to break this barrier. The young player said he needed to be strong enough to fight back when taunted. Rickey responded, "I'm looking for a ballplayer with the guts *not* to fight back." Robinson took the field, first in Montreal and then in Brooklyn in 1947. He faced exclusion from his own teammates, taunts from opposing players and fans, and pitches that were thrown at his head. As difficult as it was, and it was extremely difficult, Robinson had the courage "not to fight back" with the result that he achieved a remarkable victory, a different kind of victory. At a cost to himself, Robinson opened the door for other black athletes to play this game and other professional sports.[12] The cross is this kind of victory. Jesus willingly and knowingly faced his death. He had the courage not to fight back, but to absorb the taunts, rejections, misunderstandings and death. In so doing, unjust violence was taken into the life of the triune God. It is this absorbing of evil's worst into the life of God that turns it into a victory. It is a victory of courageous love, God's love for the whole world.[13]

It is a Christian conviction that in the person of Jesus Christ we come to know God who has fully entered the world of suffering

Another way of viewing the cross as atonement is to recognize its *solidarity in suffering*. In the depths of suffering people can feel alone, whether when they experience dementia or flee a country prone to violence. It is a Christian conviction that in the person of Jesus Christ we come to know God who has fully entered the world of suffering. God has not remained on the sidelines of history, but has personally entered it. The Old Testament portrays God as being vulnerable to suffering. He grieves humanity's sinfulness, hears the cries of people in slavery, laments Israel's failure to be a productive vineyard and produce the fruit of justice, and suffers through the rejection of prophetic words to the nation. As the biblical story narrates the life of Jesus, we sense his own lament: "Jerusalem, Jerusalem ... How often have I desired to gather your children together as a hen gathers her brood under her wings, and you were not willing!" (Luke 13:34). His sense of abandonment is likely one of the greatest moments of pain in the life of Jesus: "My God, my God, why have you forsaken me?" (Mark 15:34). One New Testament writer captures this aspect of solidarity: "For we do not have a high priest who is unable to sympathize with our weaknesses, but we have one who in every respect has been tested as we are, yet without sin" (Hebrews 4:15). This is not to minimize the pain of any human situation, but in response to Dietrich Bonhoeffer's claim that "only the suffering God can help,"[14] the cross points to God who understands our suffering and who suffers in solidarity with us.

A third perspective places an emphasis on the atonement as *costly reconciliation*. The Bible narrates the story of God who seeks to reconcile individuals and nations with each other, and the human family with the earth. Above all, God seeks reconciliation of humanity with God. In the life of Jesus we see God's reconciling purposes in action. Thus he speaks forgiveness of sins to an unnamed woman, with the benediction, "Go in peace" (Luke 7:50), go in wholeness. A demoniac is healed and Luke says he was "clothed and in his right mind" (Luke 8:35). The ministry of Jesus creates wholeness, reconciliation. But it is a costly reconciliation. He is misunderstood, opposed and eventually crucified. This reconciliation does not end with God, but is intended to move into all spheres of life. In Paul's words, "All this is from God, who reconciled us to himself through Christ, and has given us the ministry of reconciliation" (2 Corinthians 5:18). The cross seeks to reconcile all peoples: racially, sexually and economically. Christian community is shaped by the cross.

Each year Canadians hold sacred the day of November 11, Remembrance Day. On this day Canadians honour the lives of those given in service for this country during the wars of the 20th and 21st centuries. Services take place in the nation's capital, Ottawa, and in schools across the country. In 2010, a unique moment took place, largely unobserved by those participating at the Remembrance Day service at the University of Toronto. At an important moment in the service, bells from the university's carillon tower played out. What people didn't know was that its musician was a Japanese doctor, studying medical education at the university. Dr. Uchino accepted an invitation to play this instrument in order to retain her love for music. As she prepared for her part, Dr. Uchino learned about Japan's part in defeating Canadian troops at the Battle of Hong Kong in 1941. She also learned about Canada's confinement of Japanese-Canadians during the war simply because of their race. With her music, Dr. Uchino became an agent of reconciliation. Her love for medicine and music helped a nation to remember.[15]

Practising the Doctrine

The cross of Jesus Christ is central to any understanding of the Christian faith. The cross is also central—crucial!—to our understanding and practice of holiness. However, how a holy God could become associated with such an unholy event posed a great difficulty for early Christians, and remains so even for today. Paul Minear recognizes the dilemma:

> For execution by crucifixion to become the criterion of holiness, and God's holiness at that, became the supreme scandal. It created havoc (and still does) with all other ideas of wisdom, power, salvation, God—and thereby of holiness ... It is easy enough to accept, in theory, the idea of God as the sole source and criterion of holiness; but it is anything but easy when such holiness is defined by the awful dereliction on Golgotha.[16]

Let's pursue what holiness means when viewed through the lens of the cross. Both God's holiness and ours.

The Cross and God's Holiness

We begin by acknowledging that the cross leads us to a different understanding of *God*. While the whole of the biblical story contributes to our understanding of God, it is *concentrated* in the death of Jesus. What gives special importance to the cross is the conviction that, in some profound way, God was deeply involved in that death. The Apostle Paul states it boldly: "God was in Christ reconciling the world to himself."[17] Recall our discussion on the Trinity, where it was noted that while individual persons of the Trinity may have tasks appropriate to their person, they ultimately act in concert. The triune God, whom we know as Father, Son and Holy Spirit, is disclosed to be a God who suffers in the event of the cross.[18] Brengle argues: "The whole Trinity is involved in the atoning work of Jesus Christ on Calvary."[19] Charles Wesley captured its significance:

> Amazing love! how can it be
> That thou, *my God,* shouldst die for me?[20]

Christ crucified both reveals and redefines God ... God is cruciform —Michael Gorman

However, this seems so contrary to the way we normally think of God. The creeds and worship of the church draw on the language of almighty, sovereign, Lord, ruler, majestic, omnipotent to speak of God. And each of these words *is* an apt description of God. But from a Christian perspective they all need to be understood through the experience of the cross. The defining moment of God's character is found in the cross. And the cross evokes such language as shame, defeat, suffering, death, weakness, betrayal, injustice, vulnerable. Here precisely *is* the heart of God's character, the heart of the triune God's character. In the cross, God has fully entered the suffering of our world, engaged the powers of our world, embraced the shame of our world, experienced the alienation and exclusions of our world, and absorbed the evil of our world. In Michael Gorman's words, "... *Christ crucified both reveals and redefines God ... God is cruciform.*"[21] Letting the cross redefine the character of God goes against the grain of our world. The cross redefines God as cross-shaped, as cruciform. And because the cross informs our understanding of God, it also informs our understanding of God's holiness. The defining moment of holiness is found at Golgotha, the garbage site for a city. God's character has led him in love to enter fully into the darkness of our world and engage its suffering. We understand God's holiness to be a wounded holiness shaped by the cross. The Salvation Army's poet-General, Albert Orsborn, has reflected on the cross with these words:

> We worship thee, O Crucified!
> What glories didst thou lay aside;
> What depth of human grief and sin
> Didst thou consent to languish in,
> That through atoning blood outpoured
> Our broken peace might be restored![22]

The Cross and Our Holiness

If the cross shapes our understanding of God's holiness, it also shapes what holiness means for us: "... if Christ is God's holiness for us, then becoming like the crucified Christ is sharing in God's holiness and thus become like God."[23] Our holiness, too, will be cross-shaped.

A cross-shaped holiness will emphasize the holy life as a *journey*. Luke's Gospel marks an important moment when Jesus "set his face to go to Jerusalem" (Luke 9:51). This journey to Jerusalem and the cross creates a repetitive chord in the remaining chapters of Luke's Gospel. Jesus is "on the way."[24] From his testings in the wilderness to the Garden of Gethsemane, Jesus journeyed to the cross. His steps were intentional, not haphazard. But they were steps that alternated joy with tears. And it is no accident that Christians were known in the Book of Acts as people of the "Way."[25] Biblical spirituality "is not a straight road but one with ups and downs and turns like a mountain path. It includes both ecstatic joy and the dark night of the soul, both dying and rising. Its essence is not the love of power, but the power of love."[26] It involves the blindsiding experiences of broken marriages, premature deaths, joyous surprises and difficult decisions. There are many crises in the pilgrimage of faith. And this journey of holiness is never fully reached this side of eternity. Paul's perspective marks every step of the way: "Not that I have already obtained this or have already reached the goal" (Philippians 3:12). We never cease being "on the way." One discipline that helps this journey of holiness is Lent. The "40 days" journey, which begins with Ash Wednesday, need not be duplicated in the form it takes in the rest of the church. But

Salvationist spirituality does need to take Lent's journey more seriously. This is a time to draw upon our music, our artistic capacities, reflection upon our service, and our preaching in order to live inside this journey. There is freedom within Salvation Army worship to develop our own approach to this season.[27] The cross is a journey that shapes biblical spirituality, our holiness.

Holiness that is cross-shaped will impact our approach to *vocation*. The Christian faith understands our lives to be purposeful, to live out of a sense of calling. What we do with our lives, and how we do it, is important. Employment is not simply a job with which to earn money; it is a way to honour God's greater purposes with the gifts and capacities we have. But how does the cross impact the decisions we make about the kind of vocation we choose and where we choose to fulfil it? It has been said that "Something's your vocation if it keeps making more of you."[28] There is much truth in this, but if this is the only consideration it can lead to an imbalance. L. Gregory Jones notes the counterbalance: "Even as we recognize the potential for fulfillment and abundant living, Christians also recognize that the God we worship is the God who tells us that only those who lose their life will find it."[29] For this reason, Jones speaks of vocational discernment as *negotiating the tensions* "between that which gives us fulfillment and the self-emptying we are called to offer in the service of others."[30] When we consider God's callings upon our lives, it's important to recognize that there will be costs involved. It may be in the towns and cities where God places us or the tasks God gives us. Jesus' death was an atoning death, and his life was an atoning life. The cross shapes our vocational life as an expression of holiness.

Christian holiness shaped by the cross will *exercise power differently*. To enter the world of Christian faith is to enter a world of power. We sing about it, listen to biblical sermons on David's abuse of power, join in worship on Palm Sunday to celebrate Jesus' "deeds of power,"[31] and experience power in the decisions of the Army and its leaders. We live in a culture where power is exercised by CEOs, educators, team managers and the media. Power in and of itself is simply a part of our world. Salvationists are called to exercise power in a way consistent with the story of Jesus and the cross. The cross turns our notions of power inside-out. Daniel Migliore puts it this way: "... the power of God depicted by Scripture is *strange power.* It is not the power of force but the power of Spirit ... and it is made known above all in the weakness of the cross of Jesus."[32] How we exercise power in leadership and in our relationships will demonstrate our understanding of the cross.[33] We are called to exercise *strange power,* a holy power.

The sufferings of our cities and nations draw the Army into the heart of its mission. Ours is a holy mission shaped by the cross

Finally, a cross-shaped holiness will engage The Salvation Army *with the sufferings of our world.* As noted, Matthew's Gospel views the healing ministry of Jesus as an *atoning ministry* where "He took our infirmities and bore our diseases" (Matthew 8:17). Jesus engaged the sufferings of his day. General John Gowans spoke of the Army's mission "to serve suffering humanity."[34] The Salvation Army at its best has engaged the sufferings of our world: from living with convicts on Devil's Island to befriending prostitutes in the Red Light District of Amsterdam, from building a match factory for young children suffering from "phossy-jaw" to medical work with lepers and untouchables in India. There are 21st-century forms of suffering that draw us to respond: from work with victims of HIV-AIDS to the mentally ill, from the exclusion of immigrants in our communities to young people caught up in gangs, from the pain involved in a family when one of its members has taken their life, to a friend who faces the black hole of unemployment. The cross is planted firmly in The Salvation Army's name and mission. The sufferings of our cities and nations draw the Army into the heart of its mission. Ours is a holy mission shaped by the cross.

This core conviction matters! The sixth doctrine forms the centre point of Salvation Army doctrines. There is a sense in which all of the other doctrines flow into it and away from it. It has a way of concentrating Christian faith. It takes us back into Scripture to read it again and then pushes us into the world to serve it in light of the cross. Whatever the difficulties of comprehending the cross in our time, we wrestle with its meaning in order to be faithful to the triune God. Whatever the difficulties of living a cross-shaped holiness, we seek to practise its life both personally and communally. We refuse any limitation of the cross, believing that it is for "the whole world so that whosoever will may be saved." To this saving purpose of the cross we turn in the remaining doctrines.

Reflection Questions for Chapter Six

1. This doctrine focuses on the cross of Christ. In what places or events do you see the cross symbolized in our culture?
2. If you are studying this book with a group, read the chapter together.
3. What phrase or section caught your attention? Why?

Forming the Doctrine:

4. Read Luke 6:6-11. How do you see the death of Jesus anticipated in this story?
5. Of all the images that interpret the death of Jesus, which do you find *most* helpful? Why?
6. Of all the images that interpret the death of Jesus, which do you find *least* helpful? Why?

Engaging the Doctrine:

7. How do you think the word "atonement" is understood in our culture?
8. What is your response to Bonhoeffer's claim that "only a suffering God can help"?
9. Why do you think our culture finds the cross to be irrelevant or scandalous?
10. In what ways do you understand the cross to be relevant for our times?

Practising the Doctrine:

11. In what ways is the image of holiness as a journey helpful to you?
12. What are some ways that you think the cross impacts our vocational choices?
13. What difference do you think it makes to view the cross as central to the mission of The Salvation Army?

Conclude: Pray one of the songs on the cross from *The Song Book of The Salvation Army,* such as "When I Survey the Wondrous Cross" (*SBSA 1987,* No. 136).

Endnotes for Chapter Six

1 Paul Minear, "The Holy and the Sacred," *Theology Today* 47 (April 1990): 8.

2 For example, Bach's *Passion Chorale* and Marc Chagall's paintings of the crucifixion.

3 For more extensive reading into this issue, see Jerome H. Neyrey ed., *The Social World of Luke-Acts: Models for Interpretation* (Peabody: Hendrickson Publishers, 1991).

4 "... the circumstances and understanding of Jesus' death can never be torn from the fabric of the circumstances of his life, so tightly interwoven are these." See Joel B. Green, "The Death of Jesus and the Ways of God," *Interpretation* 52 (January 1998): 27.

5 Matthew Bridges, "Crown Him," *SBSA 1987*, No. 156. Emphasis mine.

6 See, for instance, 1 Peter 2:7.

7 Luke 9:31. The word is translated "departure," and the context is the Mount of Transfiguration where Moses and Elijah speak with Jesus.

8 Thus this doctrine has to do with our salvation, which will be explored more fully in the remaining doctrines.

9 See Colossians 2:15.

10 "So if ... no one other than God can make it and no one other than humanity ought to make, it is necessary for the God-man to make it." See Anselm's argument in Alister E. McGrath ed., *Theology: The Basic Readings* (Malden: Blackwell Publishing, 2008), 91-93. While Anselm emphasized the satisfaction of God's *honour*, this image in more recent times put an emphasis on the satisfaction of God's *wrath*. The cultural context had shifted from medieval concerns with honour to the modern justice system's concern with punishment for the crime. For an outline of this view of the cross, see Joel B. Green and Mark D. Baker, *Recovering the Scandal of the Cross* (Downers Grove: InterVarsity Press, 2000), 140-142. In some parts of the world, a more "Restorative Justice" system is at work, which is closer to a biblical meaning for justice and atonement.

11 *The Salvation Army Handbook of Doctrine* (London: Salvation Books, 2010), 129, emphasis mine. The emphasis on "the whole world" deals with the issue of the extent of God's grace, and will be considered in a later chapter.

12 That Jackie Robinson succeeded in this is shown when all players from Major League Baseball honour him by wearing his number 42 on the same day. See the film, *42*. Directed by Brian Helgeland. Warner Brothers, 2013.

13 "The victory is never a triumph of force, but it is a victory nevertheless, and we are redeemed. In thus winning the victory, God manifests for us both the mysterious power of love and the truth that suffering is worth the price only when it is doing love's work in moving the world toward justice." William C. Placher, "The Cross of Jesus Christ as Solidarity, Reconciliation, and Redemption" in Walter Brueggemann and George W. Stroup eds., *Many Voices,*

One God (Louisville: Westminster John Knox Press, 1998), 163.

14 "The Bible directs us to God's powerlessness and suffering; only the suffering God can help." See Dietrich Bonhoeffer, *Letters and Papers from Prison* (New York: Macmillan, 1972), 361. Migliore reminds us of the danger of turning this phrase into a slogan, "but the suffering God is the triune God whose holy, self-giving, victorious love is at work from the creation of the world to its completion." See *Faith Seeking Understanding*, 132.

15 See Anthony Reinhart, "For Remembrance Day, a Tower of Song," *The Globe and Mail*, November 10, 2010— http://m.theglobeandmail.com/news/national/for-remembrance-day-a-tower-of-song/article4182456/?service=mobile. Accessed February 8, 2013.

16 P. Minear, "The Holy and the Sacred," *Theology Today* 47 (April 1990): 8.

17 2 Corinthians 5:19; see *NRSV* footnote.

18 Arthur Peacocke, "The Cost of New Life" in John Polkinghorne ed., *The Work of Love: Creation as Kenosis* (Grand Rapids: Eerdmans Publishing, 2001): "If Jesus is indeed the self-expression of God in a human person, then the tragedy of his actual human life can be seen as a drawing back of the curtain to unveil a God suffering in and with the sufferings of created humanity and so, by a natural extension, with those of all creation, since humanity is an embedded, evolved part of it. The suffering of God ... is in Jesus the Christ concentrated into a point of intensity and transparency that reveals it as expressive of the perennial relation of God to the creation."

19 Samuel Logan Brengle, *The Guest of the Soul* (London: Marshall, Morgan and Scott, 1935), 32.

20 Charles Wesley, "And Can It Be," *SBSA 1987*, No. 283, emphasis mine.

21 Michael J. Gorman, " 'You Shall Be Cruciform for I Am Cruciform': Paul's Trinitarian Reconstruction of Holiness" in Kent E. Brower and Andy Johnson eds., *Holiness and Ecclesiology in the New Testament* (Grand Rapids: Eerdmans Publishing, 2007), 157, emphasis mine.

22 A. Orsborn, "We Worship Thee," *SBSA 1987*, No. 135.

23 Gorman, " *'You shall be cruciform,'* " 158.

24 See, for instance, Luke 9:52; 9:57; 13:33; 17:11.

25 Acts 9:2.

26 Clark H. Pinnock, "The Role of the Spirit in Redemption," *Asbury Theological Journal* 52 (Spring 1997): 61.

27 For instance, on several occasions I have partnered with an officer colleague to create a Lenten Digital Community, where several Salvationist congregations from across the Canada and Bermuda Territory participated in a digital community that preached and learned from the same texts. It should also be noted that the word "Lent" comes from an old English word "lengten," which refers to the lengthening of daylight hours approaching Easter, at least as experienced in the Northern Hemisphere.

28 Quoted in L. Gregory Jones, "Negotiating the Tensions of Vocation" in L. Gregory Jones and Stephanie Paulsell eds., *The Scope of Our Art: The Vocation of the Theological Teacher* (Grand Rapids: Eerdmans Publishing, 2002), 212.

29 Jones, "Negotiating the Tensions," 215.

30 Jones, "Negotiating the Tensions," 216.

31 Luke 19:37.

32 Daniel L. Migliore, *Faith Seeking Understanding* (Grand Rapids: Eerdmans Publishing, 2004), 56, emphasis mine.

33 The international Salvation Army has spelled this out more fully in a Position Statement: "The Use of Power." See http://www.salvationarmy.org/ihq/ipspower. Accessed February 8, 2013.

34 His complete statement was: "The Salvation Army exists to save souls, grow saints and serve suffering humanity."

Holiness as Working Out an *Immense* Salvation

We believe that repentance towards God, faith in our Lord Jesus Christ and regeneration by the Holy Spirit, are necessary to salvation.—Doctrine 7

Therefore, my beloved ... work out your own salvation with fear and trembling; for it is God who is at work in you, enabling you both to will and to work for his good pleasure.—The Apostle Paul[1]

FROM THE EARLIEST YEARS OF MY LIFE, I RECALL ASSOCIATING salvation with something *big*. Whenever William Booth's anthem was sung, both the music and the words conveyed a "boundless salvation."[2] On those occasions when I actually listened to sermons as a young person, my ears picked up on the language of "full salvation" or "great salvation." Without comprehending its full meaning, I understood myself to be part of an Army of Salvation. It was with some puzzlement that I later discovered the church's ancient creeds said little about salvation. What seemed to me primary and critical was largely passed over in the earlier core convictions of the church. It can be argued that all doctrines are related to a Christian view of salvation.[3] But with this seventh doctrine we begin to explore more intentionally a Christian understanding of salvation. I want to demonstrate in the next few chapters that our view of salvation dramatically impacts our understanding and practice of holiness. Salvationist doctrines express the conviction that God's gracious initiatives *and* our appropriate responses are "necessary to salvation." Let's begin our work with this seventh core conviction, and draw out its implications for biblical spirituality.

Forming the Doctrine

In order to create some perspective, we best begin with the biblical meaning of *salvation*. This is because our understanding of salvation will impact what we think is "necessary to salvation." And as will become evident, there has been a tendency to reduce salvation in such a way as to lose sight of its immensity.

Israel's story forms the background to our understanding of salvation. Having heard the cry of his people in slavery, God acts to deliver them from Pharaoh's oppressive power. In response, Moses and Israel sing God's praises: "The LORD is my strength and my might, and he has become my salvation" (Exodus 15:2). This national deliverance from bondage is called salvation. At a more personal level, many of the psalmists depict salvation as deliverance from threats to their lives or to their integrity. For instance, when faced with personal adversaries, one psalmist professes, "The LORD is my light and my salvation; whom shall I fear?" (Psalm 27:1). As the prophet Jeremiah struggles with Israel's unfaithfulness, and feels their taunts personally, he prays, "Heal me, O LORD, and I shall be healed; save me, and I shall be saved" (Jeremiah 17:14). These few texts begin to show the richness of the Old Testament's view of salvation. It has to do with deliverance and healing; it can be both personal and communal; and it primarily has to do with God's actions in this world. It is God who saves, who liberates and heals.

When we turn to the New Testament, we find that three of the Gospels call Jesus "Saviour." After Mary gave birth to her firstborn, the child was named Jesus—which means, *Yahweh saves*—"for he will save his people from their sins" (Matthew 1:21). Shepherds near Bethlehem were jarred by the sudden appearance of "an angel of the Lord" and told not to be afraid, for "to you is born this day in the city of David a Saviour ..." (Luke 2:11). And when the adult Jesus encountered a Samaritan woman at a well, they jostled about the meaning of water and living water. But as her own townspeople meet Jesus, they conclude: "... we know that this is truly the Saviour of the world" (John 4:42). While Jesus bore other titles, he was certainly known as *Saviour.*

Luke's Gospel in particular pays close attention to what it means for Jesus to be Saviour. Jesus proclaimed forgiveness to an unnamed woman saying, "Your faith has saved you; go in peace." He addressed another woman whose body was restored to health and she to the community, "Daughter, your faith has saved you; go in peace." One of ten lepers returned to give Jesus thanks for the healing of his body, and Jesus responded, "Get up and go on your way; your faith has saved you." And when the chief tax collector, Zacchaeus, welcomed Jesus into his home and promised to restore money to anyone he had defrauded, Jesus said to him, "Today salvation has come to this house." This incident is framed with words that many believe to be the climax of Luke's Gospel: "For the Son of Man came to seek out and to save the lost."[4] In Luke's Gospel, salvation includes the healing of the body, mind and community; it involves forgiveness and economic restoration. Thus the early church proclaimed that "God exalted [Jesus] at his right hand as Leader and Saviour that he might give repentance to Israel and forgiveness of sins" (Acts 5:31). In his life, death and resurrection, Jesus announced and embodied salvation to all people.

A similar "great salvation" can be found in other New Testament writings, especially in those of Paul the Apostle. When he strikes the initial chords of his Epistle to the Romans, Paul defines the gospel as "the power of God for salvation to everyone who has faith" (Romans 1:16).[5] As Paul develops this key epistle, and his other writings, he uses many images and concepts to unfold his understanding of salvation, such as adoption, justification, forgiveness, redemption, new creation, and reconciliation. With respect to time, salvation has past, present and future dimensions. In one instance, Paul says that "you *have been* saved."[6] He also writes "to us who are *being* saved."[7] And he speaks of its future experience, "Much more ... *will we be* saved."[8] The gospel creates not only new individuals but a new humanity,[9] and ultimately a new creation.[10]

The salvation offered in Christ is huge, like the Atlantic Ocean. It is in William Booth's words, a "boundless salvation! deep ocean of love." Within its depths lie the notions of justification, reconciliation, forgiveness, new creation, citizenship in the kingdom, participation in the divine nature, ransom, sanctification, and the defeat of principalities and powers. These concepts are best understood as *aspects* of salvation, not as something different from it. "Simply put, 'salvation' is the comprehensive term for all of the benefits that are graciously bestowed on humans by God."[11] Salvation in the biblical world is an *immense* concept.

Simply put, "salvation" is the comprehensive term for all of the benefits that are graciously bestowed on humans by God —Joel Green

With this boundless salvation in mind, let's take a closer look at the human responses this core conviction says are "necessary to salvation."

> *We believe that repentance towards God, faith in our Lord Jesus Christ ... is necessary to salvation.*

Among those human elements "necessary to salvation" are repentance and faith. As the Apostle Paul summarized his ministry among the believers at Ephesus, he noted that he "testified to both Jews and Greeks about *repentance toward God and faith toward our Lord Jesus Christ*."[12] Paul anticipated the Army's seventh doctrine! The words "repentance" and "faith," however, carry a lot of baggage in western culture, so let's look at their biblical background more carefully.

The ministry of Jesus began with a call to *repent*: "The time is fulfilled, and the kingdom of God has come near; repent, and believe in the good news" (Mark 1:15). Repentance essentially means to change direction. It's as if people are walking in one direction and exhorted to do an about-face towards its opposite direction. The call of Jesus envisions humanity living with our backs to God; we have oriented our lives to something other than God. The call to repentance is an invitation to change that orientation back towards God in Jesus Christ. In response to his critics, Jesus says, "Those who are well have no need of a physician, but those who are sick; I have come to call not the righteous but sinners to repentance" (Luke 5:31-32). It's important to keep in mind that the capacity to repent itself is a gift of God's grace.[13] And it's important to realize that repentance is not a once-for-all turning. The intrusion of sin into the totality of life means that we are in constant need of change, of re-orienting ourselves to the magnetic north pole of God's grace.

Another element "necessary to salvation" in this doctrine is *faith in our Lord Jesus Christ*. If repentance emphasizes the change of direction, faith emphasizes the dynamic of trust. We have already noted occasions where Jesus turned to individuals with the words: "Your *faith* has saved you." Faith in its biblical sense is neither blind nor simply intellectual assent but an expression of trust. The woman who lavished her tears on the feet of Jesus took a risk of trust. The woman who stepped out from the anonymity of a crowd to touch the hem of Jesus' garment trusted his response. The Samaritan leper who returned to give thanks after being healed trusted the welcome of Jesus. Saving faith is not empty of content. It is directed to "our Lord Jesus Christ." Such faith is necessary because God will not coerce our response to his love. We are invited to trust the love of God expressed in the life, death and resurrection of Christ. And this involves a lifetime of trust.

We believe that regeneration by the Holy Spirit ... [is] necessary to salvation.

With this phrase we are introduced to language that emphasizes another aspect of God's role in our salvation. Salvation is about many things, but it is primarily concerned with life. And this life is expressed in the Bible with many images and concepts. It is new birth, eternal life, new creation, participation in the divine nature, a branch grafted into the vine. Here it is expressed as "regeneration by the Holy Spirit." Paul's Letter to Titus expresses this conviction: "But when the goodness and loving kindness of God our Savior appeared, he saved us ... according to his mercy, through the washing of rebirth and renewal by the Holy Spirit" (Titus 3:4-5).[14] The Bible envisions salvation through the image of renewal or regeneration, like a forest that is regenerated after a fire.

Thus the Bible creates a portrait of salvation that requires a huge canvass. The biblical mural draws on images of deliverance, reconciliation, adoption, justification, new creation, eternal life and regeneration among others. It is deeply personal and has profound social dimensions, even cosmic dimensions. The Bible portrays salvation as already realized, as presently being realized, and as yet to be fully realized. It's for good reasons that Salvationists sing their anthem lustily:

> O boundless salvation! deep ocean of love,
> O fullness of mercy, Christ brought from above,
> The whole world redeeming, so rich and so free,
> Now flowing for all men, come, roll over me![15]

Faith is an evil precisely because it requires no justification and brooks no argument
—Richard Dawkins

Engaging the Doctrine

Despite the richness of the biblical concept of salvation, our contemporaries have difficulty hearing it. For instance, the western world has difficulty with the church's call for *repentance* when the church itself is in need of repentance. Its clergy has brought shame on the church in far too many instances, such as its scandals and cover-ups. Another reason this doctrine has difficulty being heard in the 21st century is because of its emphasis on *faith*. One contemporary critic is blunt in his denunciation: "Faith is an evil precisely because it requires no justification and brooks no argument."[16] These are important accusations, and need to be heard. And responded to!

Let's begin with the accusation that faith has little place in a world full of scientific explanations. First, it helps to recognize that religious faith and modern science share a number of things in common. For instance, both science and religious faith employ *models* to help understand realities beyond our grasp. Scientists have devised the Big Bang model by which to make sense of the beginnings of the universe, or the double helix model to understand genetics. They trust these models until such time as evidence points in other directions. Similarly, Christian faith employs models as a way of understanding God who is ultimately beyond our comprehension. Through the story of Christ, Christians understand God who chooses to engage humanity in a mutual, loving relationship. This story of grace functions as a lens through which Christians seek to understand God's ways with this world. "Christian faith can be characterized accordingly as *faithful imagination*—living in conformity to the vision rendered by the Word of God in the Bible."[17] Imagination is a way of *seeing*. Imagination looks through a model or paradigm in order to understand something beyond itself. Like science, Christian faith is always open to conversation, to counter arguments, to course correction. Anselm expressed it concisely: Christian *faith seeks understanding*. Christian faith however emphasizes faith as *trust*, including the doubts that accompany the risks of faith. In the Oscar-winning film, *The King's Speech*,[18] the future King George VI seeks to overcome his speech impediments with the help of Lionel Logue. The future king is not wholly convinced of Logue's ability to help because of the Australian's unorthodox ways. At one point in the story, Logue turns to the British Empire's monarch and says, "If I am to be of any help to you, you will need to *trust* me." The unfolding story is one of trust, where a stammering king eventually and clearly addresses his people at the outbreak of war in 1939. That is the essence of biblical faith, where we are invited to trust God who heals, who works with us to bring fluency to our stammering lives. It is this faith as risky trust that is necessary to salvation.

If our contemporaries have difficulty with the word *faith*, they also question the concept of *salvation*. It is true that journalists refer to an emerging politician as the "saviour" of the party, or a gifted athlete as a team's "saviour." But any thought of God so participating in our world's history as to accomplish its salvation is rejected out of hand. As the western world experienced the profound impact of scientific and technological developments it felt less need of God to accomplish salvation. The kinds of changes envisioned were within the abilities of humanity. If anything, the word *progress* came to define salvation for the West. In fact, there was much reason to celebrate these developments and to hope. However, the early 20th century brought many of those hopes to the ground with a thud. The First World War, followed soon after by the Second, raised important questions about humanity's ability to bring about needed change. As the 20th century came to a close, there came with it the realization that science and technology is two-edged. Computers can enable the severely handicapped to communicate; they can also facilitate traffic in child pornography. The tools used to excavate oil can also deplete the earth of its resources. Science and technology have important but limited roles to play. Something beyond the capacities of science is needed to bring about real transformation in our world. This is what the Christian community means by salvation.

If our contemporaries are to be open to a Christian understanding of salvation, it will help to *retrace its journey* within the life of the church. The concept of salvation has changed over time. We have seen that the Scriptures depict a great salvation, but as the church developed into its eastern and western expressions, each had a way of emphasizing different aspects of salvation, like a river that divided into two separate branches.[19] It is here that the Salvationist's Wesleyan heritage takes on importance. Raised in the Church of England, and educated at Oxford, John Wesley was also influenced by the theologians of the Eastern Orthodox Church. Without denying his indebtedness to Reformers like Luther, Wesley sought to integrate the eastern emphasis into his understanding of salvation. His benchmark sermon, "The Scripture Way of Salvation," begins this way:

> What is *salvation*? The salvation which is here spoken of is not what is frequently understood by that word, the going to heaven, eternal happiness ... It is not a blessing which lies on the other side of death ... it is a present thing ... [It] might be extended to the entire work of God, from the first dawning of grace in the soul till it is consummated in glory.[20]

Wesley sought to unite a salvation that had become polarized during the story of the church. However, while William Booth deeply appreciated his Wesleyan heritage, it took time before he broadened his more revivalist understanding of salvation to incorporate this Wesleyan understanding of salvation. Roger Green argues that it was during the late 1880s that Booth underwent changes in his thinking: "The most significant and dramatic change in the later theology of William Booth was an evolution that included an understanding of salvation as not only personal, but social as well."[21] As Booth became aware of the many social expressions of this emerging Army, such as a centre devoted to the care of alcoholic women in Toronto, he wrote an article for the 1889 publication of *All the World,* in which he expressed his growing insight: "But with this discovery ... which has been growing and growing in clearness and intensity from that hour to this; which was that I had two gospels of deliverance to preach—one for each world, or rather, one gospel which applied to both."[22] Booth gradually came to the realization that salvation was both personal and social. Our contemporaries will appreciate Christian salvation to the degree that we fully understand *all* its dimensions.

Thus, in order for a Christian understanding of salvation to be heard again, we need to recover its immensity. As has already been argued in this chapter, salvation has many dimensions. It includes justification, but it also opens up the rich images of regeneration, eternal life, new creation, reconciliation and others. Each of these images speaks to some reality of life, and thus is a very flexible way of connecting God's saving ways with humanity. Similarly, while the salvation offered by God has a focus on Christ's atoning death, it is not limited to his death. Salvation also includes his atoning life, his resurrection and his *parousia* or coming again. There is no need to crawl into a defensive posture when speaking of salvation. There is no need to reduce William Booth's "boundless ocean" to a prairie creek in July. In order for our generation to hear this immense salvation, we need to recover its fullness ourselves.

Practising the Doctrine

The Apostle Paul wrote from prison to the young community of Christians in the Roman colony of Philippi. He wrote to them as "saints in Christ Jesus who are in Philippi" (Philippians 1:1). He addressed them as those who lived both "in Philippi" and "in Christ Jesus." Christian believers have a dual address. We are located squarely in the cities and nations in which we live, with the sense of identity that comes with that location. We are also located "in Christ

Jesus," in that his story also creates our identity and shapes our lives. Early in the letter Paul draws out implications of being "in Christ Jesus" with the exhortation to "live your life in a manner worthy of the gospel of Christ" (1:27). He then concludes: "Therefore, my beloved ... *work out your own salvation* with fear and trembling; for it is *God who is at work in you,* enabling you both to will and to work for his good pleasure" (2:12-13, emphasis added). Paul portrays holiness as the working out of salvation in our personal and communal lives. What then are the implications of this immense salvation for Salvationist spirituality? An important contribution of this doctrine to the practice of holiness is that it grounds the shape of holiness in the richness and depths of Christian salvation. An immense salvation will necessitate an immense holiness. This core conviction matters!

First, we will work out our salvation to the degree that we worship *the God of an immense salvation.* Who God is will determine the way we relate to God. If we envision God to be remote and distant, we will find it difficult to imagine his concern with our personal lives. If we envision God to be a judgmental tyrant, we will live in fear of that judgment. And if we imagine God to be a doting parent who gives the children everything they ask for, we will resist God's discipline. It's important that we let the full biblical story inform our understanding of God, rather than one that is shaped too easily by cultural and personal tastes. Partial truths about God run the risk of unhealthy portraits of God, thus unhealthy relationships with God. For this reason, "The doctrine of salvation is vital for our understanding of the nature of God. It shows that we worship a saving God, one who understands our human situation and comes to rescue us."[23] The care with which we approach God in worship is critical. It requires the disciplined attentiveness of an airplane pilot, not the casual stroll of a tourist. For those who lead worship, it is instructive to think about the choice of music. Over a period of time, do our songs emphasize only certain aspects of salvation, such as forgiveness? Or do they include the breadth and depth of salvation's vocabulary? Mary's prayer after her visit to Elizabeth offers a model for Salvationist worship: "My soul magnifies the Lord, and my spirit rejoices in God my Saviour" (Luke 1:46-47). An awareness of a boundless salvation magnifies the God we worship.

When we practise an immense salvation, there will be evidence of *healthy congregations*. Salvation is deeply connected to healing and health, and Paul's words are addressed to a congregation, not simply individuals. We can speak of the health of a congregation, and of its toxicity. A congregation can become a toxic community when unhealthy patterns of relating become embedded over generations. In his Letter to the Philippians, Paul portrays a healthy community as one that looks to the interests of others thus reflecting the mind of Christ (see Philippians 2:4-5). In other places, the Christian community is encouraged to speak truth in love, encourage one another and bear one another's burdens. But its writers don't wear blinders. One church was warned to see that "no root of bitterness springs up and causes trouble" (Hebrews 12:15). There are times when it is necessary to confront toxic behaviour in a congregation. This has implications for a congregation's leadership structure and pattern of communication. A congregation shaped by salvation will include both confidentiality and transparency. At all times the goal is to be a healthy community.

The scope of salvation—however we define salvation—determines the scope of the missionary enterprise —David Bosch

Holiness as the working out of our salvation will *shape our mission*. David Bosch has stated this most clearly when he argues that "the scope of salvation—however we define salvation—determines the scope of the missionary enterprise."[24] When we take seriously the whole of Christ's saving ministry, we will begin to grasp this "boundless salvation" and the ways it may shape our mission as an Army of *Salvation*. For instance, when salvation functions as a guiding force for a congregation's mission, it will have some emphasis on health for the wider community. During times of pandemics, Salvationist congregations can become centres of truthful information rather than conjecture. As populations age in the western world, the phenomenon of dementia takes on importance. A congregation can play a vital role in helping its members understand the nature of dementia and overcome some of the fears and stigma attached to it. Congregations can also help its young people become aware of health issues related to sexuality. Some congregations have included a parish nurse on their staff. This person is a qualified nurse, and seeks to build bridges between the congregation and the community. This may take the form of helping street people caught in the bondage of drugs. It may also take the form of helping new immigrants work their way through the maze of the public health system. When we widen the lens of mission, it leads us to inquire about ways that a Salvation Army division or territory may engage in issues of health. Historically, the Army has been in the forefront of creating medical centres, whether HIV-AIDS clinics in developing nations or general hospitals.[25] During the SARS crisis in Toronto in the winter of 2003, Salvationists delivered food to people who had been quarantined by the crisis. New diseases and pandemics, however, have begun to emerge in our time. And with them will be the need for the Army to ask in what ways it might respond to concerns for health as they impact a nation. Dean Pallant asks the appropriate question: "What characterizes faithfully oriented Salvation Army health ministry in the twenty-first century?"[26] As we keep the concept of salvation in the forefront it will help us to shape the way we do mission in our time.

Another image that is reflected in the biblical concept of salvation is *hospitality*. Salvation makes room for people who are different. A paradox of Luke's Gospel is that the child for whom there was "no room in the inn," publicly made room for others. He welcomed tax collectors and sinners at the table. He invited himself into the home of Zacchaeus and made room for this chief of tax collectors. When facing Simon the Pharisee with his lack of hospitality, Jesus made room for him to see things differently by telling a parable. In his death, Jesus welcomed a companion on a cross beside him. In his life and death, Jesus expressed hospitality. September 11, 2001, is a day stamped on the imaginations and memories of so many North Americans. Soon after the first of the Twin Towers collapsed, air traffic controllers began diverting traffic from airports on the east coast of North America. One of the places willing and able to accept diverted planes was Gander, a community in Newfoundland and Labrador. Passengers on the planes sensed something was wrong when they landed at the Gander airport, but they found out why only when they were released hours later and taken into the terminal. Then they began to see the horror that created the havoc in New York and Washington. It didn't take long before the passengers on these flights were escorted to food, and eventually to billets, in Gander. Its citizens opened up their homes to strangers, and the community went about creating meals for the stranded passengers. The Salvation Army was deeply involved with other citizens in Gander in this expression of hospitality, of expressing salvation. When the 10th anniversary of this tragic event was acknowledged, New York firefighters sent a gift to the Town of Gander. It was a steel beam taken from one of the Twin Towers. This symbolic gesture expressed the thanks of Americans to this Newfoundland community for their hospitality in a moment of darkness. A holy people will be a hospitable people.

A holy people will be a hospitable people

The Christian gospel proclaims that in Jesus of Nazareth God has acted to restore humanity's relationship with God. It is a relationship where trust replaces suspicion, where hope has a basis, where community is built through grace and God's vision of a healed world begins to take effect. We are saved. And with this realization we begin to "work out" this salvation; we are being saved. Like a newly married couple, the implications of this new covenantal relationship require time and hard work. We begin to see that "repentance," "faith in our Lord Jesus Christ" and "regeneration by the Holy Spirit" are *constant necessities* in order to work out our salvation. Holiness is the working out of the character of this relationship, the character of this immense salvation. Holiness will be shaped by our continual repentance; new situations will require new expressions of trust; the renewing power of the Holy Spirit will transform not only personal lives but the organizational life of The Salvation Army. Holiness shaped by salvation reaches beyond the present moment to God's greater goal: "I press on toward the goal for the prize of the heavenly call of God in Christ Jesus" (Philippians 3:14). We will be saved. Working out our salvation invites us to the practice of salvation-shaped holiness.

Reflection Questions for Chapter Seven

1. What are some situations in life where you have had to choose what is *essential*?
2. If you are studying this book with a group, read the chapter together.
3. What phrase or section caught your attention? Why?

Forming the Doctrine:

4. How has your understanding of *salvation* changed over time?
5. Read Luke 8:40-48. What do you learn about faith and salvation from this story?
6. Read Titus 3:4-5. When you think of *regeneration*, what images come to mind?

Engaging the Doctrine:

7. What do you think makes it difficult for the present generation to hear the term *salvation* in its biblical sense?
8. In what ways do you experience faith as trust?
9. If salvation has to do with *healing*, how important is this word for our times?

Practising the Doctrine:

10. What helps your worship to envision this God of immense salvation?
11. What are some healthy expressions of life in your congregation?
12. What are some needs in your community where hospitality could be expressed to those who feel they are outside the community?

Conclude: Pray or sing a verse of William Booth's song, "O Boundless Salvation" (*SBSA 1987*, No. 298).

Endnotes for Chapter Seven

1 Philippians 2:12-13.

2 William Booth, "O Boundless Salvation," *SBSA 1987*, No. 298.

3 The centrality of salvation in relation to all the doctrines is argued by Carl Braaten: "Salvation is not one of the many topics, along with the doctrine of God, Christ, church, sacraments, eschatology, and the like. It is rather the perspective from which all these subjects are interpreted, for the sake of the church's mission in the world." See Carl E. Braaten, "The Christian Doctrine of Salvation," *Interpretation* 35 (April 1981): 117.

4 See Luke 7:50; 8:48; 17:19; 19:9-10.

5 The Greek wording literally says, "the power of God *into* salvation."

6 Romans 8:24; Ephesians 2:9, emphasis mine.

7 1 Corinthians 1:18, emphasis mine.

8 Romans 5:9, emphasis mine.

9 Ephesians 2:15.

10 Romans 8:18-25. Note that the language here is "redemption" which is another of Paul's concepts for salvation.

11 Joel B. Green, *Salvation* (St. Louis: Chalice Press, 2003), 9. For a more complete treatment of the breadth of salvation, see Brenda B. Colijn, *Images of Salvation in the New Testament* (Downers Grove: IVP Academic, 2010).

12 Acts 20:21, emphasis mine.

13 When Peter's critics listened to his story about the inclusion of Gentiles in the church, "they praised God, saying, 'Then God has *given* even to the Gentiles the repentance that leads to life'" (Acts 11:18, emphasis mine).

14 The translation used here draws on the footnote in the NRSV. For an extensive treatment of the concept of regeneration see "I Am About To Do A New Thing" in Brenda B. Colijn, *Images of Salvation in the New Testament* (Downers Grove: IVP Academic, 2010).

15 *SBSA 1987*, No. 298.

16 Richard Dawkins, *The God Delusion* (New York: Houghton Mifflin Books, 2008 edition), 347.

17 Garrett Green, *Imagining God: Theology and the Religious Imagination* (Grand Rapids: Eerdmans Publishing, 1989), 134.

18 Lionel Logue played by Geoffrey Rush and the future King George VI played by Colin Firth, *The King's Speech*. Directed by Tom Hooper. The Weinstein Company, 2011.

19 The early Orthodox Church in the Greek-speaking East emphasized the *life* of Christ, and depicted salvation as participation in the life of God. The words of Athanasius express this conviction: "He became human in order that we might

become divinized." The process by which this happened was through the education of the soul. The Latin church in the West, however, put its emphasis on the death of Jesus, and depicted salvation as forgiveness from the guilt of sin. As Randy Maddox has pointed out, "While these two approaches are not mutually exclusive, the emphases are determinative." *Responsible Grace: John Wesley's Practical Theology* (Nashville: Kingswood Books, 1994), 142.

20 This sermon was published in 1765, and is considered by at least one student of Wesley "as the single best homiletical summary of his soteriology, or doctrine of salvation." See Richard P. Heitzenrater, *Wesley and the People Called Methodists* (Nashville: Abingdon Press, 1995), 220.

21 Roger J. Green, *War on Two Fronts: The Redemptive Theology of William Booth* (Atlanta: The Salvation Army Supplies, 1989), 76.

22 Quoted in Roger J. Green, *War on Two Fronts*, 99.

23 *The Salvation Army Handbook of Doctrine 2010*, 152.

24 David J. Bosch, *Transforming Mission: Paradigm Shifts in Theology of Mission* (Maryknoll: Orbis Books, 1992), 393.

25 Salvationists in Winnipeg have been instrumental in establishing a palliative care facility for patients diagnosed with incurable illnesses. This facility reflects a commitment to surround people with care as they die.

26 The issue of different models of health is explored in Dean Pallant, *Keeping Faith in Faith-Based Organizations: A Practical Theology of Salvation Army Health Ministry* (Eugene: Wipf and Stock Publishers, 2012).

CHAPTER 8

Holiness and the Bedrock of Grace

We believe that we are justified by grace through faith in our Lord Jesus Christ and that he that believeth hath the witness in himself.—Doctrine 8

Grace is the substructure on which everything else is built.—T. Runyon[1]

FOUNDATIONS ARE CRITICAL TO THE STRUCTURE OF BUILDings. Construct an inadequate foundation and storms or earthquake tremors will bring the building down. Some buildings last long because they have been built on solid foundations. The Salisbury Cathedral was constructed in the 13th century, and remains an active place of worship and service in England to this day, even if its spire is leaning at an angle! This important cathedral has been built on a unique and strong foundation. Among the images for salvation employed in the Bible is that of a building.[2] And among the images created by Christ to depict the Christian life is the story of two construction workers, one who built a house on sand while the other built a home on rock. With dramatic results![3] This eighth doctrine draws attention to salvation's foundation, which is God's grace. This is a bedrock conviction, with important relevance for the 21st century and the practice of holiness.

Forming the Doctrine

The various phrases of this doctrine have a long history. Some put us smack in the middle of the European Reformations of the 16th century.[4] Other phrases have their basis much more in the time of the Wesleys in the 18th century. But all of them are grounded in the Bible itself. The Apostle Paul anticipated this eighth doctrine when he wrote, "For by grace you have been saved through faith" (Ephesians 2:8). Let's start by paying close attention to the doctrine's respective phrases beginning with, "We are justified by grace through faith."

We are Justified ...

With the word *justified,* we come to a watershed moment in the story of the church. In the eye of the hurricane is Martin Luther and his personal breakthrough with God. Instead of hearing the phrase "righteousness of God" (Romans 1:17) through the fear of his own inadequacies, he came to understand it as God's provision of grace. There was nothing Luther could do to stand before this righteous God, but he could accept God's gift of justification to him. From this realization the Lutheran Reformation developed its emphasis on justification by grace through faith.

The church is indebted to Luther and others for recovering this important dimension of Christian faith. However, at present there is an intense debate as to whether Luther's understanding of justification is precisely what was intended by the biblical writers. It has been noted by some that the *doctrine* of justification has taken on shades of meaning different from its *biblical* image.[5] It's a complex discussion, so let's turn to the biblical roots of justification in order to examine it.

First, while the concept of justification can relate to an *acquittal of pardon* in court, it is more properly a *restored relationship.* Notice, for instance, how Paul parallels justification with reconciliation in his Letter to the Romans: "Much more surely then, now that we have been *justified* by his blood, will we be saved through him from the wrath of God. For if while we were enemies, we were *reconciled* to God through the death of his Son, much more surely, having been reconciled, will we be saved by his life."[6] The relational aspect of reconciliation is important if we are to understand justification. If there is value in viewing justification through the image of pardon in a court room, Brenda Colijn argues that we are best to think of it as a family court where the restoration of relationships is the important thing, and not simply a verdict of acquittal.[7] In fact, our contemporary usage of the word justification in connection with computers is helpful. When we justify a text, we *align* it. Biblical justification has primarily to do with our realigned relationship with God and, through it, to others. Note, too, that while justification is tremendously important, it is *one among many* aspects of Paul's understanding of salvation. Recall that his keynote in Romans 1:16 stands as a prism through which to view the different dimensions of salvation: "For I am not ashamed of the gospel; it is the power of God for salvation to everyone who has faith, to the Jew first and also to the Greek." His unfolding of salvation in Romans and other Epistles includes justification, but also reconciliation, new creation, regeneration and adoption among others. The biblical image of justification is tremendously important, but it is not intended to carry the whole weight of our understanding of salvation. It is one important component of the building, but it is not the whole structure. Justification emphasizes our realigned relationship with God.

Biblical justification has primarily to do with our realigned relationship with God and, through it, to others

We are justified *by grace* ...

Luther's discovery has impacted our reading of the Bible. Salvation is a gift, "For *by grace* you have been saved through faith" (Ephesians 2:8). We need to be careful not to pass over this too quickly. In order to appreciate that we are justified by grace it is necessary to give more thought to the biblical world of grace.

Grace is fundamental to Israel's faith. A central conviction of the Old Testament is that the Lord is "a God merciful and gracious, slow to anger, and abounding in steadfast love and faithfulness." God's gracious character is affirmed by Moses, the Psalmists, Lamentations and even the reluctant prophet Jonah![8] This "confessional statement ... cuts across the Old Testament as a statement of basic Israelite conviction regarding its God."[9] And the New Testament bears witness to its conviction that God's grace became visible in the person of Christ: "In the beginning was the Word, and the Word was with God, and the Word was God ... And the Word became flesh and lived among us ... full of grace and truth."[10] For this reason it can be argued that if the Bible has a single thread in its plot it is "that God is essentially, characteristically, and fundamentally *gracious*."[11] The whole of the Bible characterizes God as gracious, a God of distinctive grace.

In grace, God takes initiative "to seek out and to save the lost."[12] In grace, God responds to humanity in ways not deserved. In grace, God's saving love is offered to all. Grace is the unbounded love of God offered to all humankind, and Jesus made it visible. Grace incarnate! Thus when this Salvationist doctrine states we are "justified by grace" it acknowledges that justification is a gift not deserved. By grace God has taken the first step in restoring our relationship. By grace God offers justification to all. By grace God accepts us into his covenantal community.

We are justified by grace *through faith in our Lord Jesus Christ ...*

Because justification comes through grace, it can only be received as a gift. The appropriate response is *faith*. There are, however, inadequate ways of thinking about faith in relation to this gift of grace. This awareness introduces a feature of Reformation faith that became problematic. There were those following Luther who so emphasized God's role in justification that it came to be expressed as "justification through faith *alone*." While appreciating the need to keep God's actions in the forefront, this wording can negate the appropriate human response to God's grace.

Two observations are in order. First, it is important to realize that faith itself is made possible by God's grace. A term used to speak of this is "prevenient grace." The word "prevenient" is related to a Latin word which means "to go before." This dimension of grace emphasizes the way God's grace through the Holy Spirit goes before us even prior to intentional and conscious faith. The Book of Acts can be read as God's grace going before, giving men and women the capacity to repent and believe the gospel: "Then God has given even to the Gentiles the repentance that leads to life" (Acts 11:18). It is because God's salvation is not imposed on us that we are invited to respond with freedom and integrity. Grace can be resisted. But grace makes possible our trust in the redemptive work of Christ.[13] Second, the active nature of faith can best be translated with the word *faithfulness*.[14] In Romans 3:26, Paul argues that God "justifies the one who has the *faith of Jesus*."[15] This phrase parallels his argument in Romans 4:16, referring to "those who share the *faith of Abraham*." Abraham's journey of faith is best expressed as faithfulness, as is Jesus' life of obedience. In Brenda Colijn's words, "The gospel reveals God's covenant faithfulness through the faith(fulness) of Christ, to benefit all those who have the same faith(fulness) as Christ."[16] Faith, best understood as faithfulness, is the appropriate response to God's grace.

Thus far we have considered the phrase, "We are justified by grace through faith in our Lord Jesus Christ." This is followed by a phrase in the doctrine that seems at first glance unrelated:

... and the person who believes has the witness in herself/himself.

What does this have to do with all that has gone before in this doctrine? It helps here to keep our Wesleyan roots in mind. The journey of John and Charles Wesley has a role in the phrasing of this doctrine, and is of importance to Salvationists.

While in their 20s, the Wesleys agreed to serve the emerging British colony of Georgia in the New World. On many fronts, however, their brief time there was a disaster. John tripped himself up over a failed romance, and Charles' health couldn't cope with living conditions. Their faith was at a low ebb when they returned on separate voyages to England. But one thing they took from their sense of failure was an introduction to Moravian Lutherans. During their initial voyage across the Atlantic, a severe storm shook the Wesleys, but not the Moravians. John and Charles witnessed a calm faith amidst turbulent waters and this evoked their interest. Conversations with Moravians on their return to England, and a timely reading of Luther, led both Wesley brothers to an experience of faith in the spring of 1738 that profoundly shaped their lives. John Wesley later journaled his Aldersgate experience: "... I felt my heart strangely warmed. I felt I did trust in Christ, Christ alone for salvation; and an assurance was given me that he had taken away *my* sins, even *mine*, and saved *me* from the law of sin and death."[17] Wesley understood this moment as his *grasp* of justification, and a note of *assurance* that he had indeed been pardoned by God. It didn't take long though before he began to question this strong note of assurance. According to his Moravian friends, true Christian faith would be absent of questions and doubts. But Wesley had questions in full measure. A way was needed to acknowledge his doubts but not to be defined by them. He found this in Paul's conviction that "all who are led by the Spirit of God are children of God. For you did not receive a spirit of slavery to fall back into fear, but you have received a spirit of adoption. When we cry, 'Abba! Father!' it is that very Spirit bearing witness with our spirit that we are children of God."[18] The source of assurance for faith is not to be found within ourselves, but through the Spirit's presence enabling us to experience the intimacy of God as Father. This, too, is by grace through faith.

Thus this eighth doctrine concentrates our thinking on key terms and their relationship to salvation. The argument put forward here is that salvation has many facets to it, a primary one of which is justification. We might put it this way: By grace you have been saved, that is: justified, adopted, reconciled and forgiven by faith in our Lord Jesus Christ! Basking in his new-found joy, Charles Wesley penned a song soon after his own grasp of this assurance. The song voices his conviction:

> No condemnation now I dread;
> Jesus, and all in Him, is mine.
> Alive in him, my living head,
> And clothed in righteousness divine,
> Bold I approach the eternal throne
> And claim the crown, through Christ, my own.[19]

Through the life, death and resurrection of Christ, God realigns us in a relationship of covenantal love which was intended for us from the beginning of creation. And through the Holy Spirit this relationship is made assuredly real to us.

Engaging the Doctrine

While this doctrine has played a key role in the life of the church, it is not so obvious how it connects with life in the 21st century. Martin Luther's struggles to be accepted by God don't easily resonate with a culture that wants God "on demand." Even the language of "justification" and "grace" create dissonance. But when we look carefully at the meaning of these words and the thrust of the doctrine, we can begin to see just how relevant they are for this generation.

For instance, one of the important issues in our time is to know what it is that *validates the worth of our lives*. Our culture in the West tends to value us because of what we accomplish. Our lives are justified by the medals we win or the celebrity status we achieve. This is not to minimize important achievements. But when our life is measured only by them we set ourselves up for tragedy when we can no longer achieve that kind of success. One of the tragedies in our time is the number of former athletes who find life empty after the spotlight is removed due to retirement or injury. Similarly, the contemporary search for acceptance is viewed by some as a contributor to a life of addiction. This is a complex issue, but there is sufficient evidence pointing to the need for acceptance by others as a factor in the pursuit of prescription or illegal drugs. When the Christian faith proclaims that we are "justified by grace through faith" it is stating the conviction that our lives are valued by God apart from any personal achievement or accomplishment. The justification of our lives lies not with what we do but with what God has done for us. God has acted in the life, death and resurrection of Jesus to secure our justification, realignment, validation with God.

A second way this doctrine relates to life in the 21st century is its emphasis on *grace as gift*. Some have argued that in a market society the very notion of gift has become problematic. A glance at the newspaper or Internet postings leads us into a world where goods and services are bought and sold. From cars to homes, from schooling to service clubs, from fashion to food, we become aware that much of life has become a commodity that is bought and sold in the marketplace. When most human transactions are governed by economics, can there really be such a thing as a gift? Margaret Visser has explored the phenomenon of gifts and gratitude in her book, *The Gift of Thanks*. In it she notes that the exchange of gifts and gratitude is very much coloured by the culture in which it takes place and often functions to create bonds in a society. Gifts and our responses to them are not incidental. From a Christian perspective, Visser argues that "a gift to another person is at the deepest level a response to grace, which is a gift already received."[20] God is known in the Bible as the gift-giving God. God's creative and redeeming work is God's gift to us. It is an expression of grace. This core conviction, which is grounded in the concept of grace, has significant implications for a culture characterized by commodity. Community is built on the foundation of gifting, of grace. This realization is part of the dynamic in the musical version of *Les Miserables*. Valjean had been arrested and imprisoned for stealing bread to feed his hungry nephew. Upon his release from prison years later, he finds refuge for a night's sleep in the home of a bishop. Valjean however takes advantage of the bishop's hospitality to steal some silverware. When the constables re-arrest Valjean, the bishop intercedes and provides him with an alibi. Valjean is taken back by this gesture of grace, and sings:

A gift to another person is at the deepest level a response to grace, which is a gift already received
—Margaret Visser

> Yet why did I allow that man
> To touch my soul and teach me love?
> He treated me like any other
> He gave me his trust
> He called me brother
> My life he claims for God above
> Can such things be?[21]

A bishop's gesture of grace sets in motion a story of grace. Grace transforms the relationship between Valjean and the bishop. And this transformation works its way into the relationships Valjean forms with others that come into the circle of his life.

Finally, a Christian view of grace has an important contribution to make to the way The Salvation Army *partners with other individuals and organizations* to carry out our mission. The Army's mission is huge and often requires Salvationists to work with others. It is important to retain organizational integrity when working with others, but it is also important to realize that Salvationists do not have a monopoly on God's grace. The opening of John's Gospel contributes to this conviction: "The true light, *which enlightens everyone*, was coming into the world."[22] The active grace of God through the Holy Spirit is not limited to Salvationists, or even Christians. When we take this dynamic view of grace seriously it will enable us to recognize that God's holy love is at work in the whole world, not simply our corner of it.[23] This realization enables us to partner with businesses to bring toys to children at Christmas, to work with the Muslim community to help our prisons become more humane, and to partner with governments to alleviate human suffering during a rail disaster. Salvationists look for what is shared in common, and work together on matters of common concern, all the while holding to a full trinitarian commitment of grace.

So this important doctrine reflects watershed moments in the story of the church. It is a conviction whose judgment has been formed over time. But it also bears witness to important issues in the 21st century. What then might it mean for this core conviction to inform our understanding and practice of holiness?

Practising the Doctrine

As we have seen, this doctrine has been constructed from strong materials. Each phrase is important, and each phrase points to some aspect of the practice of holiness. At the heart of this doctrine is the conviction that the Christian life is constructed on *grace*. The importance of this is captured by Ted Runyon when he argues that "Grace is the substructure on which everything else is built."[24] Not too far from our house is a large urban park. Recently the park officials decided to expand its duck pond and erect an educational centre. While this centre was being constructed, my wife and I took our young grandson to watch the workers put in the foundation. He watched with delight as steel beams were driven into Manitoba's shifting soil. Today we can see the centre's structure above the ground, but we can't see the foundation beams that were driven into the ground. Holiness builds upon the sometimes hidden foundation of God's grace. If we build our lives on the foundation of grace they will also *take the shape of grace*. Let's consider some of the ways we can live out a holy life shaped by the bedrock of grace.

We will be characterized by grace as we *learn to view life through the lenses of grace*. The Gospel of Mark narrates the story of a woman who anointed Jesus just prior to his arrest and crucifixion.[25] The reaction of many present in the room was one of severe criticism: "Why was this ointment wasted in this way?" They had a point. It was a costly gesture and money from it could have been used to help the poor. These critics viewed this gesture through one set of lenses. Jesus viewed the woman's gesture through other lenses: "Let her alone; why do you trouble her? She has performed a good service for me." Jesus goes on to explain how her act of kindness has really "anointed" his body for its burial. Everyone in the room witnessed the same gesture, but Jesus interpreted it by grace. The reality of interpreting by grace came to me when our kids were in their teens. On one occasion Cathie and I prepared to move from Toronto to Winnipeg. Our three kids wanted a final time with their friends. The house was stacked with boxes because the movers were scheduled to arrive the next day. But we agreed to their request on condition that they clean up after their friends left. When I got up the next morning, I went downstairs to make a cup of coffee. Instead of a moment of relaxation I was faced with pizza boxes and Coke cans that littered our living room. I was furious. Moments later Cathie came into the kitchen and looked at the same scene, and said: "Isn't this special? Our kids think so much of their friends that they want to have them over one last time!" We both viewed the same mess. I viewed it through the lens of broken promises and inconvenience, but Cathie viewed the scene through the lens of friendship. How we interpret a situation impacts how we respond to it, for "only when we interpret by grace will we live by grace."[26] Grace offers a set of lenses through which to view life around us.

When we view life through grace we will *learn to see the sacramental* in the world around us. The Christian faith understands Jesus as one whose life conveyed grace, who made grace visible. Thus he is named The Sacrament.[27] On one occasion Jesus became aware of the hunger of crowds as they listened to his teaching in the wilderness. Taking five loaves and two fish, "he looked up to heaven, and blessed and broke them, and gave them to the disciples to set before the crowd" (Luke 9:16). Later, on the night Jesus was arrested, "he took a loaf of bread, and when he had given thanks, he broke it and gave it to them" (Luke 22:19). On the road to Emmaus, the risen Christ conversed with two puzzled followers. He agreed to stay with them for the evening, and "When he was at the table with them, he took bread, blessed and broke it, and gave it to them" (Luke 24:30). Took. Blessed. Broke. Gave. Walter Brueggemann argues, "These are the four decisive words of our sacramental existence." The Salvation Army's poet General, Albert Orsborn, understands their sacramental nature: "My life must be Christ's broken bread ... That other souls, refreshed and fed, May share his life through mine."[28] As Salvationists we often take what is given to us in order to meet the deep hungers around us. As we take the resources of others we give thanks, we break them for others and we give to others. Salvationists have a way of viewing sacramental grace through meals for the homeless, care for the sick, our preaching and our music.[29] Holiness shaped by grace appreciates the sacramental.

Finally, as a community that practises grace, we will be *characterized by thanksgiving*. Canada's season of Thanksgiving is in the month of October. The harvest is in, the autumn leaves are in their glory, and we begin to brace ourselves for winter's onslaught. Before we do we offer thanks, usually with a well-cooked turkey and pumpkin pie. It's one of my favourite weekends. The cultivation of gratitude is something that should extend beyond this Canadian holiday into the whole of the year, but it's not easy in a consumer society. I have enjoyed watching my two daughters teach their children to say thanks. Some have argued that the expression of thanks is one of the more difficult tasks for a child to learn.[30] And when it is expressed as adults it can catch people off guard. I was on a flight to New York City that was diverted because of a summer storm. Most passengers were not happy campers. When the flight finally resumed, flight attendants came along and offered refreshments. I took a cold drink and expressed thanks. The attendant turned to me and said, "You may not realize it but you are the only person on this flight that has said thank you." The Army's divisional staff in our city has looked for opportunities to express thanks to different levels of government for the work they do. On one occasion we hosted a coffee break in the large rotunda of our provincial legislative building. As I stood there an executive secretary approached me, seeing me in Salvation Army uniform. "Why are you doing this?" she asked. I responded, "We simply want to say thanks for all you folks are doing on behalf of the Province of Manitoba." "That's remarkable," she replied. "Nobody ever thanks us for the work we do." Martin Luther once portrayed worship as "the tenth leper returning to give thanks." Holiness is the cultivation of gratitude into the whole of our lives, both personal and communal.

Holiness is the cultivation of gratitude into the whole of our lives, both personal and communal

Finally, the practice of graced holiness will shape the church as a *community of grace*. As the body of Christ the church is intended to make God's grace visible. The difficulty, of course, is that while grace is visible in the story of Christ, it is not always visible in the story of the church. In fact, there are times when the church displays anything but grace. We might be inclined to dismiss the church, but God doesn't. Grace creates community because God's love moves beyond Father, Son and Spirit to the world God loves. The salvation, the healing, that God offers the world is to be realized in the community of salvation, which is the church. And The Salvation Army, with all its flaws, is intended to be one expression of God's saving grace. For this reason we gather together to hear our story of grace in the Bible. We sing and play the music of God's sovereign grace. We speak and listen to each other in order to live as a graceful community. And we engage the world beyond ourselves knowing that grace is not contained but seeks the welfare of the city in which we live.[31] When we fail, we repent and seek forgiveness. When we come close to embodying God's grace, we rejoice and celebrate. We engage in the hard work of creating a community of grace. If The Salvation Army has a visible presence in the community, it is often felt most at Christmas. We put out the Christmas kettles, sing and play Christmas music in the streets, deliver food and toy hampers to families. Christmas is a busy time for Salvationists. It's also a season when we tune into God's grace. We structure our worship around the season of Advent with the conviction that underlying all of our activity is a gift. One biblical writer puts it this way: "Thanks be to God for his indescribable gift!" (2 Corinthians 9:15). God's grace forms this community so that we might embody God's grace in the wider world.

This eighth doctrine points to a bedrock conviction about our salvation. This core conviction matters! Its deep foundation lies with the grace of the triune God. Upon that grace we can begin to construct the edifice of salvation that includes justification and regeneration. As noted, these gifts are named in our doctrines but are not the only blessings. We are "ransomed, healed, restored, forgiven."[32] Salvation is deeply personal and it is also communal, even environmental. And the faith that begins to grasp this salvation is best characterized as faithfulness. It's a lifetime of trust and obedience. For that depiction of faith we turn to our ninth doctrine.

Reflection Questions for Chapter Eight

1. This chapter draws on the image of foundations. What observations have you made about the importance of foundations?
2. If you are studying this book with a group, read the chapter together.
3. What phrase or section caught your attention? Why?

Forming the Doctrine:

4. Read Exodus 34:6; Psalm 103:8, 17; Lamentations 3:22-23; Jonah 4:2. What do you make of this emphasis on grace in the Old Testament?
5. How helpful do you find the argument that justification is like the term used in computer language?
6. What are some ways you have witnessed God's grace going *before* you?

Engaging the Doctrine:

7. What are some unhealthy ways you think people seek to validate or justify their lives?
8. How important is the experience of gifts to you? Why?
9. What are some ways you see grace to be at work in people who would not claim Christian faith?

Practising the Doctrine:

10. Read Mark 14:1-9. How have you experienced a moment when you and a friend looked at the same situation but viewed it differently?
11. In what ways do you experience your congregation as a "community of grace"?
12. Why would you consider grace so essential for the life of holiness?

Conclude: Pray Ephesians 2:1-10.

Endnotes for Chapter Eight

1 Theodore Runyon, *The New Creation: John Wesley's Theology Today* (Nashville: Abingdon Press, 1998), 212.

2 See, for instance, 1 Corinthians 3:9-17.

3 Matthew 7:24-27.

4 I am using the word "Reformations" in the plural because of the awareness that there were many reformations in 16th-century Europe, each with their own distinctive features. See Diarmaid MacCulloch, *Reformation: Europe's House Divided* (Toronto: Penguin Books, 2003).

5 For a discussion of the issues surrounding justification, see "Justification by Faith(fullness)" in Brenda B. Colijn, *Images of Salvation in the New Testament* (Downers Grove: IVP Academic, 2010). Alister McGrath contends that the doctrine of justification "has come to develop a meaning quite independent of its biblical origins," quoted in Colijn, 197. See also N. T. Wright, *Justification: God's Plan & Paul's Vision* (Downers Grove: InterVarsity Press, 2009), 37: "For too long we have read Scripture with nineteenth-century eyes and sixteenth-century questions. It's time to get back to reading with first-century eyes and twenty-first-century questions."

6 Romans 5:9-10, emphasis mine.

7 For this insight and a helpful introduction to issues surrounding the current debate about justification see, Colijn, "Justification by Faith(fullness)."

8 Exodus 34:6. See also Psalm 103:8, 17; Lamentations 3:22-23; Jonah 4:2.

9 Terrence E. Fretheim, *Exodus* (Louisville: John Knox Press, 1991), 302. Fretheim continues: "It thus constitutes a kind of 'canon' of the kind of God Israel's God is, in the light of which ongoing involvement in its history is to be interpreted."

10 John 1:1, 14.

11 J. Clinton McCann, Jr., "The Hermeneutics of Grace," *Interpretation* 57 (January 2003): 5.

12 Luke 19:10.

13 "God seeks us before we even desire to seek him ... The term 'prevenient grace' describes this preparatory work of the Holy Spirit. It is the grace that comes before conversion. Our moral sense, or conscience, although imperfect because of ignorance and sin, can act as a stimulus to spiritual awakening." See *The Salvation Army Handbook of Doctrine 2010,* 164-165.

14 The word is *pistis,* and the context best determines which translation is used.

15 The translation "the faith of Jesus" instead of "faith in Jesus" is based on the Greek text, and used in the *NRSV* footnote.

16 Brenda Colijn, 207. This awareness will be spelled out more fully when dealing with the phrase, "continued obedient faith" in Doctrine 9.

17 See http://www.gbgm-umc.org/aldersgate-wheaton/aumcname.html. Accessed March 2, 2013.

18 Romans 8:14-16. See Theodore Runyon, *The New Creation*, 58-70.

19 Charles Wesley, "And Can It Be," *SBSA 1987*, No. 283.

20 Margaret Visser, *The Gift of Thanks* (Toronto: HarperCollins Publishers, 2008), 208.

21 http://www.allmusicals.com/lyrics/lesmiserables/prologuewhathaveidone.htm. Accessed November 1, 2012. The song, "What Have I Done?" has been set to music by Claude Schonberg with lyrics by Herbert Kretzmer. The musical, *Les Miserables*, is based on a book by the same title written by Victor Hugo, which is based on events in France in the early 19th century. The filmed version of the musical features Hugh Jackman, Russell Crowe and Anne Hathaway, directed by Tom Hooper and produced by Universal Pictures, 2012.

22 John 1:9, emphasis mine.

23 With respect to non-Christian religions, Theodore Runyon argues, "Wherever we go and whomever we reach with the message of Christianity, the Spirit has preceded us. We can be assured that there is no one in whom the Spirit has not already been at work. The openness of persons is often because of the operation of this prevenient grace in their lives, causing them to raise questions and making them receptive to new sources of meaning." T. Runyon, *The New Creation*, 218-219.

24 T. Runyon, *The New Creation*, 212.

25 See Mark 14:1-9.

26 J. Clinton McCann, "The Hermeneutics of Grace," *Interpretation* 57 (January 2003): 15.

27 "Christ has been described as the one, true, original Sacrament." *The Salvation Army Handbook of Doctrine 2010*, 270.

28 Albert Orsborn, "My Life Must Be Christ's Broken Bread," *SBSA 1987*, No. 512.

29 See, for instance, Paul du Plessis, *The Sacrament of Music: A Selection of Poetry* (Upper Norwood, England: Privately Published, 1987).

30 "Children who have been brought up to say these words ['thank you'] do not manage to produce them spontaneously until sometime between the ages of four and six. In our culture thanking is believed to be, for most children, the last of the basic social graces they acquire." Margaret Visser, *The Gift of Thanks* (Toronto: HarperCollins Publishers, 2008), 12.

31 See Jeremiah 29:7.

32 Henry Francis Lyte, "Praise My Soul the King of Heaven," *SBSA 1987*, No. 17.

CHAPTER 9

Holiness as "Long Obedience in the Same Direction"

We believe that continuance in a state of salvation depends upon continued obedient faith in Christ.—Doctrine 9

There is a great market for religious experience in our world; there is little enthusiasm for the patient acquisition of virtue, little inclination to sign up for a long apprenticeship in what earlier generations of Christians called holiness.—Eugene Peterson[1]

The longest running sports event in North America is held in St. John's, Newfoundland and Labrador. It's the annual regatta, held at Quidi Vidi—a small inland lake located just before the water flows out to the Atlantic Ocean. This event goes back 500 years to a time when fishermen raced each other as part of their summer excursion for cod in the North Atlantic. These days the race is held in August, and contestants come from all over the province. The boats are lined up, a starter signals the beginning, and the scullers row to markers down the course and then back to the finish line. It's a grueling race, one that exhausts the rowers. Strength and perseverance are needed to complete the race. As with other sports, it's not just how you begin but how you finish that really matters. This ninth doctrine pays particular attention to the whole of the race, or the whole of the game. Its focus is on "*continued* obedient faith." And while an emphasis on "obedient faith" may encounter a difficult reception in the 21st century, we may be surprised to discover that it resonates with important insights in education. This core conviction makes a significant contribution to our understanding and practice of holiness.

Forming the Doctrine

It's important that we keep this core conviction connected with *salvation*. "*Continued* obedient faith" is linked with "*continuance* in a state of salvation." Christian salvation describes our renewed relationship with God. It is a justified, realigned, reconciled, forgiven relationship. It is also a covenantal relationship whereby the regenerating power of the Holy Spirit brings the presence of God to bear upon us personally and communally. However, relationships are anything but static. They involve risk and trust. God's gracious influence through the Spirit of Christ is always at work in our lives to deepen that trust. But God does not coerce our response. At all points we are respected and trusted by God. Some expressions of the Protestant church after the European Reformations argued that God's grace was "irresistible," and that those chosen by God for salvation would "persevere" in their Christian walk. This had a way of presuming upon God's grace. In the words of a later German Lutheran, it tended to create a "cheap grace."[2] Countering such a view prompted an emphasis on our relationship with God as dynamic. This awareness helps us to understand the formation of the doctrine's emphasis upon "continued obedient faith in Christ."

There are many New Testament texts that depict the Christian life as obedient faith. For instance, the Apostle Paul begins his Letter to the Romans with the claim that his vocation was "to bring about the obedience of faith among all the Gentiles" (Romans 1:5). Paul wouldn't detach faith from obedience, nor obedience from faith. However, this insistence on faith's obedience is also grounded in the life of Christ himself. It has been argued by Richard Longenecker that it is Christ's obedient faith that in fact stands as a "foundational conviction" for the early church.[3] Let's look more fully into this claim.

While each Gospel in the New Testament narrates Jesus' life of obedience, the Gospel of Luke gives it centre stage. During his family's annual pilgrimage to Jerusalem for the Passover, the young Jesus stays behind to engage the temple's teachers with his inquisitive questions. His parents finally catch up with him and express their exasperation. His response jars them: "Did you not know that I must be in my Father's house?" (Luke 2:49). Two things catch our attention. First, Jesus is conscious of a claim of obedience upon his life: "I must." Second, Jesus is also conscious of a special relation to God such that God is "Father." This relationship is affirmed at his public baptism, when a voice from heaven declares, "You are my Son, the Beloved; with you I am well pleased" (Luke 3:22). Just prior to his public ministry, Jesus is led by the Holy Spirit into the wilderness where he is tempted. At issue in the temptations is the seed of doubt: "If you are the Son of God ..." (Luke 4:3, 9). What follows in Luke is the story of Jesus who lived a life of faithful obedience as a Son to the Father. At numerous moments in the story, Jesus affirms his loyalty, especially when he acknowledges that he "must undergo great suffering,"[4] and be rejected by the nation's leaders. We find this coming to its climax on the Mount of Olives just prior to his arrest. Withdrawing from his closest disciples, he "knelt down, and prayed, 'Father, if you are willing, remove this cup from me; yet, not my will but yours be done'" (Luke 22:41-42). The Gospel of Luke narrates Jesus' life of faithful obedience.

While several New Testament texts draw attention to Christ's life of obedience, Paul's Letter to the Philippians is among the most significant. As he encouraged these new believers to "seek the interests of others," Paul sketched the mind "that was in Christ Jesus, who, though he was in the form of God ... emptied himself, taking the form of a slave ... And being found in human form, he humbled himself and *became obedient to the point of death—even death on a cross*."[5] This passage in Philippians compacts the story of Christ into critical elements. In his life of obedience "Jesus shows what it is to be most human, most like what a human being is supposed to be, living in full obedience to God. Such obedience turns out to mean the truest kind of freedom, in which one has chosen the life that meaningfully fulfills one's destiny."[6] And if this is true of Christ, how much more it is meant to be true for his followers!

The Book of Hebrews makes an important connection between

Christ's obedience and ours. This sermon is addressed to a congregation that seems to be tottering between moving forward in their allegiance to Christ and a return to their old life. In response to this, its author holds Jesus up as the "pioneer of their salvation" (Hebrews 2:10). And although this Christ "was a Son, he learned obedience through what he suffered; and having been made perfect, he became the source of eternal salvation for all who obey him" (Hebrews 5:8). It's instructive to recognize that obedience is something learned; obedient faith requires teachability. Obedience is also connected here to suffering, but this suffering is related to the cost of living the Christian life with integrity. Hebrews contains a number of warnings to its readers about the dangers of falling back in faith instead of moving ahead. In one instance the dangers are spelled out in dramatic terms: "Therefore let us go on toward perfection, leaving behind the basic teaching about Christ ... For it is impossible to restore again to repentance those who have once been enlightened, and have tasted the heavenly gift, and have shared in the Holy Spirit ... and then have fallen away, since on their own they are crucifying again the Son of God" (Hebrews 6:1-6). The warnings are real, but the emphasis of Hebrews is its look to the future with a more athletic image: "Therefore ... let us run with perseverance the race that is set before us, looking to Jesus the pioneer and perfecter of our faith" (Hebrews 12:1-2). The Christian life is like a long-distance race, a muscle-depleting regatta. Sprinters may impress with their speed, but what is needed is perseverance. What is needed in this race is "continued obedient faith."

While the Bible affirms this emphasis on "continued obedient faith in Christ," some notes of caution are needed. First, biblical faith always begins with God's gracious actions. Faith, including persevering faith, is a response to God's grace. The New Testament certainly emphasizes the imperatives of faith: "Bear one another's burdens, and in this way you will fulfill the law of Christ"; "Be subject to one another out of reverence for Christ"; "Do nothing from selfish ambition or conceit"; "clothe yourselves with compassion, kindness, humility, meekness, and patience"; "Discipline yourselves, keep alert."[7] All of these imperatives for continued obedient faith mark the landscape of scripture. But we need to recognize that they come in response to God's prior actions: "We love because he first loved us."[8] When we consider God's relationship with Israel, this grace/response rhythm is obvious. For instance, we may look to the Ten Commandments as an exercise in obedient faith. However, it is important to keep in mind that these obligations begin with God's actions: "I am the Lord your God, who brought you out of the land of Egypt, out of the house of slavery." Only when God's relation to Israel has been established does the word of God proceed: "... you shall have no other gods before me."[9] In fact, the grace of God creates a new sense of identity in those whom God liberates. God's deliverance has made of Israel "a priestly kingdom and a holy nation."[10] In similar fashion, those who have been set free by the life, death and resurrection of Christ also have a new sense of identity. Paul writes to believers: "To ... those who are sanctified in Christ Jesus, called to be saints"; "Now you are the body of Christ and individually members of it"; "For freedom Christ has set us free"; "So then you are no longer strangers and aliens, but you are citizens with the saints and also members of the household of God."[11] Continued obedient faith responds to the continued faithfulness of God's grace.

All right knowledge of God is born of obedience
—John Calvin

A second note of caution is that we likely hear the word "obedience" with overtones of mindless obedience to rules. If so, we would be missing its biblical intent. As has already been noted, Jesus' obedience is grounded in his relationship to God as Father. Obedient faith is directed to persons, not rules. Obedience is another way of talking about faithfulness. It is Christ's faithfulness that characterizes obedience. John Calvin was on track when he said, "All right knowledge of God is born of obedience."[12] In fact, this is how the disciples of Jesus learned. They responded to his invitation to "Follow me" without knowing the full implications of the invitation. Obedience was grounded in their relationship with Christ: they were "with him" (Mark 3:14). It was only as they followed, as they continued in their obedient faith, that they gradually began to understand. And even here, the full grasp of his life, death and resurrection became a lifelong journey. Only as Peter and the others carried out their leadership roles and practised their faith, did they grasp a little more of Christ's curriculum. Continued obedient faith in Christ involves the deliberate, intentional, practice of faith based on the relationship we have with God through Christ.

Thus, far from being a secondary aspect of faith in the Bible, obedience is central. From Abraham and Sarah's obedience in leaving their home to Peter's leaving his nets, faith is marked by obedience. Obedient faith is important not simply because believers are instructed to obey, but because our Lord was characterized by obedience.[13] Our calling to continued obedient faith is grounded in Christ's obedient faithfulness.

Engaging the Doctrine

The word "obedience" can evoke a wide range of reactions in our times. When our three kids were younger, they pressured Cathie and me into getting a dog. As one daughter framed it, "How can I possibly be a veterinarian if we don't have a pet in the house?" We caved in and arranged to adopt a dog, a Collie-German Shepherd. One of the first things Cathie did was to take Tobie to an "obedience school." Poor Tobie! She could never quite figure out who was supposed to be the instructor and who the student. Our attempts as a family to train this dog were fuel enough for any cartoonist's sketches. We eventually worked out an understanding between us, but Tobie would never be what could be called an "obedient" dog. When it comes to people, we are very careful how we use the word "obedience." And for good reason. The horrors of the Nuremburg Trials following the Second World War disclosed the painful reality of Nazis like Albert Speer who committed unthinkable atrocities in the name of "duty" or "obedience to orders." The movie, *A Few Good Men*, portrayed an American military cohort who silenced the truth in the name of "obeying orders." So when this doctrine expresses the conviction that our salvation "depends upon continued obedient faith in Christ" all kinds of red flags go up. However, there is an opposite danger of dismissing the notion of obedience altogether. As we become a market society where more and more goods and services are bought and sold, the concept of obedience has little place. Jonathan Sacks argues that the language of consumerism has "eroded our moral vocabulary." According to Sacks, "It is difficult to talk about the common good when we lose the ability to speak about duty, obligation and restraint, and find ourselves only with desires clamouring for satisfaction."[14] Perhaps in our fears about the misuse of obedience we have thrown the baby out with the bath water. How then can we approach the concept of obedient faith in such a way that is it faithful to the biblical story and helpful to our times?

Let's begin by exploring the relationship between obedience and learning. Dogs aside, we are inclined to think that obedience makes it difficult to learn. If an instructor requires me to obey, I may do so, but at the expense of forming my own convictions. In education it's called "rote learning." Students are required only to feed back the information "poured" into them. It's not good education.[15] Neither is it the way obedience works in learning. When teaching students to play a brass instrument, I don't hesitate to ask for their obedience. I instruct them to hold the mouthpiece correctly to produce a buzzing sound; I require them to hold the instrument in a proper manner; and I demonstrate breathing techniques with the expectation they will follow. Only gradually will the students begin to get it. Only with time and obedience will they begin to produce a sound that actually sounds like a trombone or trumpet. I agree with Charles Wood in this respect: "Obedience is not a substitute for knowledge, nor a way of getting over one's desire for knowledge, nor a way of convincing oneself of something. It is, simply, *a way to knowledge*."[16] Donald Schön adds to this perspective: "When someone learns a practice, he is initiated into the traditions of a community of practitioners and the practice world they inhabit."[17] Brass students are initiated into the tradition of music; science students are initiated into the tradition of astronomy; nursing students learn their craft in the practice of medicine; theological students are initiated into the tradition of faith seeking understanding. Initially this requires the following of authority, or obedience to the insights and skills of the discipline. Learning a skill requires obedience in the authority of that tradition.

Obedience has several dimensions, one of which is *obligation*. Parents feel deep affection for their children, and they also feel obligated; to act out of obligation for a child creates a sense of family. Canadian soldiers have been known to help build bridges with Afghan citizens because they believe themselves to be obligated to these people of another nation. When we introduce the language of obligation or duty, we may find ourselves asking about freedom. When a parent acts out of obligation is he really free? When a soldier fulfils a duty is she acting freely? Richard John Neuhaus expresses his conviction that, "It is the highest exercise of freedom to decide on what is our duty."[18] When we speak of "the obedience of faith" we are speaking of an obligation freely chosen. Another dimension of obedience is *accountability*. As James Read has commented, "An accountable person is one who can be depended upon to act as they ought. Essentially, they can be 'counted' on." And they are prepared to "give an account."[19] Universities that receive government grants are answerable to that government for the way the funding is spent. The Salvation Army receives public money and is accountable for that money. One of the issues here is whether businesses are accountable for anything beyond making a profit for investors. Is there such a thing as the "common good"? It's encouraging to see some companies move beyond their commitment to the profit line to "give back" to the community.[20] In their own way they have taken seriously the "common good," and recognize accountability to the larger society. Obedience then recognizes something greater than the individual and is willing to be answerable to that greater good.

Let's bring some of these strands of thought together. This ninth doctrine contends that we come to understand Christian faith by doing it. It's as we do, as we obey, that we come to know. It's as we "follow Christ" that we come to understand who Christ is and what discipleship means. When Jesus instructed Peter to put out his nets again despite having nothing to show from his fishing, he obeyed. He did what Jesus instructed.[21] And this teachability enabled Peter to begin to understand what it meant to follow Christ, even to a cross and beyond. It's important to keep in mind the kind of relationship of which Jesus speaks. Obedient faith is not primarily obedience to rules, but to a person. Obedience is not a substitute for knowledge; it is through obedience that we come to know. Through obedience Peter and the other disciples came to view the world through God's grace expressed in Christ. By following him they came to understand God's covenantal love as extending to the excluded, the outcasts. This was new. And the Teacher engaged them in the task of reflecting on their doing. They were being trained in the ways of saving grace. There is no short cut in this apprenticeship. The comprehensive salvation of which biblical faith speaks requires "continued obedient faith." It is a faith that acknowledges legitimate authority and accountability. "Knowledge of God is born of obedience." This conviction matters!

Thus, while there may be legitimate resistance to faith that is characterized by obedience, our times and our culture have developed convictions about the importance of *doing*. As we practise our convictions we come to understand them! Let's consider ways this doctrine contributes to our understanding and practice of holiness.

Practising the Doctrine

In my early years of Salvation Army officership, I came across the writings of Eugene Peterson. Most of the North American church knows him as the author of *The Message,* a contemporary paraphrase of the Bible. For me, however, Peterson became a kind of mentor in congregational leadership. This "Presbycostal"[22] from Montana had put down roots with a Presbyterian congregation in the suburbs of Washington, D.C. While going through a time of questioning in his calling—he named it the "badlands"—Peterson came across a phrase from the German philosopher, Friedrich Nietzsche: "the essential thing 'in heaven and earth' is ... that there should be a long obedience in the same direction; there thereby results, and has always resulted in the long run, something that has made life worth living." Peterson resonated with this statement, and later incorporated it into a book on the Psalms called, *A Long Obedience in the Same Direction.*[23] In his view, "There is a great market for religious experience in our world; there is little enthusiasm for the patient acquisition of virtue, little inclination to sign up for a long apprenticeship in what earlier generations of Christians called holiness."[24] He feared a generation of Christians who wanted to use the Bible like a toolbox to repair their lives or inspire a dull day. In his view, we can't be trusted to do that. Instead,

> The Holy Spirit is writing us into the revelation, the story of

salvation. We find ourselves in the story as followers of Jesus. Jesus calls us to follow him and we obey—or we do not. This is an immense world of God's salvation that we are entering; we don't know enough to use or apply anything. Our task is to obey—believingly, trustingly obey. Simply obey in a 'long obedience.'[25]

The idea of conversion as conversion to teachableness is an important one for us to reclaim —Richard Osmer

Holiness is characterized by a long obedience in the same direction.

Holiness shaped by continued obedient faith will require a *teachable spirit*. At the heart of Christ's invitation to discipleship comes an invitation to learn: "Come to me, all you that are weary and are carrying heavy burdens, and I will give you rest. Take my yoke upon you, and *learn from me*; for I am gentle and humble in heart, and you will find rest for your souls."[26] Richard Osmer argues that "The idea of conversion as conversion to teachableness is an important one for us to reclaim."[27] We interpret or make sense of things through our key assumptions, which are formed over time. Transformative learning often takes place when life's experiences *question* those assumptions. The Twelve Disciples had to examine their assumptions when Jesus put a child in their midst and said, "This is what the kingdom of God looks like."[28] They had to question their assumptions when he washed their feet with a basin and towel and said, "This is what leadership looks like."[29] Their trust in him enabled them to eventually reframe their assumptions and learn obedience, thus to learn holiness. What is true of individuals is also true of congregational holiness. "Jesus' call to discipleship is an invitation to participate in a learning community where people continually reframe their experiences and challenge their fundamental assumptive frameworks."[30] A Salvationist congregation brings together people of different backgrounds. We might find it difficult to imagine that God's grace is at work in *all* of us because we assume what is acceptable behaviour within a congregation. We might assume that Salvationist identity can only be expressed in certain ways. We might wonder whether our mission can only take certain forms to be truly Salvationist. A commitment to be a holy Salvation Army requires that we bring a teachable spirit to our institutional life. Holiness is learned and therefore requires our teachability.

The language of "continued obedient faith" keeps the importance of *perseverance* before us in the practice of holiness. It draws attention to *long* obedience in the same direction. One way of considering this aspect of holiness is to pay attention to some of the athletic images used in the New Testament. As Paul bids farewell to the elders of the church at Ephesus, he discounts his own life but prays that "I may finish my course and the ministry that I received from the Lord Jesus" (Acts 20:24). He hoped that his ministry "was not running, or had not run, in vain" (Galatians 2:2). And when he acknowledges that he has not reached the goal of the Christian life, he states his goal: "forgetting what lies behind and straining forward to what lies ahead, I press on toward the goal for the prize of the heavenly call of God in Christ Jesus" (Philippians 3:13-14). The ancient Olympic Games became a way of understanding the disciplined response needed to grace. As noted above, the Letter to the Hebrews turns to these same games: "Therefore, since we are surrounded by so great a cloud of witnesses ... let us run with perseverance the race that is set before us" (Hebrews 12:1). In January 2011, our son, Colin, stood at the top of Signal Hill in St. John's, Newfoundland and Labrador. He looked out over the North Atlantic, turned around to face the city, and began to run. His goal was to run across Canada along the Trans-Canada Highway, all 7,600 kilometres. The personal dream of running across Canada was important, but Colin also ran with conviction. He was aware of the impact of computer and television screen time on Canada's youth. Some have called it an epidemic. Colin was determined to draw attention to the concern, and eventually spoke to more than 20,000 students during his run. I joined him as a vehicle support driver for a few weeks in the summer. It was one thing to follow the run through his website; it was another thing to be in the vehicle and sense the toll this run was taking on his mind and body. There were mornings when he simply had to push himself out of the vehicle and put one foot in front of the other. But he did it. He ran with perseverance the race set out for him. Nine months after that day on Signal Hill, Cathie and I stood at the bottom of a hill in Victoria, British Columbia. Accompanied by students from a nearby school, Colin reached the Pacific Ocean and put his foot in the water while his parents stood nearby with tears in their eyes. The Salvation Army has a race set before us. It may not be the same as other expressions of the church. And the race set before Salvationists in the 21st century may not be exactly the same as the race of our Founders. But it's ours. And we run it with perseverance as an expression of holiness.

Any ecclesiastical system that has no structural means of clergy supervision of clergy seems an odd and ethically dangerous arrangement
—William Willimon

Finally, the practice of obedient faith in Christ has implications for *ordained leadership in the church*. In contrast to our culture's emphasis on individualism, John Kavanaugh believes that "Obedience is the willingness to be ... held responsible as an interdependent social being."[31] The Army is blessed with volunteers, employees and soldiers whose lives express this commitment to something greater. The Army's ordained leadership assumes this commitment. When a person becomes an officer, he or she enters a covenant. It is a sacred moment. Its language begins with the words: "Called by Almighty God to proclaim the Gospel of our Lord and Saviour Jesus Christ as an officer of The Salvation Army, I give myself to God and here and now bind myself to Him in a solemn covenant."[32] The covenant of an officer includes many commitments, and it is not a straitjacket. It is done in freedom, and may be terminated in freedom. Among other things, officership entails a willingness to be supervised in ministry, much like an athlete who is coached in a sport. Scandals that have rocked the church have prompted William Willimon to argue, "Any ecclesiastical system that has no structural means of clergy supervision of clergy seems an odd and ethically dangerous arrangement."[33] The Salvation Army's supervision includes an officer's use of time, finances, computers, and loyalty to doctrine and the Army's symbolic life. This does not mean that an officer simply parrots what has gone on before. In order to be loyal to the deep principles of the Army, it is necessary at times to push us into new ways of thinking and acting. But as an officer lives out his ministry covenantally, he will not be exploring vocational possibilities with other organizations. She will provide the Army with a degree of stability in difficult times by virtue of her promises. The religious market may be a way to sell books and CDs, but it is not the way for officers to relate to the Army. The practice of Salvation Army officership is a long obedience in the same direction. This, too, is holiness.

The place of continued obedient faith has come to expression in many of our beloved songs. One of these was composed by Charles Wesley under difficult circumstances. During her marriage to Charles, Sally Wesley gave birth to eight children, only three of whom survived childhood. The first child born to Sally and Charles died of smallpox at the age of 16 months. Out of such painful experiences Charles penned a song that touches on this ninth doctrine, and is loved by the church:

Gentle Jesus, meek and mild,
Look upon a little child,
Pity my simplicity,
Suffer me to come to thee.

Now I would be as thou art;
Give me an obedient heart;
Thou art pitiful and kind,
Let me have thy loving mind.[34]

At this point in our work we are going to make a change. Thus far we have examined the doctrines in order. Normally the 10th core conviction would be considered next. But as mentioned in the Introduction, this doctrine will be kept in harness until the end. In fact, we are really engaging the 10th doctrine with all the others, so it is not out of sight. In order to stay our course, however, the next two chapters will focus on the 11th doctrine, and an additional chapter on the church. Then we will come back to Doctrine 10.

Reflection Questions for Chapter Nine

1. When you think of *obedience,* what images or stories come to mind?
2. If you are studying this book with a group, read the chapter together.
3. What phrase or section caught your attention? Why?

Forming the Doctrine:

4. Read Mark 3:14. In what ways do you think the relationship of Jesus with his disciples was important for the way they learned to follow Christ?
5. What happens to your view of Christ when you think of him "learning obedience"?
6. What songs come to mind that speak of obedience?

Engaging the Doctrine:

7. What are some unhealthy ways obedience is experienced in our culture?
8. In what ways have you learned a skill before you really understood what you were doing?
9. In what ways do you consider *duty* an important concept for our times?

Practising the Doctrine:

10. How important do you think it is to be teachable? Why?
11. What has helped you to be teachable over the years?
12. In what ways have you learned the practice of faith through obedience?

Conclude: Pray the song of Charles Wesley quoted at the end of the chapter.

Endnotes for Chapter Nine

1 Eugene H. Peterson, *A Long Obedience in the Same Direction: Discipleship in an Instant Society, 2nd ed.* (Downers Grove: InterVarsity Press, 2000), 16.

2 This phrase comes from the writings of Dietrich Bonhoeffer.

3 See Richard N. Longenecker, "The Foundational Conviction of New Testament Christology: The Obedience/ Faithfulness/ Sonship of Christ" in *Jesus of Nazareth: Lord and Christ*, Joel B. Green and Max Turner eds., (Grand Rapids: Eerdmans Publishing, 1994).

4 Luke 9:21.

5 Philippians 2:5-8, emphasis mine.

6 William C. Placher, *Narratives of a Vulnerable God* (Louisville: Westminster John Knox Press, 1994), 15.

7 See Galatians 6:2; Ephesians 5:21; Philippians 2:13; Colossians 3:12; 1 Peter 5:8.

8 1 John 4:19.

9 Exodus 20:1-2.

10 Exodus 19:6.

11 See 1 Corinthians 1:2; 12:27; Galatians 5:1; Ephesians 2:19.

12 Quoted in Charles M. Wood, *An Invitation to Theological Study* (Valley Forge: Trinity Press International, 1994), 35.

13 In Longenecker's view, "all the titles ascribed to him in the NT and all the metaphors used in description of the nature and effects of his work are founded ultimately on the early Christians' conviction regarding the full obedience and entire faithfulness of Jesus of Nazareth." See Longenecker, "Foundational Conviction," 475.

14 Jonathan Sacks, *The Dignity of Difference* (New York: Continuum Books, 2002), 32.

15 A critique of this form of education has been expressed by Paulo Freire, *Pedagogy of the Oppressed* (New York: Continuum Publishing, 1990).

16 Charles M. Wood, *An Invitation to Theological Study*, 37.

17 Donald A. Schön, *Educating the Reflective Practitioner* (San Francisco: Jossey-Bass Publishers, 1987), 36.

18 Richard John Neuhaus, *Freedom For Ministry* (San Francisco: Harper and Row Publishers, 1979), 136.

19 James E. Read, "Accountability: Talking the Walk," Unpublished Paper. (Winnipeg: Salvation Army Ethics Centre, May 2011).

20 See, for instance, "Corporation with a Conscience," in *Salvationist* (September 2011): 20-21.

21 See Luke 5:1-11.

22 This is his own word to describe his Pentecostal roots and Presbyterian ordination!

23 Eugene H. Peterson, *A Long Obedience in the Same Direction: Discipleship in an Instant Society, 2nd ed.* (Downers Grove: InterVarsity Press, 2000). The Psalms of Ascension are grouped in the Psalter for pilgrims on their journey to festivals in Jerusalem – Pss. 120 to 134.

24 Eugene H. Peterson, *A Long Obedience*, 16.

25 Eugene H. Peterson, *The Pastor: A Memoir* (New York: HarperOne, 2011), 248. Peterson lived out his ordination vows within the same Presbyterian congregation for many years, until he eventually accepted a teaching position with Regent College in Vancouver.

26 Matthew 11:28-29, emphasis mine.

27 Richard R. Osmer, *A Teachable Spirit: Recovering the Teaching Office in the Church* (Louisville: Westminster/ John Knox Press, 1990), 52.

28 See Mark 10:13-16.

29 See John 13:1-15.

30 Thomas R. Hawkins, *The Learning Congregation* (Louisville: Westminster John Knox Press, 1997), 123.

31 John F. Kavanaugh, *Following Christ in a Consumer Society* (Maryknoll: Orbis Press, Revised edition 1991), 153.

32 For the full text of the officer covenant, see: https://www.salvationist.org/poverty.nsf/vw_sublinks/BD3B682EB177EEF680256ABE002DD930?openDocument. Accessed Mar 3, 2013.

33 William H. Willimon, *Calling and Character: Virtues of the Ordained Life* (Nashville: Abingdon Press, 2000), 71.

34 Charles Wesley, "Gentle Jesus," *SBSA 1987*, No. 793.

CHAPTER 10

Last Things: Holiness as the Practice of Hope

We believe in the immortality of the soul; in the resurrection of the body; in the general judgment at the end of the world; in the eternal happiness of the righteous; and in the endless punishment of the wicked.—Doctrine 11[1]

If I knew tomorrow that the world would end, I would still plant an apple tree today.—Martin Luther[2]

My youngest daughter and I sat in the upper seats of Toronto's baseball stadium. The game progressed with powerful hits and good defensive plays. After nine innings, one of the teams won the game, but the victory had little meaning. Weeks later, the players went on strike. Because there was no proper ending to the season there was no real purpose to this particular game. How a sport ends determines the significance of the season's games. How history ends impacts its meaning in the present, thus to our lives. This 11th doctrine gives voice to Christian convictions about our world's ending.[3] A danger when approaching this doctrine is to get sidetracked by secondary matters, such as trying to predict when and how the end will come. The conviction expressed here is that God's character and purposes shape the ending of our world. This purposeful ending gives meaning and hope to the present. As noted in the previous chapter, we are going to leave our exploration of Doctrine 10 until the final chapter in the book. With this in mind, let's sketch the essential outline of this 11th core conviction, and engage it with issues that need to be considered for an adequate hearing in our times. We will finally consider its contribution to the practice of holiness in the present moment. What we believe about the future matters.

> Your kingdom come
> —The Lord's Prayer

Forming the Doctrine

Christians the world over join in the prayer taught by Jesus: "Our Father in heaven, hallowed be your name. Your kingdom come. Your will be done, on earth as it is in heaven."[4] This formative prayer is concerned with the kingdom of God, the active reign of God in our world. We pray this prayer believing that in Jesus of Nazareth, God's future has already broken into the present; the "light has dawned."[5] We also pray this prayer believing that God's purposes are not yet fully realized; we continue to see that children are abused and the environment has become toxic. There is yet to be the "end of the age."[6] The Lord's Prayer is prayed in hope.

The public ministry of Jesus begins in Matthew's Gospel with the proclamation, "Repent, for the kingdom of heaven has come near" (Matthew 4:17). In Matthew's Gospel, the first thing Jesus does to give substance to the kingdom is to teach.[7] The Sermon on the Mount becomes a lens through which to view the character of the kingdom. Matthew then draws attention to the way Jesus embodies the character of the kingdom by healing a Roman centurion's slave, demoniacs and a paralytic, and by eating socially with outsiders. In the public ministry of Jesus, God's future has broken into the present. And yet this future is not fully realized. When teaching in parables, Jesus imagines the reign of God to be like a field that grows both grain and weeds. Rather than uprooting the weeds, however, the householder instructed the workers to "Let both of them grow together until the harvest."[8] When explaining this parable privately to his disciples, Jesus speaks of the harvest as "the end of the age." Later in Matthew's Gospel, the disciples press Jesus as to "when will this be, and what will be the sign of your coming at the end of the age?" Jesus assures them that he will return, but cautions them about trying to calculate the end because "about that day and hour no one knows, neither the angels of heaven, nor the Son, but only the Father."[9] The followers of Christ live in the tension between the kingdom of God already realized and yet to be fully realized.

The New Testament draws upon several images to reflect the conviction that God's purposes have not yet been fully realized. For instance, the risen Christ is the "first fruits" of a greater harvest to come.[10] This agricultural image is drawn from Israel's worship at Passover, when the early fruits of the harvest were presented to God in anticipation of the greater harvest yet to come. Another image is employed when the cross is viewed as a victory already accomplished, and a victory yet to be fully realized: "Then comes the end, when ... [t]he last enemy to be destroyed is death."[11] What we experience in our relationship with Christ in the present moment is profound, and yet there is more.

The future as envisioned by biblical writers includes personal, social and cosmic dimensions. At a personal level, we each experience death. But death is not the end of our personal existence. Christian hope is based on the resurrection of Christ and the conviction that "this mortal body must put on immortality" (1 Corinthians 15:53). These words at Christian funeral services speak to the world's suffering: "he will wipe every tear from their eyes. Death will be no more; mourning and crying and pain will be no more" (Revelation 21:4). But God's future is not simply for personal salvation. The Bible's vision is for the "healing of the nations" (Revelation 22:2). This social and political healing is envisioned by Isaiah when nations "shall beat their spears into pruning hooks; nation shall not lift up sword against nation, neither shall they learn war any more" (Isaiah 2:4). God's future embraces all peoples. The promise that through Abraham and Sarah God would bless the families of the earth (see Genesis 12:1-3) finds it realization here. These personal and social hopes are complemented by the more cosmic dimensions of salvation when God will "gather up all things in [Christ], things in heaven and things on earth" (Ephesians 1:10). Elsewhere Paul says "that the creation itself will be set free from its bondage to decay and will obtain the freedom of the glory of the children of God" (Romans 8:21). The destruction of fish stocks, the rape of the world's forests and the damage done to the earth's atmosphere will one day experience its own healing. God's purposes will be done on earth as in heaven.

It is clear from these few biblical texts that a Christian view of the future is concerned with a living hope in the present: "For in hope we were saved" (Romans 8:24). It expresses the conviction that without turning humanity into robots, God will bring his purposes to complete realization. We have been created to experience a genuine give-and-take relationship between ourselves and this triune God. God has made himself vulnerable in our world in order to achieve this relationship, but God's sovereign purposes will one day be completely realized. With this in mind, let's touch on some of the phrases in this 11th doctrine:

We believe ... in the immortality of the soul. How we hear the word "immortality" is important. Biblically, the soul is not some invisible part of the person, trapped in a body. Soul is the biblical way of speaking about the whole person, not a part of the person. This phrase "affirms that we are whole persons, originally brought to life by God (Genesis 2:7), and because of God's action there will be no loss of integrated, embodied personality in the life beyond present existence."[12] Each human life is of utmost importance now, and into eternity. Death is not the end of persons, but neither are we absorbed into the divine life like a drop of water into a cosmic ocean.

We believe ... in the resurrection of the body. Life is fragile. Our bodies and minds often bear the marks of decay and suffering. Christian hope is based on the resurrection of Christ and with it the hope of life after death. The resurrection of Christ is our pattern; his resurrection body shows continuity with this life, but it is also different. The grain that is sown develops into the stalk of wheat. "What is sown is perishable, what is raised is imperishable. It is sown in dishonor, it is raised in glory. It is sown in weakness, it is raised in power. It is sown a physical body, it is raised a spiritual body" (1 Corinthians 15:42-44). Our embodied life will be transformed.

We believe ... in the general judgment at the end of the world. Care needs to be exercised when thinking about judgment. God's judgment is not one of vindictive revenge. The character of final judgment will be consistent with the character of God's ways expressed in the life, death and resurrection of Christ. Yet judgment expresses hope. It means that the world will not end with a shrug of indifference. The injustices of Auschwitz or cyber-bullying or the effects of Ponzi schemes will not end up in a black hole. We will all face judgment where "the work of each builder will become visible, for the Day will disclose it" (1 Corinthians 3:13).

We believe ... in the eternal happiness of the righteous. The Bible has numerous images of God's future. It is depicted as a city (see Revelation 21-22) and a great banquet to which peoples of the world come, especially "the poor, the crippled, the blind, and the lame" (Luke 14:15-24). The parables of Jesus speak of "joy in heaven" when one sinner repents (Luke 15:7). This joy characterizes the presence of God with humanity where sin's presence and power has been eliminated, and "where righteousness is at home" (2 Peter 3:13).

We believe ... in the endless punishment of the wicked. As with the note of judgment, care needs to be exercised when talking about "the endless punishment of the wicked." We can too easily try to determine who the wicked might be and what form their punishment might take. Daniel Migliore gives a healthy perspective: "Hell is not an arbitrary divine punishment at the end of history. It is not the final retaliation of a vindictive deity. Hell is self-destructive resistance to the eternal love of God ... but neither in time nor in eternity is God's love coercive."[13]

This 11th doctrine has been developed organically from its biblical roots. It expresses the belief that the world as we know it will end, it will come to a finish. But its ending will be shaped by the purposes and character of God. Such an ending creates hope, "For hope is what you get when you suddenly realize that ... the rich, the powerful, and the unscrupulous do not after all have the last word."[14] This conviction matters! How then can this 19th-century doctrine be heard adequately in the 21st century? Let's turn to some contemporary issues that impact our hearing of this doctrine of hope.

Engaging the Doctrine

One of the contributions this 11th doctrine makes to the present moment is its conviction that there is hope for *meaningful lives now.* Lesslie Newbigin argues, "Meaningful action in history is possible only when there is some vision of the future goal."[15] The biblical vision of this goal is captured in images of the lion and the lamb lying down together, of the healing of the nations, of the blessing of all the families of the earth, of a future "where righteousness is at home" (2 Peter 3:13).[16] This understanding of "last things" enables us to live hopefully now. This hope, however, has been challenged from several directions in recent history.

Meaningful action in history is possible only when there is some vision of the future goal
—Lesslie Newbigin

One challenge comes from the tendency to think that humanity can create a certain and peaceful future with its own resources. This was the case as the 20th century dawned. In the early years of that century, there was much optimism. A growing awareness of technological accomplishments and educational institutions led to a belief in humanity's *progress*. Some would even argue that the western world developed a *doctrine of progress*.[17] With the right application of understanding and tools, humanity could eliminate disease and poverty, and usher in a golden age. There is much to be grateful for in the development of these tools. Unfortunately two world wars, subsequent ethnic cleansings around the world and economic tsunamis have undermined any confidence in a doctrine of progress. And if this confidence in humanity's abilities needed to be shaken even more, a new threshold was crossed on September 11, 2001. Optimism faded. But hope is not the same as optimism.

If recent history has undermined a doctrine of progress, recent *science points to a sure ending* of our world. For instance, we know that asteroids and meteorites have occasionally crashed into the earth's surface with quite astounding effects. It is quite possible, even likely, that these objects from space will crash into our planet again. Even if we keep free from such collisions for a few hundred million years, the continents will continue to shift so that the Atlantic Ocean will disappear as an ocean.[18] And assuming life still exists in some form, we will need to face the extinction of our universe about four billion years from now. Either the sun will consume our planet or life will freeze to death as our universe expands beyond the sun's ability to give life. So from a scientific perspective, an ending to our world is certain. However, Christian hope expresses the conviction that God will bring this world and this universe to God's *purposeful* ending. That it will be a meaningful ending is the substance of faith.

If our society has cast its doubts on Christian hope, the church has too often undermined hope by the way it reads the Bible. A preoccupation with prediction has led the church astray. Some have turned biblical texts into detailed maps for the future. But the Bible is not a GPS! Attempts to predict the time of Christ's return embarrass not only the false predictor but the larger church. A preoccupation with Christ's Second Advent may also prompt us to bury our heads in the sand and avoid responsibilities in the present. It's important, in this respect, to read the Book of Revelation with integrity. John of Patmos writes as a pastor to churches under pressure. He writes as an artist, painting images with words that are alive and evocative. Its heart is a vision of a throne encircled by creatures at worship. And between the throne and the creatures John sees "a Lamb standing as if it had been slaughtered" (Revelation 5:6). Revelation's vision claims that when life seems most chaotic, *there is a centre*. There is a place which can hold life together. Based on Revelation's imagery, the church sings:

All thy works with joy surround thee,
Earth and heaven reflect thy rays,
Stars and angels sing around thee,
Centre of unbroken praise.[19]

Another challenge that confronts this conviction about the future is that it seems to unfairly view *those who do not share Christian faith.* What happens in the end to those who do not hold Christian convictions? Is everyone saved, or only those who profess faith in Jesus Christ? In our global world this is an important issue and cannot be swept under the carpet. First, let's remind ourselves that *God's love is a holy love.* God's love has spilled over into the world which God created, inviting our free response of love in return. God's love is for all creatures. God's love is not a coercive love, therefore it can be rejected. And God's holy love can be counted on to bring our world to a finish in ways consistent with that love. Second, God's holy love is active in our world through the Holy Spirit in *ways we cannot limit.* The Bible itself includes mention of those individuals who were not part of the community of Israel or the church, but who nonetheless experienced something of God's grace. Think, for instance, of Moses' father-in-law, Jethro, or Ruth the Moabite who demonstrated faithful loyalty to Naomi, or the Magi who came to the child Jesus with gifts of worship. The prophet Amos hints at God's liberating work beyond Israel: "Did I not bring Israel up from the land of Egypt, and the Philistines from Caphtor and the Arameans from Kir?" (Amos 9:7). And when Isaiah envisions God's future, "On that day Israel will be the third with Egypt and Assyria, a blessing in the midst of the earth, whom the LORD of hosts has blessed, saying, 'Blessed be Egypt my people, and Assyria the work of my hands, and Israel my heritage' " (Isaiah 19:24-25). Imagine: Israel, Egypt and Iraq all within God's vision for the future. The saving grace of God is expressed in particular ways, but we need to be careful that we don't limit God's holy love only to those ways. Finally, *judgment at the end of history belongs to God.* We are not in a position to make that judgment. When we read about judgment in the parables of Jesus, those who are welcomed into his presence are surprised, and those who are excluded from his presence are surprised. What functions as the bar for judgment is the degree to which we have fed the hungry, given drink to the thirsty, clothed the naked and welcomed the stranger (see Matthew 25:36-46). We are not in a position to judge who is and who is not doing this. We leave any final judgment to God with whom it belongs. The song of Frederick Faber is important to grasp:

> There's a wideness in God's mercy
> Like the wideness of the sea;
> There's a kindness in his justice
> Which is more than liberty.

For the love of God is broader
Than the measure of man's mind;
And the heart of the eternal
Is most wonderfully kind.[20]

Thus while this doctrine has its critics, it is a critical conviction for navigating treacherous currents in our times. This core conviction offers hope in the present because it portrays a purposeful future. God's future.

In response to this gospel, we are called to practise hope, to make God's future in our present wherever possible

Practising the Doctrine

The Ohio River in the United States winds its way between Ohio and Kentucky. In the early 1800s, it was a most important river. If black slaves from Kentucky were able to cross the river into Ohio, they stepped into a different world because Ohio did not endorse slavery. Blacks could begin a different life, if they were not caught. Many factors prompted black slaves to flee Kentucky, but among them were rumours of hope. They began to hear of a land called Canada where blacks fought alongside whites and aboriginal peoples in the British Army. They didn't know it, but in what is now Ontario, Lord Simcoe had passed a law prohibiting the practice of slavery. Black slaves heard rumours of hope, and some of them fled their bondage for the Underground Railroad and freedom.[21] The Christian gospel evokes rumours of hope. It spreads rumours about a day when "Death will be no more; mourning and crying and pain will be no more" (Revelation 21:4). And God's gift of life will accomplish "the healing of the nations" (Revelation 22:2). In response to this gospel, we are called to practise hope, to make God's future in our present wherever possible. Martin Luther understood the practice of Christian hope when he said, "If I knew tomorrow that the world would end, I would still plant an apple tree today."[22] Holiness is characterized by the practice of hope.

Paradoxically, the *practice of hope often begins by accepting the reality of loss and death*. Life has many kinds of endings, and each ending is unique. A personal loss occurred shortly after Cathie and I moved into our home in retirement. A summer storm deluged our part of the city just after its maintenance crews had closed a valve in the sewer system. The rain had no place to go, except to back up with the sewage into our neighbourhood. Sixty-five homes had their basements flooded, ours included. We lost many personal belongings, but when I was able to assess the damage, it became evident that close to 40 years of personal journals had been destroyed. There was nothing that could be done to retrieve them. My sense of loss was profound. (The only consolation lay in the observation that I wouldn't have to read 40 years of my own handwriting!) Mitchell and Anderson have drawn attention to the different kinds of losses we can experience.[23] We may lose a physical object, such as a house from a fire or flood which contained many personal memories that will not be replaced. An important personal relationship may come to an end, either through divorce or the death of one of the persons in that relationship. Sometimes a personal dream dies, a dream to which we have attached our sense of worth or identity. Military conflict has too often resulted in the loss of the functioning of a soldier's body or mind; she or he can no longer do what they used to do. Retirement may bring with it the loss of significant vocational purpose. And families may experience the loss of how they work together when one member of the family moves to another place in the nation. These are all very real losses, real deaths. The practice of hope begins by acknowledging the depth of these losses. We have been created by God to live in this good world of objects, cities, houses, families and work. They combine to form our sense of identity, and when we lose someone or some aspect of our life, a death has occurred. Hope begins as we learn to accept that death, not by denying it. In Paul's words, we do "not grieve as others do who have no hope" (1 Thessalonians 4:13). But we do grieve what has been lost. Grief is an expression of hope.

If there are times when we need to accept loss, there are also times when *the practice of hope means a refusal to accept things as they are*. God's future is not characterized by children living in poverty, or certain ethnic groups being demonized, or rivers being poisoned. Holiness may evoke dissatisfaction with the present. Things are not as they should be and we need to do something. It was this holy dissatisfaction that prompted William Booth to turn to his son, Bramwell, the day after he had observed men sleeping under the bridges of London, England, and ask his son if he knew this was happening. Bramwell's vague response was met with: "Go and do something! Get hold of a warehouse and warm it and find something to cover the poor fellows. But mind, Bramwell, no coddling!"[24] William Booth's agitation with what he witnessed reflects the conviction that the streets of London did not embody the kingdom of God. His was a holy dissatisfaction with present social conditions. It was this refusal to accept things as they were that shaped Booth's final words to Salvationists: "While women weep, as they do now, I'll fight; while children go hungry, as they do now, I'll fight; while men go to prison, in and out, in and out, as they do now, I'll fight; while there is a poor lost girl on the streets, while there remains one dark soul without the light of God, I'll fight, I'll fight to the very end!" The practice of hope may begin with a refusal to accept things as they are.

We learn to *make the future in the present with small gestures of hope*. Recall the story of Jeremiah when Israel was in Babylonian captivity. The real estate market in Jerusalem had crashed; property was without value. And Israel was without hope. But the word of the Lord came to Jeremiah with the instruction that he was to purchase family land. This gesture in the face of hopelessness signaled God's intention that "Houses and fields and vineyards shall again be bought in the land" (Jeremiah 32:6-15). Jeremiah made the future in the present with a small gesture that conveyed hope. We learn to gesture hope within the Christian community. Children learn the meaning of hope as they give Gifts of Hope to other children at Christmas. These Gifts of Hope come in the shape of a well for clean water or books for school. Congregational musicians learn the meaning of hope when their rehearsals take the chaos of a first reading and eventually create sounds of beauty and integrity. They understand that hope requires rehearsal and teamwork. It doesn't just happen. Community care ministries learn the meaning of hope when its workers visit a corps member suffering from dementia, since they value that person made in the image of God and loved by God. We learn hope as we develop small projects to bring healing to a groaning creation. The commitment to a *green* centre of worship anticipates the healing of Earth's wounds. Giving hope necessitates entering the world of suffering. As Paul puts it, "[Love] bears all things, believes all things, *hopes all things*, endures all things."[25] Holiness involves learning hope. And it is learned in the context of a Christian community that worships and serves this God who makes the future in the present.

The practice of hope doesn't just happen; it is *nurtured in corporate worship*. Salvationists gather as a worshipping community each Sunday. We come from places where hopelessness is often at work: families get stuck in unhealthy communication, jobs are threatened and medical diagnoses rob us of a future. When we meet with others who bend the knee to Christ, we enter a world of hope. We read the Bible together and are invited to hear again the stories where hope is at work. We listen to the story of Ruth and marvel at the way she provided a future for her bereaved mother-in-law, Naomi. We join with others in reading Esther's story and the risks she took to evoke hope in a situation of potential genocide. As we hear again the stories of our faith, we step inside them and hope is nurtured. We also sing the songs of hope. One of us may come to our worship thinking life has reached a dead end, but then we are invited to sing, "Don't assume that God will plan for you no more, Don't assume that there's no future to explore."[26] Concerned about the place of the church in our society, we conclude a time of worship with these words: "Make the future in the present, Strong of heart, toil on and sing: God is with us, God is with us, Christ our Lord shall reign as King!"[27] And when we come to the season of Advent, we are reminded that while Christ's First Advent helps us to understand his Second Advent, the opposite is also true. Christ's Second Advent informs our celebration of Christmas; the ending—the eschaton—is a place to begin. When rehearsing brass ensembles, I have often found it helpful to give good attention to a composition's ending. As the musicians gain a sense of how the music concludes, it helps them to envision the various sections that come before. Corporate worship is where we rehearse our faith's finish so that we make the future in the present. The practice of corporate worship helps us to learn the meaning of hope.

While this doctrine points to the practice of hope, it's important that we not lose the tension of hope's now and not yet. Lesslie Newbigin claims that "This vision of a real horizon, a goal toward which we move, is what gives to the whole New Testament its most distinctive character, the character of hope which is both alert and patient."[28] Hope is patient because not every Christian project accomplishes its goal. It is also patient because the depths of evil in our world are profound. There are yet tragic deaths that rob families of joy. There are yet injustices that will never be corrected within this world. But within this tension we practise hope now:

> Because we ground our faith in the risen Christ, we practise hope.
> Because we believe God will bring his good work to completion, we practise hope.
> Because we look forward to the city whose architect and builder is God, we practise hope.
> Because we look forward to the reconciliation of all things, we practise hope.
> Because God's future will vindicate God's character, we practise holiness now.
>
> Your kingdom come. Your will be done on earth as it is in heaven.

Reflection Questions for Chapter Ten

1. How might there be different kinds of endings to an event? What difference does this make?
2. If you are studying this book with a group, read the chapter together.
3. What phrase or section caught your attention? Why?

Forming the Doctrine:

4. What are some ways you see Jesus expressing hope in his public ministry?
5. What biblical image of the future ignites your imagination? Why?
6. Read Romans 8:18-25. What is the character of hope in these verses?

Engaging the Doctrine:

7. How do you see our culture concerned with the future?
8. What role does hope play in our times?
9. What are your hopes for The Salvation Army?

Practising the Doctrine:

10. What kinds of losses have you experienced in your life? What brought you hope?
11. In what ways can Salvationists be people of hope in our times?
12. What connections do you make between hope and holiness?
13. How is the season of Advent a time of hope for you?

Conclude: Pray the Lord's Prayer.

Endnotes for Chapter Ten

1 As noted in the previous chapter, we are delaying our treatment of Doctrine 10 until the last chapter.

2 Quoted in Daniel L. Migliore, *Faith Seeking Understanding: An Introduction to Christian Theology*. (Grand Rapids: Eerdmans Publishing, 2004), 352.

3 A more technical word for this doctrine is *eschatology*, or study of last things.

4 This prayer is most often prayed using the language from Matthew 6:9-13.

5 Matthew 4:16.

6 Matthew 28:20.

7 The first block of five teaching sections in Matthew is the Sermon on the Mount, 5:1-7:29. This is followed by his healing ministry in chapters 8-9. It should be noted that Matthew's language, "kingdom of heaven," reflects the Jewish tendency to avoid using the name, "God." Mark and Luke use the language, "kingdom of God."

8 Matthew 13:24-30.

9 Matthew 24:36.

10 1 Corinthians 15:20-23; see also Romans 8:23. This and other images are explored more fully in N.T. Wright, *Surprised by Hope* (New York: HarperOne, 2008), 98-106.

11 1 Corinthians 15:24-26.

12 *The Salvation Army Handbook of Doctrine* (London: Salvation Books, 2010), 225.

13 D. Migliore, *Faith Seeking Understanding*, 347.

14 N.T. Wright, *Surprised by Hope*, 75.

15 Lesslie Newbigin, *The Gospel in a Pluralist Society* (Grand Rapids: Eerdmans Publishing, 1989), 114.

16 See Isaiah 11:6; Revelation 22:3; Genesis 12:3. See also Donald E. Burke, "Shalom: The Biblical Vision in a Broken World," *Word and Deed* 15/2 (Spring 2013): 47-63.

17 "The myth of progress has sometimes served us well—those of us seated at the best tables, anyway—and may continue to do so. But ... it has also become dangerous. Progress has an internal logic that can lead beyond reason to catastrophe. A seductive trail of successes may end in a trap." See Ronald Wright, *A Short History of Progress* (Toronto: Anansi Press, 2004), 5.

18 See Simon Winchester, *Atlantic* (New York: HarperCollins Publishers, 2010), 441ff.

19 Henry van Dyke, "Joyful, Joyful," *SBSA 1987*, No. 10.

20 Frederick Faber, "Souls of Men," *SBSA 1987*, No. 265.

21 The story of Thornton and Lucie Blackburn who fled Kentucky for Ontario is explored in Karolyn Frost, *I've Got a Home in Gloryland: A Lost Tale of the Underground Railroad* (Toronto: Thomas Allen Publishers, 2007). Thornton

Blackburn started Toronto's first public transit service! By pointing to this story it is not intended to imply that Canada is without its racial difficulties. Canada's history has its own tragic share of racial tensions and prejudices.

22 Quoted in Daniel Migliore, *Faith Seeking Understanding*, 352.

23 See Kenneth R. Mitchell and Herbert Anderson, *All Our Losses, All Our Griefs: Resources for Pastoral Care* (Philadelphia: The Westminster Press, 1983), Chapter Three.

24 Robert Sandall, *The History of The Salvation Army: Volume Three 1883-1953* (New York: The Salvation Army Supplies and Purchasing Department, 1953), 67-68.

25 1 Corinthians 13:7, emphasis mine.

26 John Gowans, "Don't Assume," *SBSA 1987*, No. 44.

27 Walter John Mathams, "God is With Us," *SBSA 1987*, No. 158.

28 Lesslie Newbigin, *The Gospel in a Pluralist Society*, 110.

CHAPTER 11

The Church: God's Holy Character in Community

We believe ...—Salvation Army Doctrines

Throughout the biblical story ... the people of God are expected to embody God's holy character publicly in particular social settings.—Kent Brower and Andy Johnson[1]

THE SALVATION ARMY WAS GIVEN ITS NAME IN 1878. Barely had the ink dried on the posters when a most remarkable event took place in the new nation of Canada. It was the autumn of 1883, in the town of Kingston, Ontario. Salvationists met for a Sunday evening service with their officer, Captain Abby Thompson. They noticed a man standing in the doorway, and gasped. He was Canada's first prime minister, Sir John A. Macdonald! His opponents later accused Sir John A. of being taken in by the beauty of Captain Abby. Actually, Canada's prime minister came to learn "about the effects of the depression of Canada's new class of urban workers."[2] The leader of this young nation had come to The Salvation Army to learn about the people of his nation!

The Salvation Army is a unique expression of the church. Many Salvationists have resisted being called a church. George Scott Railton, for instance, claimed that "We are an Army of Soldiers of Christ, seeking no church status, avoiding as we would the plague of every denominational rut."[3] And yet Bramwell Booth argued that, "Of this

Great Church of the Living God, we claim and have ever claimed, that we of The Salvation Army are an integral part and element—a living fruit-bearing branch of the True Vine."[4] In 1978, General Frederick Coutts wrote a pamphlet entitled, "The Salvation Army in Relation to the Church." It was not, however, until the publication of *Salvation Story* in 1998, and reaffirmed in the present *Handbook of Doctrine*, that something close to a doctrine of the church appears:

> Salvation Army doctrine implies a doctrine of the Church. Each doctrine begins: 'We believe ....' 'We' points to a body of believers, a community of faith—a church .... Salvationists are members of the one body of Christ. We share common ground with the universal Church while manifesting our own characteristics. As one particular expression of the Church, The Salvation Army participates with other Christian denominations and congregations in mission and ministry. We are part of the one, universal Church.[5]

There is a growing awareness that The Salvation Army is an integral expression of the church. But contemporary reservations about the church, along with uncertainties about the meaning of holiness, have combined to make any thought of a *holy church* difficult to imagine. As we have done thus far, let's explore how core convictions about the church were formed over time and consider their importance within the 21st century. Then we will be in a position to appreciate their contribution to our understanding and practice of holiness.

Forming the Doctrine

In order to understand the formation of this conviction about the Army as an expression of the church, we best begin with the ministry of Jesus. It's evident in all the Gospels that Jesus created a community around himself. Luke's Gospel shows this happening almost from the beginning. As Jesus attempted to teach along the shore of a lake, the pressure of the crowd prompted him to commandeer a fishing boat. It belonged to Simon Peter. It may have seemed a little presumptuous for Jesus to do this, but Simon made no objection. When the class was finished, Jesus instructed Peter to take the boat out further into the water. Peter was humming to himself, "Fished all night but we caught no fishes, out on the deep blue sea," when he realized something had happened. The boats came ashore with a catch of fish that staggered Peter. He fell to his knees, but Jesus said to him, "From now on you will be catching people." While this incident involved Simon Peter and Jesus, Luke's Gospel continues, "When *they* had brought the boats to shore, *they* left everything and followed him."[6] Simon Peter, James and John followed Jesus. A community formed around Jesus and his mission. Embryonic church! As we follow Luke's Gospel, we watch this community as it followed Jesus and learned from him. They observed Jesus responding to criticism about his table fellowship. They sometimes found themselves acting as go-betweens for the complaints of Pharisees. And they sometimes found themselves the object of criticism for not living up to the expected piety of the day. As the small group of three grew to 12, they were sent out on a field practicum and then reported back to Jesus. Their personal ambitions became a subject in the curriculum when they argued among themselves who was the greatest. When others were excluded from the healing of Jairus's daughter, only Peter, James and John were permitted into the privacy of the moment. Together they feared for their lives when their boat threatened to sink in a storm, but they asked the right question: "Who then is this?" Together they helped to feed a multitude with a few loaves and fish. Together they made the request, "Lord teach us to pray." Together they heard the instruction of their Teacher, "Beware of the yeast of the Pharisees ... Consider the ravens ... From everyone to whom much is given, much will be required." And when this community of Jesus heard the demands of following their Master, they wondered who could be saved. But Jesus turned to his community with the words, "Truly I tell you, there is no one who has left house or wife or brothers or parents or children, for the sake of the kingdom of God, who will not get back very much more in this age, and in the age to come eternal life." Thus it was that when Jesus came to the dark moment of his life he turned to this embryonic community and said, "You are those who have stood by me in my trials" (Luke 22:28). Whatever their flaws, and they were many, this community of disciples was learning what it meant "to leave everything" and "follow" Jesus. "By gathering the twelve around him as a microcosm of restored Israel, Jesus displayed God's intention to *form a people* who would embody God's character and draw the nations to God."[7]

As the Book of Acts picks up the story, we recognize the importance of individuals such as Peter, Philip and Lydia. But their roles are carried out in the larger context of the Christian community. The Day of Pentecost counters the fragmentation of Babel and forms a new community. Its life is shaped by the Holy Spirit, such that the community is characterized as those who "devoted themselves to the apostles' teaching and fellowship, to the breaking of bread and prayers ... and had all things in common" (Acts 2:42-44). The early church experienced the presence of God through the risen Christ and the Holy Spirit. It was a community of salvation, for "In the context of Acts ... salvation signifies incorporation into and participation in the Christ-centered community of God's people."[8] The church in Acts constitutes the people of "the Way" (Acts 19:23).[9] The New Testament writers draw on numerous images for the church, each with its own insights. Thus the church is "God's field" and "God's building" (1 Corinthians 3:9), the letter of Christ (see 2 Corinthians 3:2-3), the bride of Christ (see Ephesians 5:23-32), the body of Christ (see 1 Corinthians 12), the golden lampstands (see Revelation 2-3). Even the teaching of Jesus in the Gospels offers images such as "the salt of the earth" and "the light of the world" (Matthew 5:13-14), and in John's Gospel, believers are branches of the vine (see John 15:5). When we read the Letters of Paul we realize that while some are addressed to individuals like Timothy, most are addressed to a community of believers. The New Testament envisions Christian believers as a "new humanity" where the ancient walls dividing Jew and Gentile had been broken down (Ephesians 2:15). This led to a later description of the church as "the Third Race." No longer characterized by the designation Jew or Gentile, the church was a community composed of all ethnic diversities. God's salvation in Christ found concrete expression in this community.

As this Third Race lived out its communal life in the Roman world, it eventually found itself moving from the margins of that world to its centre. The Roman emperor, Constantine, had witnessed the cruelties of religious persecution. He wanted none of it. He had also witnessed the contributions of the church to the Empire. So from a place of suspicion, Constantine moved the church to official recognition. The community of Jesus now formed the dominant religious faith in the Roman Empire. Its position of importance and peace provided opportunities to reflect on its faith, but its integrity suffered. There were those accused of betraying the faith during times of Roman persecution. Others were suspected of nurturing convictions that led the church astray. By the fourth century, what had been pockets of believers within an empire, developed into significant communities around the shores of the Mediterranean world, centred in cities that spoke either Greek or Latin. There was much in common within this community of faith; there were also many tensions. Within the umbrella of Rome's security, the church began to hammer out its convictions in various ecumenical councils. These councils voiced the church's belief in "God the Father almighty ... And in one Lord Jesus Christ ... And ... in the Holy Spirit, Lord and Giver of life." But in this early Nicene Creed, the confession was also made: "And we believe in one holy catholic and apostolic church." Along with its affirmations of faith regarding God, the church itself constituted part of that confession. Christian faith cannot be envisioned without this community called the church.

How the church lived out its character of being one, holy, catholic and apostolic is the stuff of history. It has its heroic moments, and its too often dark and tragic moments. The community of Jesus settled into an uneasy relationship with the powers of its day. Christ's towel and basin seemed too often to be replaced by symbols of power. Different centres of gravity developed between the Byzantium East and Roman West. The church in the West eventually found itself engulfed by Reformation movements in the 1500s, such that the "oneness" of the church could no longer be assumed. And when Henry VIII sought a way out of his marriage to Catherine of Aragon, he enabled the Church *in* England to become the Church *of* England. Its reformers sought to make it the *via media*, the church of the *middle way*. When John and Charles Wesley went to study at Oxford University in the early 1700s, they could draw on the instruction of Roman Catholic mystics, Reformation writers, Puritans and the ancient Patristics from the East. But they also felt a deep calling to renew the Church of

England, and to "spread scriptural holiness over the land." Only with their death did the Methodist Movement in Britain become a separate church, with its own ordained leadership. And with their death, the Methodist Movement splintered into the formation of such groups as the New Methodist Connection. A young William Booth sought a place within this church, but the fit wasn't good. An invitation to speak in the streets of East London, England, in 1865, planted a seed from which sprang The Salvation Army. The Salvation Army's story is integrally connected to the church's story. Little did Sir John A. Macdonald realize what he was stepping into!

The church has earned its reputation for failing to characterize a gracious God

Engaging the Doctrine

If some Salvationists have difficulty envisioning the Army as a church, the western world has even more difficulty with the church as an aspect of faith. Several factors make it difficult for contemporary culture to take the church seriously. Let's engage this emerging core conviction with concerns of the 21st century.

One obstacle is the church's *flawed history*. While the church has contributed much that is good to the world, such as schools and hospitals, it has also compromised its Lord. With the exception of Europeans like Samuel de Champlain, the cross of Christ too often accompanied the conquest of indigenous peoples in the New World.[10] Canada's own history has been marred by church-sponsored residential schools that stripped First Nations people of their language and identities. The contemporary church, like the sons of Eli, is too often scandalized by its clergy engaging in financial and sexual escapades. Tragically, misplaced trust has sometimes victimized children. The church has earned its reputation for failing to characterize a gracious God. The Christian community needs to acknowledge its role in these developments. The season of Lent is an appropriate time to face these issues. Ash Wednesday begins with a reading from the prophet Joel:

> Yet even now, says the LORD, return to me with all your heart, with fasting, with weeping, and with mourning; rend your hearts and not your clothing. Return to the LORD, your God, for he is gracious and merciful, slow to anger, and abounding in steadfast love, and relents from punishing.[11]

The church will only be heard with credibility when it admits to its sinfulness and responds appropriately.

If the church is dismissed because of its flawed history, it also runs into trouble simply because it has an *institutional life*. The culture of the western world views institutions with suspicion. It is felt that institutions become an end unto themselves, and the church is not exempted from this tendency. And yet institutions are essential to life. Hospitals are designed to nurture healing, but hospitals require policies, governing bodies, licensing procedures and supervision. A hospital's institutional life is designed to support its healing practices. They are not mutually exclusive. The church is designed to nurture the life of God's grace, and its institutional life can serve that purpose. The Salvation Army, too, has its policies and positional statements, procedures for employment and termination, and local and international connections so that Salvationists in Canada and Bermuda can respond to the needs of Haiti at the time of an earthquake.[12] The Scriptures do not advocate any one structural form of the church. It is one of those areas where there is freedom to express our life together given the culture in which we live. The Salvation Army does not claim to have the final and best form of institution. It will always be open to change. But we do not put a wedge between institution and spirituality. Holiness has structure.

However, if there are objections to the church, there are also issues that make the church especially *relevant* in the 21st century. In particular, the sense of *community* envisioned for the church is most relevant for our time. The Salvation Army is a "community of faith." It has been noted throughout our study that the western world in particular has gravitated to an emphasis on the individual with a corresponding loss of community. But when we speak of the church as community, we need to ask, What kind of community? For instance, any of the following could be considered a community of sorts: a football team, a political party, a family, a corporation, a prison, a school, a city, an online discussion group and a flock of Canadian geese! (The prophet Jeremiah at least praised Canadian geese for knowing how to migrate when winter came, unlike Israel's lack of a moral compass.)[13] Salvationist expressions of community vary in different parts of the world. I would like, however, to be more personal and draw on my own experience as a Salvationist who lives in Canada. While acknowledging its flaws, I also value the experience of community within The Salvation Army.

Growing up within the Salvationist community I learned that I was *not alone*. It is true I had a family who knew me and, apart from all the jousting that goes on in a family, appreciated me. But within my church I became aware of others who knew my name, asked how things were going and kept in touch with me. It's possible to take this for granted, except that as we moved into the 21st century, loneliness has become a critical issue in western culture. Robert Putnam captured the concern with his image that instead of bowling together in leagues, like they did in the 1950s, people now tend to *bowl alone*. As Putnam researched the involvement of Americans in activities such as voting practices, community groups, religious organizations and recreational activities, he recognized a remarkable trend in the last third of the 20th century: "Without at first noticing, we have been pulled apart from one another and from our communities."[14] We bowl alone! Whatever its many faults, Salvationist congregations are communities where people know our name. We are not alone.

Within the Salvationist community, I became aware that I was *part of a larger story*. As kids, we enjoyed acting out the manger scene at Christmas or re-enacting the exodus in a sand tray. Gradually, the episodes in the story took shape as we learned the concept of time. Eventually, I heard the names of Francis of Assissi and Catherine Booth. Over time, I learned to both affirm that story and critique it. As has been noted, if we want to know who we are we need to know the stories of which we are a part. As I grew in years, I learned that I was part of a city's story, and a nation's story. In time, I learned a sense of identity within the music of the West. But my faith community created in me a sense of identity within a much larger story. It was a narrative that placed me within the story of God's ways with humanity. Within this story I have come to understand who I am.

I *learned to interpret*, to make sense of texts, within this community of salvation. Around our family table I learned the language of our sacred texts. As we met within the larger community of faith, those texts were read and interpreted. Like Ezra before a rebuilt Jerusalem, our leaders took seriously the reading of God's Word, and its interpretation.[15] The ancient words were given meaning for our times. Granted, in retrospect some of the interpretations left much to be desired. But the attempts were there.[16] Garrett Green has argued that "The examples both of modern science and the history of religion point to the same conclusion: that the most powerful way to change the world is precisely by interpreting it."[17] There are many images by which to view the church. One with which I playfully envision is the church as an "interpretive centre." For instance, as you drive up Signal Hill in St. John's, Newfoundland and Labrador, there is an interpretive centre. Once inside, the centre helps to make sense of the formation of the province, and how its eastern portion was at one time actually part of the continents of northwest Africa and Europe, while its western portion is part of North America.[18] The Salvationist community is an interpretive centre making sense of its faith story in the contemporary world. Salvationists interpret for transformation.

Within the Salvationist community I came to know people who appreciated football and music. But I also came to know people who had little interest in football, and certainly didn't like rock 'n' roll! In a limited way, I came to know people who were *different* from me. I went to camp with young people who were "other" than me. I rehearsed with musicians of a "different" generation. In time, this sense of "otherness" would bring me face to face with people of different ethnicities, languages, political persuasions and loyalties. But there was something about learning the word "we" that has never left me. In our worship we sang, "We gather together to ask the Lord's blessing." We prayed, "Our Father, who is in heaven." We. Us. Our. When my wife, Cathie, and I were appointed to a new expression of The Salvation Army in Alberta's oil sands, we found ourselves in the midst of people from other parts of Canada and the globe. They had come to northern Alberta because of the promise of work. Together we learned to appreciate our differences: Newfoundland idioms, East

Indian food, Malaysian joy, Albertan swagger. When we opened our new building, we gathered around the altar singing the Larsson and Gowans song, "They shall come from the east, they shall come from the west and sit down in the kingdom of God."[19] However inadequate, the Salvationist community has been a place where I have been privileged to learn "the dignity of difference."[20]

Finally, within the Salvationist community I have learned to *appreciate the symbolic*. Symbols function to evoke meaning. The red poppy evokes much meaning for military personnel in the West; the Olympic rings hold great meaning for athletes; the Twin Towers in New York City evoke important significance, especially for Americans. Because symbols can lose their significance over time, Avery Dulles's perspective is most important: "Any large and continuing society that depends on the loyalty and commitment of its members requires symbolism to hold it together." The Salvation Army has its own symbols, and their importance came home to me in the spring of 2013. Early in the month of April, runners in the Boston Marathon met with a tragic ending to the race. The bombs that were exploded had been strategically and symbolically placed. Later that month, I formed part of a Salvation Army brass ensemble that accompanied the singing of the American and Canadian anthems at a hockey game. The memories of the marathon were still very fresh, and the 15,000 fans at the game warmly applauded the American anthem. Then we accompanied the soloist for the Canadian anthem. The atmosphere was electric. There we were: flags, anthems, a key hockey game and Salvationists with large Red Shields on our backs. This Army's symbols belong at ice level. They evoke meaning in the life of our nations.

Thus, with all of its flaws, I have come to learn and appreciate the communal dimensions of Christian faith through The Salvation Army. Far from irrelevant, the church in its Salvationist expression is most relevant. "We believe ...." This conviction matters!

Practising the Doctrine

Communal character! A moment's pause will help us to realize that we do talk about communal character in our culture. Journalists speak of team character, or lack of it. Nations demonstrate character when they respond to a tragedy, such as a hurricane. It is the conviction of Christians that the church is intended to embody a distinct communal character—God's. Its purpose is to make holiness visible to the wider world. And yet, the connections between holiness and church have been marginalized in our times. Kent Brower and Andy Johnson frame the matter this way: In our present context, "thinking about the people of God is often reduced to how an individual is related to God and the category of holiness is either ignored, reduced to inward piety, or thought to be the preserve of legalists. *Throughout the biblical story, however, the people of God are expected to embody God's holy character publicly in particular settings.*"[21] The Salvation Army has its own contribution to make to the church's task of embodying God's holy character. On any given day, The Salvation Army may be engaged in a variety of activities. We may be advocating for the homeless, providing food for schoolchildren who lack a good breakfast, responding to a city's needs after a disastrous flood or hurricane, rehearsing music to be used in worship on Sunday, making organizational decisions regarding the financial integrity of a division, providing spiritual care in a hospital or personal care home. All of these practices express our understanding of God's character, God's holiness. Others may also engage in these activities, but Salvationists do so because we believe that in so doing we embody the character of God. And that character is cultivated locally and globally in this international Army of Salvation. How, though, is God's character actually cultivated in the Army?[22] This is a huge question, so let's consider some essential elements.

The Salvation Army has its own contribution to make to the church's task of embodying God's holy character

First, our *distinctive communal character will be cultivated as we worship God truly in the Salvationist tradition*. This is especially important in a culture preoccupied with entertainment. We become what we worship. We meet in order to get a glimpse of a holy God. This means we will bring integrity to our reading of Scripture; we will sing those songs that direct our attention to a God beyond our imagining; and together we will form a vocabulary that moves beyond "me" and "I" to "we" and "us." Salvationists welcome good worship music from many sources, but like Israel's song book shaped as the Psalter, we also count our own song book to be one way that an international Army sings from the same page. Worship of this holy God will enable us to appreciate our national and cultural heritages, but it will forbid us to idolize them. All loyalties will become secondary as we worship God with our heart, mind and strength.

Second, holiness will be cultivated in the Army through *faithful teaching*. Holy character is formed; it is not coerced. And teaching is essential to that formation. When Paul outlines the importance of gifts within the church, he draws attention to pastors/teachers who "equip the saints for the work of ministry, for building up the body of Christ, until all of us come to the unity of the faith and of the knowledge of the Son of God, to maturity, to the measure of the full stature of Christ."[23] It's helpful to note that the word used for "equip" here is the same word used to describe the disciples "mending" their nets after fishing.[24] Without realizing it we can tear apart the sacred and secular worlds in which we live; we can tear apart the institutions that give substance to our faith. Teaching mends nets. Teaching equips us in the ways of holiness, including our communal holiness.

Third, The Salvation Army's "social holiness" will embody God's character to the degree its *organizational life* reflects that character. The Army's polity and policies will be designed and implemented to reflect God's integrity as it can be embodied in the 21st century. There is no chasm here between our spiritual life and institution. They belong together. The Salvation Army has its Orders and Regulations and Operating Policies. These will always need to be considered in context, but they are intended to help the Army express our corporate character, a distinct character.

Finally, holiness will be cultivated in The Salvation Army to the degree that its *ordained leadership is distinct, holy*. Many individuals help to form Salvationist character and realize its mission, but I want to touch here on the place of ordained leadership in forming a holy Salvation Army. One of my privileges as an officer has been the many years of service in our Colleges For Officer Training. They have their beginnings with a letter from Bramwell Booth to his mother,

Catherine, in 1878. In contemplating the training of officers, he insisted that its emphasis would be the "training of the heart."[25] In other words, whatever skills and knowledge were deemed essential, matters of character were central. Officer training is an exercise in *formation*, not simply processing information. In light of this, officers are expected to exhibit the character sought in the Army as a whole. Officers are expected to work hard, to be disciplined with respect to time and finances, to be teachable, to develop skills because they are accountable, to study diligently, to be faithful with the resources entrusted to them, to join other officers in living out a shared covenant because officership is not a negotiated contract. It is a sacred moment, a holy moment, when a cadet stands before the officiating officer at a public commissioning service to hear the words: "Recognizing that God has called you, has equipped you and gifted you for sacred service, I now ordain you as a minister of the gospel of our Lord and Saviour Jesus Christ, and commission you as an officer of The Salvation Army with the rank of Lieutenant." Salvation Army officership is a privilege afforded some to help the Army as a whole become a holy community. By making a difference within the community of Salvationists, it is hoped we make a difference in our world. This difference is spelled out in the language of holiness.

You can't wage war with Salvation Army methods —Adolph Hitler

As Adolph Hitler prepared for war in the late summer of 1939, he warned his generals about the brutality that lay ahead of them. He taunted his leaders with these words: "You can't wage war with Salvation Army methods."[26] It's an intriguing question to ask how Hitler came to know this much about The Salvation Army. Yet Hitler was right to contrast Nazi ambitions with the character of The Salvation Army: they are polar opposites. This Army of Salvation is committed to the formation of community where God's gracious love is extended to all. It is a global community committed to the healing of the nations. The Salvation Army seeks to embody in its communal life the character of God, expressed most fully in the life, death and resurrection of Jesus Christ.

Reflection Questions for Chapter Eleven

1. How did you come into contact with The Salvation Army?
2. If you are studying this book with a group, read the chapter together.
3. What phrase or section caught your attention? Why?

Forming the Doctrine:

4. What observations do you make about the kind of community that formed around Jesus?
5. Read the New Testament texts that portray different images of the church. What does each image suggest to you?
6. Why do you think it is important to speak of The Salvation Army as an expression of the church?

Engaging the Doctrine:

7. What value do you believe there is in institutions? And what dangers?
8. What are some personal contributions the church, including The Salvation Army, has made to your life?
9. What vision do you have for your congregation? For The Salvation Army?

Practising the Doctrine:

10. How do you see team or corporate character expressed in different groups of people?
11. What aspect of Christ's character do you think is important for the church to express today? Why?
12. What advice would you give to somebody who is considering a life of ordained leadership in The Salvation Army?

Conclude: Pray Albert Orsborn's song, "Not unto us O Lord" (*SBSA 1987*, No. 163), which was composed for the Army's centenary celebrations.

Endnotes for Chapter Eleven

1 Kent E. Brower and Andy Johnson eds., *Holiness and Ecclesiology in the New Testament* (Grand Rapids: Eerdmans, 2007), xvi.

2 Richard Gwyn, *Nation Maker: Sir John A. Macdonald: His Life, Our Times* (Toronto: Random House, 2011), 357-359.

3 George Scott Railton, *Heathen England, 5th Edition* (London: The Salvation Army Book Depot, 1883), 145.

4 Quoted in *The Salvation Army Handbook of Doctrine* (London: Salvation Books, 2010), 247.

5 *The Salvation Army Handbook of Doctrine 2010*, 247.

6 Luke 5:1-11, emphasis mine.

7 Brower and Johnson, *Holiness and Ecclesiology*, xxii.

8 Joel B. Green, *Salvation* (St. Louis: Chalice Press, 2003), 137-138.

9 In Acts 19:32, the word "assembly" is a translation of the Greek, *ecclesia*, from which is formed the word *ecclesiology*, or the study of the church.

10 For the exploration and settlement of New France by Samuel de Champlain, see David Hackett Fischer, *Champlain's Dream* (Toronto: Vintage Canada, 2009).

11 Joel 2:12-13.

12 The "connectional" shape of The Salvation Army comes from its Methodist roots whereby each expression of the Army is viewed as connected to the greater whole. Avery Dulles makes a helpful distinction between "institutional" and "institutionalism," whereby the institution becomes an end unto itself rather than serving something greater. See Avery Dulles, *Models of the Church* (New York: Doubleday, 1987), 34-46.

13 Jeremiah 8:7. Actually the reference is to migratory birds, but Jeremiah would have concurred with this reference had he witnessed Canadian geese in flight!

14 Robert D. Putnam, *Bowling Alone: The Collapse and Revival of American Community* (New York: Simon and Schuster, 2000), 27.

15 See Nehemiah 8:1-8.

16 In retrospect, I also realize that the interpretive work of musicians also played an important role for me. There is depth in good music which requires interpretation and rehearsal. There is also depth in the biblical texts, which also requires rehearsal, study, good listening.

17 Garrett Green, *Imagining God: Theology and the Religious Imagination* (Grand Rapids: Eerdmans Publishing, 1989), 152.

18 The dividing line is at the Dover-Hermitage Fault. See Kevin Major, *As Near to Heaven by Sea: A History of Newfoundland and Labrador* (Toronto: Penguin Canada, 2001), 2-4.

19 John Gowans, "They Shall Come From the East," *SBSA 1987*, No. 170.

20 See Jonathan Sacks, *The Dignity of Difference* (London: Continuum Books, 2002).

21 Brower and Johnson, *Holiness and Ecclesiology*, xvi, emphasis mine.

22 The image of "cultivation" is implied by Paul's emphasis on the "fruit of the Spirit" in Galatians 5:22-23.

23 Ephesians 4:11-12. Based on the Greek text, the word "and" is best ignored in English translations. Pastors teach and teachers engage in pastoral work.

24 See Matthew 4:21.

25 Herbert H. Booth, "The Training Home Annual and Report of the Central Division for the Year Ending, November, 1887" (Salvation Army, n.d.), 8.

26 Quoted in Eric Metaxas, *Bonhoeffer: Pastor, Martyr, Prophet, Spy* (Nashville: Thomas Nelson, 2010), 352.

CHAPTER 12

Wholly Sanctified: Holiness Shaped by Core Convictions

We believe that it is the privilege of all believers to be wholly sanctified, and that their whole spirit and soul and body may be preserved blameless unto the coming of our Lord Jesus Christ.—Doctrine 10

We need an expanded understanding of holiness.—Phil Needham[1]

WE COME FINALLY TO THE ARMY'S 10TH DOCTRINE. In some respects it feels as if we have been holding a thoroughbred inside the starting gate until now. In fact, all along we have been putting each affirmation of faith in conversation with this 10th doctrine. We have carried out our work with the conviction that all doctrines have something important to say about holiness. The Salvation Army's doctrines do not exist in isolation from each other, but form an ecological system.[2] Thus we have asked how each individual doctrine contributes to our understanding and practice of holiness. But it's time now to give focused attention to this 10th doctrine on its own. We will turn to its biblical roots, consider reasons why its hearing in the 21st century can be problematic, and yet indicate how the wording of the doctrine itself is pregnant with meaning for our times. This core conviction matters because it is shaped by all the other core convictions.

Forming the Doctrine

It's difficult to hear the word "holy" without also hearing the cultural baggage it brings. It's a word that is easily misunderstood and sidelined in our culture; it usually carries overtones of superiority. In order to give the word a healthy hearing, let's begin with language that lets us stand on more neutral ground for a moment. When we turn to the Bible, we find that words such as different, distinct or unique help to explain the biblical meaning of "holy." For instance, Genesis tells us that God "blessed the seventh day and made it holy ..." (Genesis 2:3 *NIV*). In other words, God climaxed his creative work by making this day different or distinct. The seventh day was distinguished from the other six days in that God "rested" from the "finished" work of creation. Similarly, Moses was instructed to remove his sandals because "the place on which you are standing is holy ground" (Exodus 3:5). It's not that the soil itself was any different, but the place was distinct because of its association with God. Our contemporary world understands this meaning of the word when we speak of Ground Zero in New York City as different, even sacred, because of its association with tragedy. It's this note of distinctiveness that marks the meaning of holiness in the Bible.

The Old Testament portrays *God's* distinctiveness with the language of holiness: "Who is like you, O Lord, among the gods? Who is like you, majestic in holiness, awesome in splendor, doing wonders?" (Exodus 15:11). Israel learned the hard way not to trifle with this holy God. God could be approached only with great care and caution. The Ark of the Covenant was a symbol of God's holiness, but wrought havoc on its captors and those who approached it too casually.[3] When the prophet Isaiah witnessed "the Lord sitting on a throne, high and lofty," the seraphs in attendance cried out, "Holy, holy, holy is the Lord of hosts; the whole earth is full of his glory." The prophet's response was to become aware of his own sinfulness: "Woe is me! I am lost, for I am a man of unclean lips, and I live among a people of unclean lips; yet my eyes have seen the King, the Lord of hosts" (Isaiah 6:1-5). Indeed, Isaiah names God as "the Holy One of Israel" whose "thoughts are not your thoughts, nor are your ways my ways, says the Lord. For as the heavens are higher than the earth, so are my ways higher than your ways and my thoughts than your thoughts" (Isaiah 55:5, 8-9). And yet the staggering conviction of the Old Testament is that this Holy One risked his presence with Israel. The prophet Hosea portrays God wrestling within himself in relation to this nation that had prostituted itself to others: "How can I give you up, Ephraim? How can I hand you over, O Israel? ... My heart recoils within me; my compassion grows warm and tender. I will not execute my fierce anger; I will not again destroy Ephraim; for I am God and no mortal, *the Holy One in your midst,* and I will not come in wrath."[4] God's distinctive character is displayed precisely through his majestic presence in the midst of a flawed people. John Webster holds the tension together this way: "The holiness of God is not to be identified simply as that which distances God from us; rather, God is holy precisely as the one who in majesty and freedom and sovereign power bends down to us in mercy."[5] God is willing to get his hands dirty. This is what makes God utterly distinct, holy.

This portrayal of holiness as distinctiveness carries into the New Testament with the life of Jesus. He lived in a world where invisible boundaries guided social relationships. Recall that the heart of the temple in Jerusalem consisted of sacred space, the holy of holies. There were strict boundaries around that space so that women, Samaritans and the disfigured were less and less welcome at the heart of the temple. It was within this world that Jesus carried out his public ministry of compassionate healing. The scandal of his public ministry lay in his willingness to touch the leper, heal a hemorrhaging woman, associate with tax collectors and straighten a woman's back on the Sabbath, the holy day. His healing ministry was carried out in such a way as to violate the existing understanding of *holiness as separation*. Jesus turned his culture's understanding of holiness upside down and inside out. This brought him into disrepute with the religious leaders of his day. In their desire to protect holiness as they understood it, they brought Jesus to the Roman authorities and supported his crucifixion. In the darkness of that hour, "the curtain of the temple was torn in two" (Luke 23:45). Here is Luke's conviction that in the person of Jesus, the holy God is in the midst of flawed and sinful humanity. Michael Lodahl draws out its implication for holiness:

> … the term holy can easily erect boundaries … It is helpful, though, to recall that the word-concept of holy first of all bespeaks utter-uniqueness, distinctness, even transcendence. Hence, I would argue that the notion that God is "holy love" … ought not to be interpreted so that holy is understood as a kind of stern or wrathful qualifier; instead, it should be interpreted so as to suggest that God's love is utterly unique, totally distinct, in a "class of its own," precisely because it infinitely transcends limitations of creaturely love.[6]

> But you are a chosen race, a royal priesthood, a holy nation, God's own people
> —1 Peter 2:9

God's holiness is embodied in the person of Jesus of Nazareth. Holiness is a lived holiness. His life welcomed and embraced all. This is what contributes to a Christian understanding of God as utterly different, "in a class by himself."

Both the Old and New Testaments hold out the expectation for God's people to be holy. Israel is called a holy nation after its liberation from Egypt (see Exodus 19:6). God intended Israel to be distinct, to be different, among the nations of the world. Israel's constitution, set out in the Ten Commandments and developed in Deuteronomy, was designed to guide its distinctive life. The First Letter of Peter draws on the imagery of Exodus to mark the identity of the young church: "But you are a chosen race, a royal priesthood, a holy nation, God's own people" (1 Peter 2:9). In a most remarkable way, this community of Christians, in their own pluralistic world, is connected to the biblical story and Israel's identity as a holy people. And together with Israel, the audacious conviction is expressed that their communal character could reflect God's character: holy! In light of this we can sense the Apostle Paul working hard to make holiness real in the churches he founded. Paul understands Christian believers to have a new identity. They are saints, holy ones. While he will direct criticisms at the church in Corinth, he begins his first letter to them with the words: "To the church of God that is in Corinth, to those who are sanctified in Christ Jesus, called to be saints" (1 Corinthians 1:2). The vocabulary of "sanctification" means to "make holy." Paul's Letters to the churches and individuals show his preoccupation with fashioning a holy people, in fact. He laboured to create a distinctive people: "I am again in the pain of childbirth until Christ is formed in you" (Galatians 4:19); "I appeal to you therefore, brothers and sisters, by the mercies of God, to present your bodies as a living sacrifice, holy and acceptable to God, which is your spiritual worship. Do not be conformed to this world, but be transformed by the renewing of your minds, so that you may discern what is the will of God—what is good and acceptable and perfect" (Romans 12:1-2). In Donald Burke's words, "holiness according to Paul, and as generally taught in the New Testament, is a thoroughgoing reformation of human character that is seen in a thoroughgoing transformation of human actions."[7]

It's the conviction of the biblical story that God is utterly distinct, holy. It's also the Bible's conviction that those who know God are distinct, holy. How this distinctiveness gets worked out in the world constitutes the roller-coaster ride of the Christian church. There have been exemplary moments when Christ's character was most evident. There have also been tragic moments when the character of individual believers and the church has blurred the character of her Lord. Some Christians removed themselves from the mainstream of the church to create monastic orders in order to recover a sense of holiness. Others, like Francis of Assisi, remained in the mainstream of life. The Reformation recovered important aspects of Christian faith, but it was the Wesley brothers and the Methodist Movement that insisted on real change, real transformation in the life of believers. It was this legacy that the early Salvation Army captured with its 10th doctrine, "We believe that it is the privilege of all believers to be wholly sanctified."

Engaging the Doctrine

The vocabulary and importance of holiness has been effectively muted in the 21st century. Its language has been relegated to the private sphere of religious belief and practice. There are many reasons for its disappearance from public conversation, of course. As the public realm became more secular in the West, the sacred became more insular. This had a way of pushing any notion of transformation into a small religious pocket of life. And The Salvation Army had its own ways of reducing the breadth and depth of holiness. Let's engage these concerns in order to hear a healthy doctrine of holiness in our times.

> Issues of character have erupted all through our culture in recent years

What is the point of emphasizing this core conviction if it doesn't *make sense* to people in the 21st century? At a superficial glance it would seem that our preoccupation with holiness has little to do with parenting or the Olympics or global financial meltdowns. And yet issues of character have erupted all through our culture in recent years. The financial world of Ponzi schemes and the global collapse of banks and nations have raised concerns over integrity. The influence of performance enhancing drugs has brought team championships and personal records into question. There is a concern among educators in North America that, in an attempt to insulate young people from the experience of failure, we may have made difficult the development of necessary character traits like "grit" or tenacity.[8] Character is no longer relegated to the sidelines. It's part of the game now. The 21st century has made it possible for us to hear again the importance of character and of a people being shaped by the character of God.

If holiness is, in fact, quite relevant for our times, what is needed to recover its place within The Salvation Army? It's helpful to understand how we got to where we are. While it is true that the Army's Founders acknowledged their indebtedness to John and Charles Wesley, in reality they embraced a version of Wesleyan holiness that had its roots in American revivalism. This is not to fault this revivalist movement; the uncertainties of frontier living in America had a way of shaping Methodism's understanding of holiness, especially with its emphasis on a "second blessing." But David Rightmire is right in arguing that "The blending of American revivalism and perfectionism resulted in a stress on the *immediacy and completeness* of the 'second blessing,' received by faith and consecration."[9] As a result, a particular model of holiness took root in the early Army. Several things, however, made this model problematic: holiness came to be detached from the greater work of salvation, its scope focused mainly on the heart, and it was to be realized in a particular moment in time. Let's pick up on these themes and approach our task as a careful work of restoration.

A first task is to restore holiness to a *biblical understanding of salvation*. In the West, we have tended to speak of salvation as personal conversion and the life of holiness as something that follows later. As argued earlier in this book, however, holiness is an aspect of salvation, not different from it. Salvation is a comprehensive term for the whole of God's gracious ways with us.[10] Salvation is the "deep ocean of love"[11] in which we learn to navigate our lives. Holiness is one dimension of this boundless salvation, as is justification, adoption and new creation. The New Testament's emphasis is that Christians have a new identity; we are "in Christ." This new identity includes all the dimensions of salvation, which become visible when put through a prism of grace. Thus its writers argue that we are *already* "sanctified by the Spirit" (1 Peter 1:2), we are *already* "sanctified in Christ Jesus" (1 Corinthians 1:2). This is who we are. Given this identity, we are called to live it out in our world. Our vocation is to be different people in the cultures of our time, different in matters of character. Paul thus exhorts the Philippians to "work out your own salvation with fear and trembling; for it is God who is at work in you" (Philippians 2:12-13). Holiness is not something different from salvation, but expressive of it.

A second aspect of holiness that needs to be restored is its *social dimension*. Without losing our emphasis on "heart holiness," we need to expand it to include social, political and even ecological dimensions. In his own day, John Wesley argued that "there is no holiness but social holiness." Wesley objected to a Lutheran emphasis on justification such that our status with God came to represent the *whole* of Christian faith. In response, Wesley argued for *real change*, for holiness that had social dimensions. Among his many contributions to his social world, it was John Wesley who, in his final days, wrote to encourage William Wilberforce in his crusade to abolish slavery.[12] As the formative years of The Salvation Army took shape, personal piety was emphasized. The image of a "pure heart" or "clean heart" dominated. The Army *was* quite involved in the social dimensions of salvation, such as the match box factory, but these were not often connected to holiness. Recent years have witnessed an attempt to recover the social dimensions of holiness. During the tenure of General Shaw Clifton, the International Social Justice Commission was formed:

> The Salvation Army's strategic voice to advocate for human dignity and social justice with the world's poor and oppressed. Believing that everyone is created in the image of God but that global, economic and political inequity perpetuates human injustice, the International Social Justice Commission exercises leadership in determining The Salvation Army's policies and practices in the international social arena. Lamenting the abusive and unethical behavior imposed on vulnerable people in today's world, the Commission helps link The Salvation Army with like-minded organizations and other world forums to advocate the cause of global social justice.[13]

Without losing our emphasis on "heart" holiness, we are learning to restore its social dimensions. We are called to exhibit a distinct communal character *together* as Salvationists.

Finally, the restoration of biblical holiness will include its emphasis on *the whole journey of faith*. As the American revivalist version of holiness took root in the early Army, it became preoccupied with a particular moment in time. An early doctrine book explained it this way:

> ... we believe that after conversion there remain in the heart of the believer inclinations to evil, or roots of bitterness, which, unless overpowered by Divine grace, produce actual sin; but that these evil tendencies can be entirely taken away by the Spirit of God, and the whole heart, thus cleansed from everything contrary to the will of God, or entirely sanctified, will then produce the fruit of the Spirit only."[14]

The image of "roots of bitterness" is taken from the Bible. But what the early framers of this doctrine failed to keep in mind is that the image relates to the social interactions of God's people, not the inclinations of the individual heart. It has to do with the communal discipline needed to create a holy people, in fact.[15] It is true that sin reaches deep into the human heart, but it also impacts our closest human relationships, the structures of our cities, the policies of our corporations and the ambitions of our nations. However, because it was felt that the "roots of bitterness" could be taken away, the conviction grew that this could take place in a *moment of time*. The more common way of referring to this moment was as a "second blessing." The "first blessing" was God's forgiveness of sin; the "second blessing" was God's deliverance from the power of sin.[16] There are appropriate ways to speak of "second blessing."[17] There will be many crisis moments in faith's journey, not just one. Our consecration is to be wholehearted, but it is in Will Brand's words, "the path of consecration,"[18] not simply the commitment of a moment. Holiness is the transformation that takes place over time as we learn to love God with our heart, mind and strength, and our neighbour as ourselves. Holiness is the transformation that takes place in a community as the mind of Christ shapes it. This transformation is not a quick fix. It involves a lifetime of learning to become who we are, both personally and communally.

Holiness is the transformation that takes place in a community as the mind of Christ shapes it

In order to hear this 10th doctrine more adequately, we have engaged it with our own history, and how the Army's view of holiness has itself undergone change. Now we are in a position to unfold the implications of this doctrine for holiness understood and practised.

Practising the Doctrine

In the early 1700s, explorers of British North America huddled around the shoreline of Hudson's Bay. They were unaware of the expanse all around them. Their view of the future land of Canada remained stunted; it needed to get bigger to match the immensity of the land. Phil Needham has argued that Salvationists need a similar "expanded understanding of holiness."[19] In fact, some expansion of our understanding has taken place over time. For instance, in Rightmire's view, Samuel Logan Brengle's emphasis on holiness as "pure love" directed the Army away from some of the restricting emphases of American revivalism.[20] Generations later, Frederick Coutts did much to continue this task with his emphasis on holiness as "growth in Christlikeness."[21] And in recent years, the Spiritual Life Commission has broadened the Army's commitment to holiness even more with this statement:

> We call Salvationists world-wide to restate and live out the doctrine of holiness in all its dimensions—personal, relational, social and political—in the context of our cultures and in the idioms of our day while allowing for, and indeed prizing, such diversity of experience and expression as in accord with the Scriptures.[22]

In order to expand our view of holiness, Salvationists have increasingly found value in different streams of spiritual disciplines. Christine Faragher, for example, has explored the *contemplative* stream in our Salvationist tradition with insight.[23] It is my conviction that *Salvation Army doctrines* also offer a way to expand our understanding and practice of holiness. Through these chapters we have been asking a simple question: How does each doctrine of The Salvation Army contribute to our understanding and practice of holiness? Now the question is asked: How does this 10th doctrine inform our understanding and practice of holiness? This may seem at first glance as somewhat circular, but it's not. Let's begin by recalling the doctrine's words and then let them resonate with themes that have been expressed in these chapters:

> We believe that it is the privilege of all believers to be wholly sanctified, and that their whole spirit and soul and body may be preserved blameless unto the coming of our Lord Jesus Christ.

First, we can observe that our 10th doctrine is almost a verbatim quote from the Apostle Paul. Writing to the young church at Thessalonica, he prayed these words: "May the God of peace himself sanctify you entirely; and may your spirit and soul and body be kept sound and blameless at the coming of our Lord Jesus Christ. The one who calls you is faithful, and he will do this" (1 Thessalonians 5:23-24). Paul wrote as a pastoral leader to a Christian community. His Letter comes to the whole church now as part of the Christian Scriptures. The wording of our 10th doctrine reminds us that Christian holiness is grounded in sacred Scripture. The spirituality of which we speak is a *biblical* spirituality. This doctrine points us not simply to First Thessalonians but to the whole of the Bible. The Christian Scriptures enable us to view the ways this holy God interacts with those made in his image. Each biblical book gives us a glimpse into the huge expanse of what it means for God to be holy and for us to mirror that holiness. The whole of the Bible narrates the character of God, and the whole of the Bible paints images of the character of God's people. There are, for instance, many horticultural images. Psalm 1 contrasts those who are like fruitful trees with those who are like chaff that the wind drives away. John 15 points to God's work as gardener, including the hard task of pruning! Paul's Letter to the Galatians sketches what can be expected as "fruit of the Spirit" (Galatians 5:22-23). Holiness is *cultivated.*[24] In addition to agricultural images, the Bible sketches the distinctiveness of Christian holiness through athletic imagery. The ancient Greek games lie in the background, but biblical writers draw upon them. Athletic contexts point to the importance of self-discipline (see 1 Corinthians 9:24-27); the importance of a goal at the finish line is stressed (see Philippians 3:12-16); and the need to run with perseverance the race set before us (see Hebrews 12:1-2) sets the stage for "a long obedience in the same direction" (see Chapter 9). These are but a few of the images that are created to help understand personal and communal character shaped by the grace of God. Every page in the biblical story contributes to our understanding of holiness.

Our 10th doctrine emphasizes holiness as a *privilege*. While our work on these doctrines has kept words such as obedience, responsibility and trust in the forefront, it's important to remind ourselves that we cannot presume upon God for a holy life. To say that holiness is a privilege is to remind ourselves that the *bedrock of grace* underlies any work of transformation. The initiative for holiness comes from God. It is not something we deserve or have earned. Neither is holiness a commodity that can be bought and sold. As a Canadian citizen, I am conscious of many privileges that are mine in this world. I have freedom to travel that is not available to all people. I have the freedom to pursue learning and vocations that are not accessible to others. I have the opportunity to vote in elections that many in our world do not have. All of these opportunities come to me as a privilege. They are undeserved. They come as a gift of grace. The doctrine of holiness claims that we can reflect the character of God, and this is a privilege wholly undeserved. The conviction that we can be a transformed and transforming people is a profound privilege. Holiness requires the disciplined response of an Olympic athlete, but at all points along the way, it is a response to grace. Holiness is a privilege.

This doctrine also points to the conviction that holiness is intended to be the experience of *all* believers.[25] Holiness is not for an elite few. God intends ordinary people to embody his character in ordinary circumstances. The Christlike life is to be lived out as we coach basketball teams, drive our cars, use the Internet, pursue our studies, parent our children, care for aging parents, celebrate important civic holidays and build the church. There will be exemplars of holiness that we turn to. They may be individuals in the history of the church, such as Francis of Assisi. They may also be individuals that are not publicly known, but we have known them personally. Certainly we will look to persons within the biblical story, such as Sarah, Joshua, Hannah, Nehemiah, Martha and Timothy. The New Testament begins many of its letters by addressing the whole congregation as "saints." The biblical emphasis is that holiness involves the whole community, not just a few of its members. One of the things we could do to recover this aspect of *all* is to restore the role of personal story to our worship services. Each of us has a story of grace to share: "This is my story, this is my song."[26] It is unfortunate that testimonies have too often come to express the dramatic and spectacular. This has had a way of sidelining the many at the expense of the few. And it has given the impression that a spectacular crisis is essential for the holy life. It's not. There are many ways for us to testify to the journey of holiness, including the doubts that coincide with faith. Our belief that holiness is for all will be convincing when we hear from all.

The language of this 10th doctrine points to holiness as being *wholly sanctified.* What follows helps to explain this phrase, "and *that is* for our whole spirit, soul and body" (emphasis mine). If the word *all* points to the question of who holiness is intended for, the phrase *wholly sanctified* points to the scope of holiness. Put simply, holiness is intended for the whole of life. With the words, "whole spirit and soul and body" we are given a shorthand way of saying "all that we are."[27] We cannot understand ourselves apart from the human community in which we live and the created world in which we have our being. Holiness is not insular. It is not a private club for elite members. Becoming like God in his character touches the mind, the emotions, all relationships, including our ethnicity and national loyalties. Just as sin is total in its effects, so holiness addresses the entirety of our existence. The Christlike transformation of our lives is intended to reach the depths of our heart and extend into the whole of our world. This is William Booth's "boundless salvation" becoming a reality. Christian holiness embodies the grace of God, in our personal and communal life. Entirely!

The final phrase in this doctrine points to a life that is *blameless unto the coming of our Lord Jesus Christ.* The word "blameless" is best understood from the way Paul uses it in First Thessalonians itself. Being blameless has to do with integrity of conduct. Paul refers to it in 3:13: "And may he so strengthen your hearts in holiness that you may be blameless before our God and Father at the coming of our Lord Jesus with all his saints." Holiness implies conduct that is above reproach. That conduct is an expression of working out our salvation in the present moment. Paul puts it this way in his Letter to the Philippians: "[F]orgetting what lies behind and straining forward to what lies ahead, I press on toward the goal for the prize of the heavenly call of God in Christ Jesus" (Philippians 3:13). Holiness has a goal, a *telos.* It is the Salvationist conviction that we can experience transformation in its entirety now, but it will always be incomplete: "Not that I have already attained this or have already reached the goal" (Philippians 3:12). It is the Salvationist argument, embodied in our tradition, that holiness is a huge privilege and task. We cannot realize the scope of holiness apart from our life with each other. Holiness will take different forms and expressions in different cultures of our world. The shape of holiness in the 21st century will not necessarily reflect the form it took in Victorian England. Transformation into the character of Christ is always a matter of pressing on toward the goal.

The Salvation Army is an expression of the church rooted in living convictions, and they shape our life together

While not stated in our doctrine, *God's role* in this is implied. It is helpful to keep in mind the way Paul concludes his prayer to the Thessalonians: "The one who calls you is faithful, and he will do this" (1 Thessalonians 5:24). Holiness begins and ends with God. It begins with God because our holiness is at best a reflection of God's holiness. So we pray as we sing,

> I want thy spotless purity
> Forever in my heart to be
> *A reflex of thy holiness;*
> O live thy life in me![28]

Holiness ends with God because "when [Christ] is revealed, we will be like him, for we will see him as he is. And all who have this hope in him purify themselves, just as he is pure" (1 John 3:2-3). The biblical view of holiness invites us to imagine something much greater than ourselves. It is to live in hope and to live hopefully in the present moment because God is faithful. This is a fundamental portrayal of God in the biblical story. It works its way through the ins and outs of God's relationship with Israel: "The LORD, the LORD, a God merciful and gracious, slow to anger, and abounding in steadfast love and faithfulness" (Exodus 34:6). Paul affirms as much when he says, "God is faithful," or in the words of J. B. Phillips, "God is utterly dependable" (1 Corinthians 1:9). The realization of holiness in our lives is bound to God's faithfulness.

Conclusion

So we conclude as we began, with the importance of core convictions. I trust it has become clear that doctrines play an essential role in Christian faith. The Salvation Army is an expression of the church rooted in living convictions, and they shape our life together. With our lived experience of God in mind, we have put each doctrine into conversation with our core conviction about holiness.

We believe ...

These doctrines affirm the importance of shared belief. It is a remarkable thing that Salvationists around the world join together through these core convictions. We hold the conviction that the Scriptures disclose the holiness of the triune God, the utter distinctiveness of God. We understand ourselves to be created in the image of God, yet flawed by sin. We believe, however, that we are immersed in an immense salvation accomplished through God's grace. The life, death and resurrection of Christ are central to these convictions and hold the pattern for Christian holiness. We are convinced of a salvation that is huge in its scope and holds out a goal that enables us to be a distinct people in the present moment. Together we affirm the belief that it is a privilege to be transformed into the image of Christ through the power of the Holy Spirit. We look for real change now and for the day when this transformation will be complete. We believe this as individuals, and we believe this as a Christian community. Shared convictions help to create our global identity as The Salvation Army.

I believe ...

Actually, I believe a number of things. I especially believe that Salvationists have an important doctrinal heritage. These affirmations of faith have not been created to sit in a trophy case, but are intended to *function* for Salvationists. I believe that each doctrine is capable of creating significance beyond its time. The task of developing their meaning lies with each generation of Salvationists. We are called to engage these historic core convictions with the issues of our day. This is an ongoing task. The doctrines are also designed to interact with each other. Each doctrine has its own integrity, but each core conviction must be understood in relation to the whole. Their voices best sing together. Together the doctrines form the core convictions of the Army. And together they contribute to our understanding and practice of Christian holiness. Ours is a holiness shaped by core convictions. Convictions matter!

Reflection Questions for Chapter Twelve

1. When you hear the word *distinctive*, what comes to mind?
2. If you are studying this book with a group, read the chapter together.
3. What phrase or section caught your attention? Why?

Forming the Doctrine:

4. Read Isaiah 6:1-5 and Luke 5:1-11. What similarities do you note between the two episodes?
5. How do you respond to the phrase *holy love* when used of Jesus?
6. When you think of God as holy, what biblical story comes to mind?

Engaging the Doctrine:

7. What are some ways you think the concept of *character* has taken on importance in our times?
8. When the word *holy* is used in our congregational life, what images come to mind?
9. In what ways do you think The Salvation Army can make a unique contribution to the expression of holiness in our culture?

Practising the Doctrine:

10. Read Galatians 5:22-23. How helpful is it to think of holiness as something that is *cultivated*?
11. In what ways has this study *expanded* your understanding of holiness?
12. What conviction about holiness has become important to you during this study? Why?

Conclude: Read the 11 doctrines together and pray using 1 Thessalonians 5:23-24.

Endnotes for Chapter Twelve

1 Phil Needham, "Integrating Holiness and Community: The Task of an Evolving Salvation Army," *Word and Deed* 3 (Fall 2000): 16.

2 Speaking primarily about the muting of the doctrine of eschatology in the church, Ronald Byers argues that, "There is, or ought to be, a kind of ecological balance in which each doctrine plays its proper role, and each serves the health of the others." See "An Advent Gift: The Eschatological Promise," *Interpretation* 62 (October 2008): 374.

3 See 1 Samuel 4-6.

4 Hosea 11:8-9, emphasis mine.

5 John Webster, *Holiness* (Grand Rapids: Eerdmans Publishing, 2003), 45.

6 Michael E. Lodahl, " 'And He Felt Compassion': Holiness Beyond the Bounds of Community," in *Embodied Holiness,* Samuel M. Powell and Michael E. Lodahl eds., (Downers Grove: InterVarsity Press, 1999), 164-165.

7 Donald E. Burke, "Holiness Unto the Lord: Biblical Foundations of Holiness," *Word and Deed* 1 (Fall 1998): 26.

8 See, for instance, Margaret Wente, "Why kids need to fail in order to succeed at school." http://www.theglobeandmail.com/life/parenting/back-to-school/why-kids-need-to-fail-to-succeed-in-school/article4513436/. Accessed February 8, 2013.

9 David Rightmire, "Samuel Brengle and the Development of Salvation Army Pneumatology," *Word and Deed* 1 (Fall 1998): 39. Emphasis mine.

10 See especially Chapter 7.

11 From "O Boundless Salvation," *SBSA 1987,* No. 298.

12 See his letter to Wilberforce, http://gbgm-umc.org/umw/wesley/wilber.stm. Accessed December 20, 2012.

13 See http://www1.salvationarmy.org/IHQ/www_ihq_isjc.nsf. Accessed February 6, 2013.

14 This is spelled out in the 1925 edition of *The Salvation Army Handbook of Doctrine,* 122.

15 For a further discussion of these issues, see *The Salvation Army Handbook of Doctrine 2010,* pp. 215-218.

16 This approach tends to create a formula for achieving holiness, such as "Steps to Holiness." See William Booth, "A Ladder to Holiness," in *Boundless Salvation: The Shorter Writings of William Booth,* Andrew M. Eason and Roger J. Green, eds., (New York: Peter Lang Publishing, 2012), 101-105. That chapter in *Boundless Salvation* deals with many of the issues discussed here.

17 Michael Lodahl argues that "what occurs in entire sanctification ... is that we begin truly to recognize the implications of our having been set apart by God in our conversion to Christ. In this recognition of the deeper implications of

relationship to God and others, we actively and willingly and lovingly entrust our redeemed selves to God. The 'secondness' ... of sanctification is this deeper relationship to God that is based upon our response to His love—a response of entire consecration, a response of offering our deepest selves as a living sacrifice." See Michael Lodahl, *The Story of God: Wesleyan Theology and Biblical Narrative* (Kansas City: Beacon Hill Press, 1994), 196.

18 Will J. Brand, "When From Sin's Dark Hold," *SBSA 1987*, No. 534.

19 Phil Needham, "Integrating Holiness and Community," 16.

20 David Rightmire, "Samuel Brengle," 42.

21 In Wayne Pritchett's view, Coutts "gave holiness teaching a different flavor than had been prominent prior to his unceasing labors to present holiness in a way that was practical, Christocentric, and in keeping with modern Biblical scholarship." See "General Frederick Coutts and the Doctrine of Holiness," *Word and Deed* 1 (Fall 1998): 50.

22 Quoted in Robert Street, *Called to be God's People* (London: International Headquarters, 1999), 63.

23 Christine Faragher, *Other Voices: Exploring the contemplative in Salvationist spirituality* (Melbourne: Salvo Publishing, 2010).

24 This is explored more fully in Philip D. Kenneson, *Life On the Vine: Cultivating the Fruit of the Spirit in Christian Community* (Downers Grove: InterVarsity Press 1999).

25 It's instructive to note the emphasis of "all" in the Army's doctrines. We believe that God is the Creator, Preserver and Governor of *all* things. We believe that despite being made in the image of God, *all* humanity has become sinful. We also believe that the atoning life and death of Jesus is "for the *whole* world."

26 Fanny Crosby, "Blessed Assurance," *SBSA 1987*, No. 310.

27 For a more complete discussion of the word "sanctify" used by Paul in this Letter, see Andy Johnson, "The Sanctification of the Imagination in I Thessalonians," in Kent E. Brower and Andy Johnson eds., *Holiness and Ecclesiology in the New Testament* (Grand Rapids: Eerdmans, 2007), 289.

28 Harry Anderson, "Saviour, I Want Thy Love To Know," *SBSA 1987*, No. 455. Emphasis mine.

BIBLIOGRAPHY

Barton, Stephen C. "New Testament Interpretation as Performance." *Scottish Journal of Theology* 52 (1999): 179-208.

Begbie, Jeremy S. *Resounding Truth*. Grand Rapids: Baker Academic, 2007.

Bibby, Reginald W. *The Boomer Factor*. Toronto: Bastion Books, 2006.

Bondi, Roberta C. "Aldersgate and Patterns of Methodist Spirituality," in *Aldersgate Reconsidered*, ed. Randy L. Maddox, 21-32. Nashville: Kingswood Books, 1990.

Bonhoeffer, Dietrich. *Psalms: The Prayer Book of the Bible*. Minneapolis: Augsburg Publishing House, 1970.

Booth, Catherine. *Female Teaching*. London: G. J. Stevenson, 1861 Edition.

Booth, Herbert H. "The Training Home Annual and Report of the Central Division for the Year Ending, November, 1887." Salvation Army, n.d.

Booth, William. *In Darkest England and the Way Out*. London: International Headquarters of The Salvation Army, 1890.

Bosch, David J. *Transforming Mission: Paradigm Shifts in Theology of Mission*. Maryknoll: Orbis Books, 1992.

Braaten, Carl E. "The Christian Doctrine of Salvation." *Interpretation* 35 (April 1981): 117-131.

Brengle, Samuel Logan. *The Guest of the Soul*. London: Marshall, Morgan and Scott, 1935.

Brown, Gillian E. "Catherine Booth: Faithful Interpreter of Scripture." Master of Religion Thesis, Wycliffe College and University of Toronto, 2004.

Brower, Kent E. and Andy Johnson eds. *Holiness and Ecclesiology in the New Testament*. Grand Rapids: Eerdmans, 2007.

Brueggemann, Walter. *Praying the Psalms*. Winona, MN: Saint Mary's Press, 1986.

Bryson, Bill. *A Short History of Nearly Everything*. Toronto: Anchor Canada, 2004.

Burke, Donald E. "Holiness Unto the Lord: Biblical Foundations of Holiness," *Word and Deed* 1 (Fall 1998): 15-28.

Burke, Donald E. "Second-Class Scripture?" *Salvationist* (August 2010): 20-21.

Callahan, David. *The Cheating Culture*. Orlando: Harcourt Books, 2004.

Chapman, Robert. *In Heavenly Love Abiding*. Belleville: Guardian Books, 2001.

Charry, Ellen T. "The Moral Function of Doctrine." *Theology Today* 49 (April 1992): 31-45.

Clifton, Shaw. *Selected Writings: Volume 2 – 2000-2010*. London: Salvation Books, 2010.

Colijn, Brenda B. *Images of Salvation in the New Testament*. Downers Grove: IVP Academic, 2010.

Coutts, Frederick. *No Continuing City*. London: Salvationist Publishing, 1978.

Coutts, Frederick. *The Call to Holiness*. St. Albans: Campfield Press, 1957.

Craddock, Fred B. *Preaching*. Nashville: Abingdon Press, 1985.

Cunningham, David S. "The Holy Trinity: The Very Heart of Christian Ministry." *Quarterly Review* 22 (Summer 2002): 125-137.

Cunningham, Mary. *Faith in the Byzantine World*. Downers Grove: InterVarsity Press, 2002.

Dawkins, Richard. *The God Delusion*. New York: First Mariner Books, 2008.

Deshazo, Lynn. "Ancient Words." (C) 2001 Integrity's Hosanna! Music/ ASCAP.

Dulles, Avery. *Models of the Church*. New York: Doubleday, 1987.

Eason, Andrew M. and Roger J. Green, eds. *Boundless Salvation: The Shorter Writings of William Booth*. New York: Peter Lang Publishing, 2012.

Faragher, Christine. *Other Voices: Exploring the contemplative in Salvationist spirituality*. Melbourne: Salvo Publishing, 2010.

Fischer, David Hackett. *Champlain's Dream*. Toronto: Vintage Canada, 2009.

Freire, Paulo. *Pedagogy of the Oppressed*. New York: Continuum Publishing, 1990.

Fretheim, Terrence E. *Exodus*. Louisville: John Knox Press, 1991.

Frost, Karolyn. *I've Got a Home in Gloryland: A Lost Tale of the Underground Railroad*. Toronto: Thomas Allen Publishers, 2007.

Fulford, Robert. *The Triumph of Narrative*. Toronto: Anansi Press, 1999.

Gaventa, Beverly Roberts. *The Acts of the Apostles*. Nashville: Abingdon Press, 2003.

General of The Salvation Army, The. *The Salvation Army Handbook of Doctrine*. London: Salvation Books, 2010.

González, Catherine Gunsalus. "The Rule of Faith," in *Many Voices, One God*, W. Brueggemann and George W. Stroup eds., 95-106. Louisville: Westminster John Knox Press, 1998.

Goodwin, Doris Kearns. *Team of Rivals: The Political Genius of Abraham Lincoln*. New York: Simon and Shuster Paperpacks, 2012.

Gorman, Michael J. " 'You Shall Be Cruciform for I Am Cruciform': Paul's Trinitarian Reconstruction of Holiness," in *Holiness and Ecclesiology in the New Testament*, Kent E. Brower and Andy Johnson eds., 148-166. Grand Rapids: Eerdmans Publishing, 2007.

Green, Garrett. *Imagining God: Theology and the Religious Imagination*. Grand Rapids: Eerdmans Publishing, 1989.

Green Joel B. *Salvation*. St. Louis: Chalice Press, 2003.

Green, Joel B. "Scripture and Theology: Failed Experiments, Fresh Perspectives." *Interpretation* 56 (Jan 2002): 5-20.

Green, Joel B. "The Death of Jesus and the Ways of God." *Interpretation* 52 (Jan 1998): 24-37.

Green, Joel B. and Mark D. Baker. *Recovering the Scandal of the Cross: Atonement in New Testament and Contemporary Contexts*. Downers Grove: InterVarsity Press, 2000.

Green, Roger J. "Facing History: Our Way Ahead for a Salvationist Theology." *Word and Deed* 1 (Spring 1999): 23-40.

Green, Roger J. *War on Two Fronts: The Redemptive Theology of William Booth*. Atlanta: The Salvation Army Supplies, 1989.

Gwyn, Richard. *Nation Maker: Sir John A. Macdonald: His Life, Our Times*. Toronto: Random House, 2011.

Harris, Cathie. "Seeing God in Newfoundland." *The War Cry* (Oct 2004): 4-5.

Hawkins, Thomas R. *The Learning Congregation*. Louisville: Westminster John Knox Press, 1997.

Hays, Richard B. *First Corinthians*. Louisville: John Knox Press, 1997.

Hedges, Chris. *Empire of Illusion*. Toronto: Alfred A. Knopf, 2009.

Heitzenrater, Richard P. *Wesley and the People Called Methodists*. Nashville: Abingdon Press, 1995.

Heschel, Abraham Joshua. *The Sabbath*. New York: The Noonday Press, 1951.

Jackson, Maggie. *Distracted: The Erosion of Attention and the Coming Dark Age*. New York: Prometheus Books, 2008.

Jones, L. Gregory. "Formed and Transformed by Scripture," in *Character and Scripture*, ed. William P. Brown, 18-33. Grand Rapids: Eerdmans Publishing, 2002.

Jones, L. Gregory. "God's holiness." *Christian Century* (Oct 20, 1999): 1004.

Jones, L. Gregory. "Negotiating the Tensions of Vocation" in *The Scope of Our Art: The Vocation of the Theological Teacher,* L. Gregory Jones and Stephanie Paulsell eds., 209-224. Grand Rapids: Eerdmans Publishing, 2002.

Kavanaugh, John F. *Following Christ in a Consumer Society.* Maryknoll: Orbis Press, Revised edition 1991.

Kenneson, Philip D. *Life On the Vine: Cultivating the Fruit of the Spirit in Christian Community.* Downers Grove: InterVarsity Press, 1999.

Kuhn, Thomas S. *The Structure of Scientific Revolutions, 2nd Edition.* Chicago: The University of Chicago Press, 1970.

Larsson, John. *1929: A Crisis That Shaped The Salvation Army's Future.* London: Salvation Books, 2009.

Lodahl, Michael E. " 'And He Felt Compassion': Holiness Beyond the Bounds of Community," in *Embodied Holiness: Toward a Corporate Theology of Spiritual Growth,* Samuel M. Powell and Michael E. Lodahl eds., 145-165. Downers Grove: InterVarsity Press, 1999.

Lodahl, Michael E. *The Story of God: Wesleyan Theology and Biblical Narrative.* Kansas City: Beacon Hill Press, 1994.

Longenecker, Richard N. "The Foundational Conviction of New Testament Christology: The Obedience/ Faithfulness/ Sonship of Christ" in *Jesus of Nazareth: Lord and Christ,* Joel B. Green and Max Turner eds., 473-488. Grand Rapids: Eerdmans Publishing, 1994.

Maddox, Randy L. *Responsible Grace: John Wesley's Practical Theology.* Nashville: Kingswood Books, 1994.

Maddox, Randy L. "Spirituality and Practical Theology: Trajectories Toward Reengagement." *Association of Practical Theology Occasional Papers* 3 (Spring 1999): 10-16.

MacCulloch, Diamaird. *Reformation: Europe's House Divided.* Toronto: Penguin Books, 2003.

Major, Kevin. *As Near to Heaven by Sea: A History of Newfoundland and Labrador.* Toronto: Penguin Canada, 2001.

McCann, J. Clinton Jr. "The Hermeneutics of Grace: Discerning the Bible's Single Plot." *Interpretation* 57 (Jan 2003): 5-23.

McGinnis, Claire Mathews. " 'Yea, the Work of Our Hands, Establish Thou It': On Stability in Academic Life," in *The Scope of Our Art*, L. Gregory Jones and Stephanie Paulsell eds., 173-189. Grand Rapids: Eerdmans Publishing, 2000.

McGrath, Alister E. *Christian Theology: An Introduction, 4th Edition.* Malden: Blackwell Publishing, 2007.

McGrath, Alister E. ed. *Theology: The Basic Readings.* Malden: Blackwell Publishing, 2008.

McGrath, Alister E. *Why God Won't Go Away.* London: SPCK Publishing, 2011.

Meeks, M. Douglas. *Trinity, Community and Power: Mapping Trajectories in Wesleyan Theology.* Nashville: Kingswood Books, 2000.

Metaxas, Eric. *Bonhoeffer: Pastor, Martyr, Prophet, Spy.* Nashville: Thomas Nelson, 2010.

Migliore, Daniel L. *Faith Seeking Understanding: An Introduction to Christian Theology, 2nd Edition.* Grand Rapids: Eerdmans Publishing, 2004.

Miller, Patrick D. Jr. *Deuteronomy.* Louisville: John Knox Press, 1990.

Minear, Paul. "The Holy and the Sacred." *Theology Today* 47 (Apr 1990): 5-12.

Mitchell, Kenneth R. and Herbert Anderson. *All Our Losses, All Our Griefs: Resources for Pastoral Care.* Philadelphia: The Westminster Press, 1983.

Murphy, Nancey. *Reconciling Theology and Science.* Kitchener: Pandora Press, 1997.

Needham, Phil. "Integrating Holiness and Community: The Task of an Evolving Salvation Army." *Word and Deed* 3 (Fall 2000): 5-20.

Neuhaus, Richard John. *Freedom For Ministry.* San Francisco: Harper and Row Publishers, 1979.

Newbigin, Lesslie. *The Gospel in a Pluralist Society.* Grand Rapids: Eerdmans Publishing, 1989.

Neyrey, Jerome H. ed. *The Social World of Luke-Acts: Models for Interpretation.* Peabody: Hendrickson Publishers, 1991.

Nussbaum, Martha. *Not For Profit: Why Democracy Needs the Humanities.* Princeton: Princeton University Press, 2010.

Osmer, Richard R. *A Teachable Spirit: Recovering the Teaching Office in the Church.* Louisville: Westminster/ John Knox Press, 1990.

Pallant, Dean. *Keeping Faith in Faith-Based Organizations: A Practical Theology of Salvation Army Health Ministry.* Eugene: Wipf and Stock Publishers, 2012.

Peacocke, Arthur. "The Cost of New Life," in *The Work of Love,* ed. John Polkinghorne, 21-42. Grand Rapids: Eerdmans Publishing, 2001.

Peterson, Eugene H. *A Long Obedience in the Same Direction: Discipleship in an Instant Society, 2nd ed.* Downers Grove: InterVarsity Press, 2000.

Peterson, Eugene H. *The Pastor: A Memoir.* New York: HarperOne, 2011.

Pinnock, Clark H. "The Role of the Spirit in Redemption." *Asbury Theological Journal* 52 (Spring 1997): 55-62.

Placher, William C. "The Cross of Jesus Christ as Solidarity, Reconciliation, and Redemption," in *Many Voices, One God,* Walter Brueggemann and George W. Stroup eds., 155-166. Louisville: Westminster John Knox Press, 1998.

Placher, William C. *Narratives of a Vulnerable God.* Louisville: Westminster John Knox Press, 1994.

Polkinghorne, John ed. *The Work of Love: Creation as Kenosis.* Grand Rapids: Eerdmans Publishing, 2001.

Power, Bruce A. *Conversations with God: Psalms as a Resource for Prayer and Meditation.* Toronto: The Salvation Army, 2005.

Pritchett, Wayne. "General Frederick Coutts and the Doctrine of Holiness." *Word and Deed* 1 (Fall 1998): 49-64.

Putnam, Robert D. *Bowling Alone: The Collapse and Revival of American Community.* New York: Simon and Schuster, 2000.

Read, Edward. *In the Hands of Another: Memoirs of Edward Read.* Toronto: The Salvation Army, 2002.

Read, James E. "Accountability: Talking the Walk." Unpublished Paper. Winnipeg: Salvation Army Ethics Centre, May 2011.

Rightmire, R. David. *Salvationist Samurai: Gunpei Yamamuro and the Rise of The Salvation Army in Japan*. Lanham: The Scarecrow Press, 1997.

Rightmire, R. David. "Samuel Brengle and the Development of Salvation Army Pneumatology." *Word and Deed* 1 (Fall 1998): 29-48.

Robinson, Barbara. "Neither Fearful nor Familiar: Imaging God the Father." *Word and Deed* 4 (Fall 2001):25-42.

Robinson, Earl. "The History of Salvation Army Doctrine." *Word and Deed* 2 (May 2000): 31-45.

Runyon, Theodore. "Holiness as the Renewal of the Image of God in the Individual & Society," in *Embodied Holiness: Toward a Corporate Theology of Spiritual Growth*, Samuel M. Powell and Michael E. Lodahl eds., 79-88. Downers Grove: InterVarsity Press, 1999.

Runyon, Theodore. *The New Creation: John Wesley's Theology Today.* Nashville: Abingdon Press, 1998.

Sacks, Jonathan. *The Dignity of Difference: How to Avoid the Clash of Civilizations*. London: Continuum, 2002.

Sacks, Jonathan. *The Great Partnership: Science, Religion, and the Search for Meaning*. New York: Schocken Books, 2011.

Sandall, Robert. *The History of The Salvation Army: Volume Two, 1878-1886*. New York: The Salvation Army, 1950.

Sandall, Robert. *The History of The Salvation Army: Volume Three 1883-1953*. New York: The Salvation Army Supplies and Purchasing Department, 1953.

Sandel, Michael J. *What Money Can't Buy: The Moral Limits of Markets*. New York: Farrar, Straus and Giroux, 2012.

Schön, Donald A. *Educating the Reflective Practitioner.* San Francisco: Jossey-Bass Publishers, 1987.

Schneiders, Sandra M. "Biblical Spirituality." *Interpretation* 56 (April 2002): 133-142.

Schneiders, Sandra M. *The Revelatory Text: Interpreting the New Testament as Sacred Scripture.* New York: HarperCollins Publishers, 1991.

Slous, Julie A. *Preaching a Disturbing Gospel.* Toronto: The Salvation Army Canada and Bermuda, 2012.

Stone, Ronald H. *John Wesley's Life and Ethics.* Nashville: Abingdon Press, 2001.

Street, Robert. *Called to be God's People.* London: International Headquarters, 1999.

Tyson, John R. *Assist Me To Proclaim: The Life and Hymns of Charles Wesley.* Grand Rapids: Eerdmans Publishing, 2007.

Visser, Margaret. *The Gift of Thanks.* Toronto: HarperCollins Publishers, 2008.

Volf, Miroslav. *Allah: A Christian Response.* New York: HarperCollins Publishers, 2011.

Volf, Miroslav, Ghazi bin Muhammad, and Melissa Yarrington. *A Common Word: Muslims and Christians on Loving God and Neighbor.* Grand Rapids: Eerdmans Publishing, 2010.

Watson, Robert A. and Ben Brown. *"The Most Effective Organization in the U.S."* New York: Crown Business, 2001.

Webster, John. *Holiness.* Grand Rapids: Eerdmans Publishing, 2003.

Willimon, William H. *Calling and Character: Virtues of the Ordained Life*. Nashville: Abingdon Press, 2000.

Winchester, Simon. *Atlantic*. New York: HarperCollins Publishers, 2010.

Wood, Charles M. *An Invitation to Theological Study*. Valley Forge: Trinity Press International, 1994.

Wright, N. T. *Justification: God's Plan & Paul's Vision*. Downers Grove: InterVarsity Press, 2009.

Wright, N. T. *Surprised by Hope*. New York: HarperOne, 2008.

Wright, Ronald. *A Short History of Progress*. Toronto: Anansi Press, 2004.

Yeago, David S. "The New Testament and the Nicene Dogma: A Contribution to the Recovery of Theological Exegesis," in *The Theological Interpretation of Scripture*, Stephen E. Fowl ed., 87-100. Malden: Blackwell Publishers, 1997.